SQUADDIE

Steven McLaughlin served in the British Army for three years and is an accomplished sportsman. A former bouncer for some of Blackpool's most violent nightclubs, he holds a black belt in Shotokan Karate and is an expert-level Master Scuba Diver. He has also been awarded an associate diploma in acting from the London Academy of Music and Dramatic Art (LAMDA) and is a member of the Society of Authors. As a prominent and highly vocal 'voice from the ranks', Steven has featured as an expert military commentator on numerous international news channels, including Radio Five Live, Sky News and the BBC World Service. *Squaddie* is his first book.

SQUADDIE

A SOLDIER'S STORY

STEVEN McLAUGHLIN

MAINSTREAM
PUBLISHING

EDINBURGH AND LONDON

Reprinted 2009

First published in Great Britain in 2006 by
MAINSTREAM PUBLISHING COMPANY (EDINBURGH) LTD
7 Albany Street
Edinburgh EH1 3UG

ISBN 9781845962425

This edition published, 2007

A catalogue record for this book is available from the British Library

Typeset in Caslon and Frutiger

Printed in Great Britain by
CPI Cox & Wyman Ltd, Reading, RG1 8EX

For Rifleman Damian McLaughlin (1975–2001)
and the men of the Royal Green Jackets

Celer et Audax (Swift and Bold)

ACKNOWLEDGEMENTS

For his continued support, help and encouragement down the years, I would like to thank my father Graham McLaughlin, and I would also like to thank Phoebe McLaughlin for her generous nature and ceaseless assistance.

No man can achieve anything without the support, guidance and wise counsel of a few choice friends and mentors. The following individuals have all been a great help to me, at one time or another: Thomas and Grace McLaughlin, Paul Clayton, John Rad, my great Polish friend Zenon, Brian Hindle, Ralph Dunow, Stuart Morrison, Lee Parkinson, Jeffrey Hall and Anthony Barnes.

Last but not least, a big thank you to everybody at Mainstream Publishing for helping me to make *Squaddie* a success. In particular, I would like to thank Bill Campbell, who immediately saw the potential of this book and realised that it was a story worth telling, and Paul Murphy, whose skilful editing and helpful suggestions were always spot on and greatly appreciated.

In order to protect their identities, I have changed the names and personal details of certain individuals.

CONTENTS

Every man thinks meanly of himself
for not having been a soldier
Samuel Johnson, 1791

1

TWO TILL THE END

None of us in the patrol had been happy at getting a surprise job; we had been roughly awoken from our slumbers and told to escort two VIPs to Basra Palace for a night-time meeting. But it was over, and we headed back to base, driving along the familiar streets of downtown Basra by night and looking forward to our beds. It took an effort not to switch off and relax a little as the cooling breeze rippled through the vehicle. If you didn't know better, you would say it was a pleasant night. Then, out of the corner of my eye, I saw Norris kick the door of the Land-Rover open, and I wondered what the hell he was doing. A split second later, he slammed the butt of his SA80 A2 assault rifle into his shoulder and started putting rounds down the side streets, at the same time screaming, 'Contact left, contact left!' As the red-hot empty shell cases bounced off my forearms I gripped the wheel tighter and shoved the pedal all the way down. At the same time, I thought to myself, 'Shit . . .'

For as long as I could remember, I always wanted to be a soldier. To be a soldier, if only in my mind's eye, would be an escape from the misery and anxiety that pervaded my childhood years.

I was born into a working-class family in 1971, and if ever I am asked to describe my childhood, only one word springs to mind – short. Childhood for me was a time of fear, loathing, isolation and a desperate longing to have the power of an adult. But it wasn't always like that, and my father, a kind and gentle man, was an ever present ray of sunshine.

The good times came to an abrupt end when a stepmother, who unfortunately didn't like children, entered the lives of my brother and me. I realised things had changed when I awoke from a deep sleep to find her hovering over my bed, silently staring at me. Before she turned and left, she said she detested me and wished I would disappear from her life. What disturbed me most wasn't the ice-cold monotone in which she spoke but the calm look of blank hatred that shone in her shark-like eyes. I was nine years old and, despite my father's constant love and reassurance, never felt safe again.

Both my brother Damian and I developed psychological problems, and neither visits to child psychiatrists nor enquiries from concerned teachers helped to solve them. The trouble was, when you are constantly told you are useless, unwanted and doomed to a life of failure, you tend to start believing it, and the prophecy becomes fact. On a regular basis, our stepmother would sit us on her knee and ask us in gleeful tones to remind her why our natural mother had left us. She always forced us to reply with the same stock answer: 'Because we are rubbish, and we don't deserve a mum.' The obvious pain and distress of our prompted answer invariably caused my stepmother's face to crinkle and beam with glowing satisfaction.

It was a heavy burden for us to bear, and it should come as no surprise that we eventually cracked under the pressure. Both my brother and I left school at the age of 15 with no qualifications, and Damian had the additional problem of poor self-confidence. I am certain that if we had enjoyed a more positive and stable childhood, we would have both shone academically, but as predicted with pleasure by our stepmother, we were a couple of deserved failures and misfits.

As soon as I turned 16, I literally ran from home to enlist in the army. I had absolutely no idea about what kind of a soldier I wanted to be, only a desperate desire to escape to a better place. After a brief interview and intelligence test, the recruiting sergeant put me down as a candidate for the infantry, telling me with a nod and a wink that as an active lad it would be just what I was looking for. I was just grateful to be achieving a level of acceptance and told him with a shrug of the shoulders that I would go wherever he felt best.

The sergeant put my name down for a selection course, but before I could attend it, I had to get my parents' permission and pass a medical. Although I knew my father would support my decision, I was worried about what my stepmother's reaction would be and thought that out of spite she might refuse to let me go. Surprisingly, she backed me 100 per cent and was positively beaming when I announced my plans. When she signed her portion of my release papers, I noticed that her hands were shaking and her voice trembled. Under normal circumstances, her encouragement would have pleased me, but I actually felt saddened by it, because it underlined how unwelcome I was at home. She would still have been pleased if I had announced I was off to fight in a conflict like Vietnam.

By making the effort to become a soldier, I had gone some way to restoring my battered pride and self-esteem, and for the first time in my life, I began to feel good about myself. The fact that the army seemed to want me gave my spirits a welcome boost, and after passing the initial tests, I felt quietly confident of getting in. Several of my school friends had already joined, and none of them were particularly bright sparks or high-flyers. I really didn't think anything could stop me, and it was in that spirit that I approached the medical.

However, at the back of my mind I knew that I did have a

problem, although it was a possibility of failure that I was reluctant to acknowledge. When I was a small child I had suffered from short-sightedness, but it wasn't that big a deal and a pair of thin glasses seemed to remedy it. My eyesight remained stable until my early teens, when it took a rapid turn for the worse, and I became as blind as a bat. The temporary lightweight glasses had long since gone, and I found myself permanently wearing an ugly pair of milk-bottle-thick lenses.

As soon as the doctor saw my distinctive goggles he sent me off for an eye test, at the same time telling me not to bother coming back unless I passed. The optician was a sympathetic sort, and he helped me as much as he humanly could, but after an hour of trying every possible combination of lenses known to man, we had to reluctantly concede defeat. Not only had I failed the eye test for the infantry, but my vision was so poor I couldn't even get a position as a trainee army chef. My grand adventure was over before it had begun. I was medically unfit to serve, and, what's more, I probably always would be.

I headed home with a heavy heart and a feeling of uncertainty about my place in the world. Without realising it, I had made a huge emotional investment in becoming a soldier, and when that dream died, I began to feel worthless again. No matter how much I told myself that the failure wasn't my fault and was just one of those things, I still struggled to beat down the voice of my stepmother in my head. It was a voice that I was sick to the back teeth of hearing, and it was a voice that told me I would always be a failure at whatever I did – because I was rubbish.

At home my rejection went down like a lead balloon, and shortly afterwards, I moved out altogether. My life entered a prolonged period of drift and aimlessness. I went through a series of crap jobs and grotty bed-sits in rapid succession, before eventually winding up at the centre of Blackpool's clubland, where for three wild and hedonistic years I worked in some of the hottest nightclubs – first as a barman and then as a bouncer.

My years in clubland were amongst the happiest of my life, and I was fortunate to be a witness to the birth of the rave scene, which dominated the early '90s. It was a period during which I changed from being a boy to a man and developed a new-found confidence and independence. I spent countless hours in grimy gyms in an obsessive quest to build my body, and, at the weekends, I put it to use servicing women and chucking out drunken punters. Perhaps the most joyous discovery of all was the contact lenses that enabled me to throw away my hated glasses – and with them a hefty dose of inadequacy and self-loathing. They were crazy days, but after a brush with the law and some major-league heavies, I decided to walk away from clubland and have never regretted it since.

By that point, I was 22 years old and had put the disappointment of the army's rejection behind me, although I did think of it from time to time, and the desire to be a soldier had never really left. I rationalised it as just one of those frustrating and annoying things that I was powerless to change, so to waste time dwelling on it would be pointless. My interest was piqued again during the 1990–91 Gulf War and the media frenzy that accompanied it. I had a couple of friends fighting in the conflict, and when they returned home to brag of their adventures, I remember feeling curiously left out. It wasn't that I hungered to fight in a bloody conflict, but I did have a yearning to be involved in something meaningful on a global scale. Battling with drunken yobs on a pub door hardly compared to taking on Saddam Hussein's elite Republican Guard, did it? Nevertheless, I had to accept that I had missed my chance, and for me the opportunity to serve would remain a distant pipe dream – or so I thought.

I was watching the news in 1993 when a story appeared that literally made me jump out of my seat. A clinic had opened that was providing a revolutionary new laser surgery to cure short-sightedness. As I watched the story unfold and listened to the testimony of former patients I realised I might have stumbled upon a way of acheiving my military ambitions. I noted the phone number of the clinic and immediately rang up and arranged an appointment. Two weeks later and £3000 lighter, I had the operation, and after six months, I was given the all clear and declared fully healed. It was then I put into action the crafty plan I had been formulating – a plan that if successful would propel me into the Royal Marine Commandos.

Whilst healing from the effects of surgery, I did some research at the library and tried to work out how to kick-start my military career. The deeper I dug and the more material I read, the clearer it became that the best regiment to join was the Royal Marines. Their selection process, their basic training regime and their excellent reputation placed them head and shoulders above all rivals. But, more importantly, they were my last true hope of becoming a soldier, because the army knew about my medical history, and I couldn't go back to them.

When I visited the careers office, I was asked if I had applied to join the Marines before or had ever been rejected by them, and I truthfully replied no. I purposefully chose not to mention my army rejection, as it was a can of worms that would undoubtedly ruin my chances if opened. After a multiple choice test and an interview, I was allowed to progress to the medical.

Common sense told me that if I confessed to having had laser surgery, my application would be instantly binned – no matter how good my vision was. When I filled out the medical questionnaire, I was never specifically asked about eye surgery, but I was prompted to indicate whether I had undergone any operations on 'any part of the body'. After the briefest of pauses and momentary soul searching, I casually ticked the 'No' box.

The medical was given by a friendly old GP who seemed to belong to another century. I sailed through all his tests and even joined in with his relaxed banter and chat. The general vibe was that he wanted me to pass the test and thought it was marvellous that I was considering a career in the forces. The only time I began to worry and things got slightly awkward was when he began examining my eyes. He spent a long time shining weird lights into them and peering closely, all the while rubbing his chin and looking puzzled. After a pause, he asked me to read to the bottom of the chart, which I did with ease. He then looked even more confused.

The doctor said that I had passed the medical, but he had some questions about my eyes. Despite my stomach turning cartwheels, I tried to appear cool and nonchalant and told him to go ahead. He asked me if I had ever been a boxer or had an accident of some sort, to which I truthfully replied no. I could see he was troubled and asked him what the problem was. He said that I had the most peculiarly shaped corneas he had ever seen and that instead of being curved, they were almost triangular. I didn't know what to say to this because he was describing perfectly the results and scars of my surgery.

Rubbing his chin and staring at me intently, he concluded that I must have 'funny-shaped eyes', as some people do. As I let out a sigh of relief he casually remarked that he knew I hadn't had surgery because he couldn't see any knife strokes, which would have been a dead give-away. I laughed along nervously before leaving his office.

Once outside, I was immediately engulfed by a wave of relief and gratitude. I had secured the precious pass certificate – now it was down to me to see if I was good enough. What the doctor should have looked for were laser burns instead of knife strokes, but, luckily for me, he wasn't up to date with the latest techniques. I felt guilty about bluffing the old boy and being dishonest, but, at the end of the day, I had no choice. At the same time, I felt a smug sense of satisfaction that I had managed to beat the system and bend the rules. I was wrong, and my lies would come back to haunt me.

I was given a preparation pack by the Marines that was designed to get me into the best possible shape for the selection course. Basically, it involved endless sets of press-ups, dips, sit-ups and daily runs for a period of two months. I was pretty fit anyway but tore into it like a rabid madman, with the goal of becoming so strong that I couldn't possibly fail. The selection course was known as a PRC, or potential recruits course, and it involved a four-day stay at the Commando Training Centre in Lympston.

The PRC is an experience I shall never forget, and it's one of the most exhausting things I have ever done. From the moment we arrived on camp until the moment we left, the pressure never once lifted. We were run ragged over assault courses and thrashed through muddy fields at breakneck speed. If we weren't outside being dragged through waterlogged tunnels by screaming corporals, then we were in the gym being ground into mush by psychotic physical training instructors (PTI). I vomited on the spot more than once and came close to physical collapse several times.

Out of forty candidates only ten of us got through, and it was a huge relief to be amongst the chosen few. On the last day, we were given a talk by a sergeant-major on what we could expect as Marine recruits. Despite being covered in cuts and bruises and feeling like I had been run over by a tank, all of the pain and weariness left me when I listened to his words. What he said brought a lump to my throat, and, in a few short sentences, he crystallised everything that was motivating me to become a soldier: 'For those of you from broken homes, poor backgrounds or without families, I don't want you to worry any longer. From now on, if you work hard for us and do your best, we will become your family – the Marines will be your family.'

I felt like he was speaking to me directly, and his words deeply moved me. Several other lads confessed to feeling the same way. I made a solemn vow not to let the sergeant-major down and to live up to the sincerity of his words.

Two months later, I returned to Lympston Commando to begin my thirty weeks of basic training. I knew that the course was going to be horrendously tough, but I had prepared well, and barring a broken leg or some other crippling injury, I felt confident of passing it. The first weeks flew by in a blur of frenetic activity. We were screamed at, pushed around, flogged round the gym, and forced to iron kit and polish boots into the early hours. It was hell on earth and stretched every fibre of my body to breaking point – but, at the same time, it was deeply satisfying, and I felt privileged to be there. Whenever I felt my spirits dipping, I reminded myself that the reason it was special was because it was tough – so I cracked on with it.

The days were long and arduous, and you didn't have time to think about anything other than immediate 'Marine business'. I was so wrapped up in the constant struggle to maintain my personal kit and morale that I had completely forgotten about the fast one I pulled on the old doctor. As far as I was concerned it was a shady bit of business that I hoped would stay well and truly in the past. Unfortunately, I was wrong, and my deceit was about to return with a sting in its tail.

Week four began much the same as any other, with the usual round of torturous gym sessions, endless inspections and parade-ground bollockings. None of that worried me, because I knew it was something I could control if I put the effort in. What did send a shiver down my spine was when I was called to the medical centre for a routine check. If I had been like the other recruits and had nothing to hide, it wouldn't have bothered me, but because I had a whopping great secret lurking in my past I found myself fretting.

My medical was conducted by a surgeon lieutenant commander of the Royal Navy, and, on the surface, it was supposed to be a routine procedure. He explained that it was service policy to give new recruits a thorough medical once they had done a few weeks training, just to check if any problems had cropped up. Apparently the things they were looking for were sexually transmitted diseases, fresh injuries, damaged bones and any 'unresolved issues' that might affect ongoing training.

A chill ran through me when I heard the last phrase, and I had an uncomfortable feeling that things were about to get messy. He glanced at my records and straight away announced, 'We have a problem here. On your medical notes the doctor who examined you has written "query eyesight".' I almost fell off my chair when he said that, and I made a valiant but totally doomed attempt to bluff him, by innocently remarking that I had passed the medical without question.

The commander told me that the examining doctor had been uncertain about my eyesight, but as I could see reasonably well he had chosen to pass me, albeit with a cautionary mark against my name. He further explained that anything I said at my recruiting medical was taken on trust and face value, because they had no authority to request medical files from GPs. The bad news was that as I was now a member of the forces they could obtain my GP's notes and investigate the problem themselves.

In a last desperate gamble, I asked the commander if he couldn't just give me a quick eye test there and then, so I could prove to him that I had nothing to hide. He shook his head and said that because another doctor had raised a query he was obliged to respond. I knew the game was up when he said he was sending me to see a specialist at the Royal Naval Hospital in Portsmouth: 'One of our most senior and eminent eye surgeons.'

Within one week, I was medically discharged from the corps, as a result of my 'enlisting with an undeclared medical condition'. The specialist merely shone a light into my eyes and coolly announced that I had undergone recent surgery. The guy was so confident that he didn't even give me a chance to deny it and said he wouldn't bother writing to my GP for confirmation of what he already knew. When I tried to protest, he chided me for lying to the corps and thinking I could get away with it – but, funnily enough, he said he had a grudging admiration and respect for the reasons why I had. But, unfortunately, rules were rules, and that was me out. The surgeon said that because it was a new procedure they didn't know the long-term effects or whether the improvement would be permanent. The Marines were worried that in five years' time I could be blind as a bat again, in which case they would have to discharge me with a costly pension. Another reason was that if I shot someone in Northern Ireland and the media heard that I had previous vision problems, the MOD could be sued for negligence. Whatever, none of it mattered because I was finished as a Marine.

The unexpected discharge was an emotional hammer blow, and it took me months to recover. I had put my heart and soul into becoming a Marine, and I desperately wanted to earn a green beret. The pain was far more intense and disappointing than my initial rejection by the army – because this time the knock-back came after I had enlisted. I had been doing well as a recruit and was relishing the challenge, so to have it end so suddenly was a brutally crushing defeat.

Of course, many years have passed since the experience, but I often think about it. I only spent a month with the Marines, but what I saw in that short time convinced me that they are the best infantry troops in the world. Nothing that I encountered in my future military career altered that belief. I will confess that for a short while I felt some bitterness and resentment towards the corps, but as time passed and I grew older those feelings were replaced by affection and respect. And no matter what I achieve in my professional life, my failure to become a Royal Marine will always be my greatest disappointment.

Eventually I became comfortable with the idea that I would never be a soldier. It was a new emotion, but I felt remarkably at ease with it. I think it was because I knew I had done everything in my power to succeed, but, through no fault of my own, it simply wasn't meant to be. After two aborted attempts, nobody could accuse me of not having tried. On a deeper level, I instinctively knew that I would have made a good soldier, and that knowledge gave me a lot of confidence, drive and increased ambition.

In rapid succession, I enrolled on a Higher National Diploma course at college (which I passed with flying colours), gained a black belt in karate and became an expert scuba-diver. I then took a job in the retail world and within a year rose to management level. As my 20s rushed by I put my military disappointments behind me and racked up one achievement after another.

The most precious relationship I had throughout that time was with my brother, who was always there to pick me up after a setback and remained in the background with a quiet strength and determination. Damian knew all about failure and rejection – but also about success. He had undergone his own titanic battle to become a soldier, and his efforts would be worthy of a book themselves. As a schoolboy he had struggled tremendously and suffered horrendous emotional abuse at the hands of our stepmother. Yet despite this, he became an award-winning cadet and athlete with an impressive display of willpower and character.

Because of his academic difficulties, Damian had to work hard to pass the army entrance test, but, true to form, when he finally cracked it, he chose to take on one of the toughest jobs available: that of a combat infantryman in the Royal Green Jackets (RGJ). Damian could have chosen differently and taken a much easier route into the army, but 'easy option' didn't enter into his vocabulary.

The infantry is one of the dirtiest and toughest jobs that the army has to offer, but the RGJ was also an elite regiment that had spawned many fine soldiers, and he was grateful for the opportunity. His basic training was six months of pure hell, yet he still managed to pass it after breaking his foot twice and spending three painful months in rehab. He could have bailed out at any time, but the fact that he stuck with it was testament to his grit and determination.

When he passed out of basic training he was visibly shrunken and hobbled about like an old man, but aside from the hollow cheeks and gaunt features, his eyes were sparkling and his smile was beaming. I was incredibly proud of what he had achieved, and as far as I was concerned, he had a pair of balls like King Kong. I think that I subconsciously transferred my military ambitions onto his shoulders, and a part of me lived through him.

Damian spent six years in the Green Jackets and completed three operational tours of the Balkans at a particularly dangerous time. Whenever he returned on leave I was always fascinated by his adventures, and I insisted on hearing every last detail. He told me that the level of hatred and opposition between the warring factions was such that it would take decades for peace to emerge. The distrust between the Muslims and Serbs made the Palestinians and Israelis seem like best friends. As an example, he told me of a street through which he would regularly patrol and have to defuse troubles: on one side were Muslims who had raped and beaten their Serb neighbours, and on the other were Serbs who had murdered Muslims and torched their homes.

In 2000, he deployed to Mitrovica in Kosovo, and some of the shit he had to deal with was unbelievable. On one occasion, there was a huge demonstration by opposing Serbs and Albanians; 60,000 people attended, and it was supposed to be peaceful. Of course, as soon as the sworn enemies caught sight of each other they surged forward and became violent. Three hundred Green Jackets were deployed to quell the riots and restore order. Before they swung into action, the commanding officer said that if they didn't keep the two sides apart, there would be full-scale carnage. And so they found themselves wedged between two huge mobs intent on wreaking havoc – 'The shit in a sandwich,' were the exact words Damian used.

Miraculously, they kept the two sides apart. They had to endure nose-to-nose contact with hate-filled Serbs howling and spitting at them. Punches were thrown, knives were brandished and soldiers were half dragged into the crowd – but they held the line and kept them apart. Damian was given a special commemorative painting of the event, entitled *The Thin Green Line*, and his name was printed alongside those who had been in the thick of it.

When he returned from Kosovo, he handed in his notice and prepared to leave the army. I was disappointed at his decision and tried to persuade him to stay in, but he had earned the right to make his own choices, and I had to respect them. At that time, I still had a rather naive and childish view of just how stressful soldiering could be, probably because I had never served in an actual unit myself.

My opinions were formed from the many military memoirs I had devoured, my own childhood fantasies and my brief stint as a Marine recruit. I seemed to view it as a *Boy's Own* adventure story and was forever spouting off about the benefits of army service and how wonderful it all was. Damian would listen to my lectures with a weary and resigned patience, before doing his best to subtly change the subject. Looking back, I now realise how overbearing and presumptuous I was. He had every right to ask me, 'What would you know about it?' but, to his credit, he never did.

When Damian's final leave as a soldier was over, I shook his hand and told him to take care. He grinned back at me and told me not to worry. It was a crisp and sunny morning, and I had never seen him looking so cheerful and confident. In a few weeks, he would be out of the army for good, and I could see that the prospect of new-found freedom was buoying him up. As his car pulled away he looked over his shoulder and gave me a cheery wave. I would never see him again. Two weeks later, he was killed in a tragic car accident whilst driving through the countryside, and I had the terrible duty, alongside my father, of identifying his body.

He was laid out on a blanketed trolley, and he looked like he was blissfully asleep. The sun shone through the frosted glass so brightly I thought it would wake him up. His blond hair glinted, and his skin took on a golden hue. Apart from a tiny indentation on his forehead, there was barely a mark on him – he looked a picture of glowing health.

I grasped his hand and shook it vigorously: 'Thanks for being my brother Damian, thanks so very much.' As I spoke the words a wave of emotion washed over me. It was a pleasant feeling: a warm glow rising from my tummy and jetting towards my head. As I kissed him I peeled back one of his eyelids and stared into it. I had never realised how beautiful and alive his eyes were until that moment. The clear blue eye gazed innocently back at me – still full of hope for the tomorrow it would never see. I gripped his biceps and felt their fullness, their inert power hanging limply. He had worked so hard to build those arms, and it had been worth it. They were beautiful arms. He was beautiful. He was my beautiful dead brother, and I loved him with all my heart.

Sorting through his personal effects I found a bag of dirty clothes and came across his favourite woolly jumper. The jumper was covered in beer stains and stank of stale smoke and aftershave. Instead of washing it, I decided to leave it as it was. Before going to sleep, I would lay the jumper on my face and inhale deeply. Although in reality it smelt bloody awful, at that moment in time it seemed like the finest perfume. The smells on the jumper were the scents of Damian's life, and I drew on them as if my own depended on it. His life was now just a beautiful memory and nothing more.

I would find myself poring over his army photos and analysing them deeply. Often he would be in the middle of a muddy field with an expression of steely determination or deadly seriousness on his face. I would gaze at his eyes and wonder what they were seeing. There weren't enough pictures of him smiling, and I was only just starting to notice it. When he was alive, I would only want to see these grim action shots, but when he was dead, I wanted to see more fun and laughter. I felt guilty as I realised just how arduous his time in the army had been and how much pressure I had put on him to stay in.

For a while, I tried to force myself to become religious and imagined seeing him again in some glorious afterlife. But I knew that was bullshit. You either believe in God or you don't – and I don't. The only thing that I believe in is nature, because I can see and feel it all around me, and I know it exists. I believe in the earth, in fire and water, the soil and the birds, and for me there is nothing else.

When I was discharged from the Marines and feeling particularly low, Damian had bought me a gift. It was only a cheap watch from a market stall, but I could tell he had taken great care in choosing it. I was deeply touched because I knew he was only earning a pittance as a cleaner at that time. Although he could barely afford the bus fare, he had still made the effort to buy me a present. When he handed it to me, he looked embarrassed and apologised that it was all he could afford. I thanked him and joked that there was no need to apologise as it was a lovely watch. Now, I wish I had told him that his simple gift meant more to me than a solid-gold Rolex.

As the numbness of his loss loosened its grip it was replaced with an urgent need for action. I needed to do something dramatic in his honour, something to repay all the support he had given me over the years. The question was what could I ever do to possibly match what he had done for me? A tragic and shocking event would provide the answer.

We all remember where we were on 11 September 2001. I spent the day shopping with a pal in Preston. When I caught the train home, I heard a couple talking about some big event that would be on the news. I wasn't really paying attention and thought that maybe the Queen Mother had died. It wasn't until I got home and switched on the television that I realised what had happened. As those shocking images replayed again and again, I thought about the effect it would have on the world and, more specifically, Britain as a nation. America would unquestionably launch military strikes, and if that happened, we would get involved.

'Wait a minute,' I thought. Had I just said 'we'? Why did I use that word as if it affected me, when I was quite safe in my own cosy little world? As the commentators referred to 'our involvement' or what 'we' will do I began to grow irritated. They were talking about it as though it affected them personally, when it patently didn't.

Already the talk had turned to possible invasions of Afghanistan, Iran or some other Middle Eastern country. I spared a thought for the unfortunate soldiers that would fight those wars and the possible horrors they might face. I couldn't imagine anything worse than lying flat on your back in the desert, mortally wounded and staring at the sky, saying to yourself, 'What the fuck am I doing here?' I sighed with relief as I realised it would never happen to me.

No sooner had the sigh passed my lips than I felt a hot sting of shame. This was the exact kind of situation Damian would have had to face as a soldier. So what gave me the right to smugly congratulate myself that I wouldn't be there and react like a selfish coward? I had just been given a glimpse of the knife-edge that soldiers like Damian routinely lived on and all I could think about was my own safety. But what made me think that I was so special and was exempt from danger or had immunity from getting involved? The answer was nothing. Fuck it, I was going to do it, and this time I would let nothing stop me. Supposedly, I wasn't medically fit, and by that point I was too old as well, but I would find a way around the rules. If my life ended in a desert wasteland, so be it.

I took a day off work to visit the Blackpool army careers office. The last time I had been there was in 1987, when I was a fresh-faced 16-year-old boy just out of school. As I caught sight of the familiar building an uncomfortably surreal feeling gripped me. I stopped in my tracks and turned to study my reflection in the nearest shop window to reassure myself that this was what I really wanted to do. The face that peered back seemed not to belong to me – my hairline was receding and fine lines decorated the corners of my eyes. I had always considered myself young at heart and rosy cheeked, but there was no escaping the fact that I now had the face of a 30-year-old man.

What the hell was I doing back there after all those years? How stupid was I to be once again tempting fate and inviting disappointment, ridicule even? It was 2001, another century for God's sake; I should have been thinking about retiring from the army – not joining up!

For the first time in 14 years, I entered the building. A bulky sergeant asked if he could help me, and I could tell from his matey tone that he didn't think of me as a possible recruit. Clearing my throat, I nervously stepped forward and said, 'Well, yes, I think perhaps you can.' He gestured to a chair opposite him, and I sat down heavily. 'I'm thinking about joining the Royal Green Jackets,' I said.

An awkward silence hung in the air before he finally asked the inevitable question: 'Just how old are you?' When I told him I was 30, he made a point of looking down at his sergeants stripes before replying, 'I'm 30, and I've been in the army for 12 years – in any case, the maximum age for an infantryman is 26 on entry.' To add insult to injury, he then gave me a funny look that gave the impression that he thought someone of my age ought to have known better and that I should stop wasting his time.

Flushing red with embarrassment and feeling ever more foolish, I asked him if he would at least listen to my story before dismissing me out of hand. As I began telling him of my struggles to become a soldier I could see his eyes glazing over and a frown forming on his face. He at least gave me the courtesy of listening, but as he looked out of the window and began shuffling papers I could see I had lost him. At the end of my story, he shrugged his shoulders and muttered that it was all very sad, but, like he said, I was too old.

Getting up to leave, I asked him one last time if he was certain there was no way he could help me. 'Absolutely 100 per cent certain mate,' he replied.

Feeling pissed off and angry, I stalked out of the office muttering a silent, 'Fuck you too, mate.'

I went to the nearest café and ordered a strong coffee. The caffeine seemed to have a calming effect on me, and as I sipped the hot liquid I mulled over my options – or lack of them. The problem I had was trying to get someone to take me seriously and to persuade that person to back me up a bit. What had really annoyed me was how the sergeant had treated me as if I was 100 years old. I realised that the army had age limits for good reasons, but I was only four years out, not fifty! I wasn't about to let one surly sergeant put me off, so I decided to look elsewhere until I got the response that I wanted.

A week later, I found myself sitting on a bench in the Liverpool army careers office, waiting to speak to a recruiter. I drew the same funny looks as before, and it seemed that every soldier in the building was casting me a second glance. The rest of the potential recruits seemed to be about 17 years old and dressed in garishly coloured tracksuits and trainers. I stuck out like a sore thumb.

As the hours dragged by and I continued to be ignored, I took the time to study the young lads streaming in and out. They reminded me of my own failed enlistment back in 1987. It was a different time then and most of those lads would have been mere babies with dads only a few years older than me – and here we were competing to be rookie soldiers. I grinned at the sheer absurdity and ridiculousness of it all. I should have been one of the sergeant-majors interviewing the would-be soldiers – not hoping to go through basic training with them!

The generation of soldiers that I would have belonged to had patrolled the hostile streets of Northern Ireland and fought in the Gulf War against Saddam's armies. These lads knew nothing of those conflicts, but I had grown up with them on the nightly news.

A few of them came and sat by me, and we made small talk. I

could see the curiosity and surprise in their eyes. For the first time, I felt like an impostor trying to fit in with a generation to which I didn't belong. The lads were friendly enough and wished me well, but I couldn't deny the huge cultural gap that separated us.

I like to think of myself as a good judge of character, and I perked up the moment I met Sergeant (Sgt.) Street. Before I even spoke, he said that he knew my application wasn't an ordinary one and could be problematic, so, for the moment, all he wanted to know was the complete story of why I wanted to enlist. I made sure not to leave anything out, telling him about my previous botched attempts and the laser surgery I had tried to keep hidden.

After I had finished, he said he understood and respected why I wanted to be a soldier, but he needed to know why I wanted to be a Green Jacket specifically. I told him the answer was quite simple – because my late brother had been one. His ears pricked up at my reply, and I could sense immediately I had struck a chord with him. As I told him of my brother's journey he began to smile broadly, before telling me he had known him and served in the same battalion.

Sgt. Street said he would make detailed enquiries about my medical status and getting the age barrier lifted, and when he knew a bit more, he would give me a call. He said it would take a few weeks, and he couldn't make any promises, except that he would personally push my application as hard as he could and support me all the way.

The next few weeks were tense and difficult. Every time the phone rang I dashed to pick it up, hoping and praying it was good news. Finally, it was. Sgt. Street told me that subject to passing all the relevant tests (which was by no means guaranteed), I would be considered for entry into the Green Jackets, despite being four years over age. He said that under normal circumstances the age rule would have instantly barred me, but thanks to my short Marine service, he had found a way around it. Because I had served a mere month in the Marines it meant that the army could treat me as a 're-enlisting soldier' and offer me a special three-year contract. All of a sudden, I felt a lot better about my time in the Marines, and I reflected that everything happens for a reason, although sometimes it is not clear to us at the time.

The next piece of news was even better: recruits who had undergone laser treatment could now join the army. The surgery was now accepted as a safe and permanent alternative to glasses, and the MOD decided it was foolish to turn people away because of it. In one fell swoop, the two biggest hurdles to my becoming a soldier had been removed. It seemed like an unseen hand of fate was guiding me, clearing away the obstacles in my path.

By the time the selection course came round, I was raring to go. I got a train to Lichfield and was given instructions to await army transport. A coach pulled up and out of it bounded an impossibly fit-looking PTI. Despite the freezing weather, he wore only a flimsy white vest and blue tracksuit bottoms, and strutted up and down the pavement like a peacock, looking at us with an expression of disdain. I had a silent chuckle at this as I could see his little charade was already spooking some of the younger recruits. One of the advantages of being an older man was that I was wise to such blatant bullshit and could see it for what it was. I played along anyway and stared straight ahead as he stalked past.

After a quick roll call, we were ordered onto the bus and driven to the selection centre. Once there, we were marched into a lecture theatre, ordered to sit still and told to remain deathly quiet. It was a simple enough instruction, but it seemed some of the lads couldn't even cope with that. As we took our seats, a nervous chatter swept the room, and rude jokes began flying back and forth. What amazed me was that our PTI escort was still with us, and despite his reddening face, the noise persisted. Eventually he exploded: 'Silence you fucking wankers!' It certainly seemed to have an effect, and the room became pin-drop quiet.

The crisp squeak of highly polished boots pierced the air, as a senior officer marched briskly to the dais in order to address us. I had no idea what rank he was, but his shoulders had more pips on them than an orange, so it must have been high. In a ludicrously posh voice, he welcomed us to the centre and outlined the wonderful careers the army had waiting for us, but only if we managed to impress him over the next few days. I visibly bristled when he said some of us would struggle physically: 'Especially the younger lads, and probably the 30 year old, too.' All heads swivelled to face me, and for the first time, I felt self-conscious and embarrassed about my age.

A gang of PTIs were placed in charge of us, assisted by a few sergeants who were there to shout and holler. The course itself was remarkably simple and consisted of two days of fitness tests and lectures, followed by a final day of leadership and initiative tasks. Anytime a recruit wanted to quit he could opt out by simply raising his hand, and if anyone was particularly crap, the PTIs would sling them off anyway. The whole time we would be observed and cajoled, pushed around and screamed at, and generally made to feel like shit.

I managed to catch the eye of the instructors early on, not because I was outstanding in any way, but because I was, as they put it, 'a bald-headed old bastard'. A sergeant took me aside and informed me that I could expect no favours due to my age. I was pleased about that because I realised the instructors would be underestimating me. They were assuming that because of my age I would struggle to keep up. I would take a perverse pleasure in ramming my fitness down their throats and embarrassing some of the younger 'speed demons' amongst the recruits. Being expected to fail would mean my success would shine all the brighter.

For the final phase, we moved onto leadership skills. We were placed in teams and told that we had to move across obstacles comprising planks of wood, oil drums and other such bits and bobs. It was bloody hard work as some of the obstacles seemed impassable. The mistake most teams made was to dither about and spend too much time trying to work it out, when the best policy was to just start moving and learn by failure. A lot of the time we ended up slithering around on our arses in the wet mud or falling off totem poles and landing in messy heaps. It must have been funny to watch because we drew a crowd of non-commissioned officers (NCO).

I was anxious not to appear bossy or like a bully that always has to take over. I decided to play it by ear and just try and put in a solid performance, rather than be team leader. The problem with that plan was the lads in my group insisted I be in charge, on account of my age and maturity. So, for the whole of the last day, I was placed reluctantly in the position of team leader. Once I had been made captain, I pushed like hell, shouting myself hoarse until victory was in the bag. After the leadership tests were finished, we faced the final hurdle of a selection interview with a senior officer.

The officer conducting my interview seemed positively ancient: he must have been at least 60, and a thick walrus-like moustache decorated his upper lip. Without doubt, he was the archetypal old-school 'British Officer Gentleman', and he glowered with establishment authority. But despite his high-society aura, he had a bit of the 'kindly uncle' about him, and his eyes told me he wished me to succeed.

And so I told him of my childhood ambition to be a soldier – and how I was embarrassed to be still clinging on to it but could deny it no longer. I told him of my experience with the Marines and why I had felt compelled to deceive them about my eyes. And, finally, we moved on to Damian and discussed his army career. While I told him all this, he nodded sympathetically and rocked in his chair, his hands folded across his considerable belly.

'A sad story young man, a sad story no doubt, and I admire you for being true to yourself after all these years. Your performance on this course has been outstanding – especially considering your age. So, on reflection, I have no doubt in recommending you for armed service. Hopefully you can help some of the weaker lads in basic training, because they will cling to you like a big brother in times of stress. But I do have one concern, and it's something I've got to ask you about.'

An awkward pause followed, and the old man looked around as if searching for the right choice of words. I could tell he was worried about offending me and felt it was a delicate matter. 'I do hope, young man, that you are not on some sort of personal crusade in honour of your brother. I am concerned you may feel obliged to serve in the army in his memory, because, as you say, you encouraged him to join up. And the reason I say this is not to cause pain but to advise you that if this is the case, you would be best to leave it well alone. The army is a serious business, especially in light of recent events. We could be at war in the near future, and you might be involved. The army is no place for making sentimental journeys, so please bear that in mind, and I am sorry I have had to say this.'

At the end of his speech, he fixed me with a piercing glare to reinforce his point, and I felt like a little boy sat in front of the headmaster. He had cut right to the core of why I wanted to be a soldier, and I couldn't deny my true reasons to him. I hadn't realised my motivations were so transparent, but he had seen through me as if I was an open window.

'Well, Sir, I am surprised you've asked me that, and I won't deny that a large part of it is about wanting to see the world through my brother's eyes. To feel and experience life as a soldier, just as he did, through good times and bad. But, equally, I have to say that I'm joining up for me – because now I'm 30 it's my last ever chance, and if I don't become a soldier, I'll always feel a bit hollow and empty. This is it for me, Sir, I've waited for 15 years, and now it's my time.' The passion of my reply surprised us both, and I embarrassed myself by feeling my eyes moisten when I mentioned Damian.

They say life comes down to a few key moments – and that was definitely one of them. The officer stood up from behind his desk and straightened his tie. I did the same. With a cheery smile and a swift movement, he thrust out his hand over the desk separating us. 'Welcome to the army. I am recommending you for service in the Royal Green Jackets. Just remember what I said. This isn't about your brother but about you, and it's not a game. Now go away and do yourself proud.'

There was an expectant atmosphere in the theatre, and as I walked in the waiting lads gave me a cheer. We had got to know one another well over the week and wanted one another to succeed. I couldn't help standing out thanks to my age, and because it was my last chance, the youngsters were willing me on to succeed. Even the hard-as-nails sergeant gave me a pat on the back as I walked by.

Taking my oath of allegiance proved to be a suitably solemn affair. It was actually pretty inspirational stuff, and we took the whole affair deadly seriously. Once the oath was completed, we were given an elaborate certificate commemorating the event, and each man had to shake hands with the man at his side. From that moment on, we were members of the army and subject to military law.

I thought a lot about taking the oath and what changes it signified in my life. It felt like I was making my own little piece of history and was taking a pivotal step by embarking on an unknown journey. Looking at the faces around me, I wondered what adventures lay ahead for us and what challenges we would face. Some of them would be enjoyable and rewarding, but, no doubt, some of them would not. Would we all live to tell the tale? Only time would tell.

Despite my obvious joy and pride at taking the oath, it also stirred some ambivalent feelings in me, because I have always been a republican. The whole idea of bowing and scraping to an unelected elite strikes me as being profoundly absurd, and I find the concept of royalty and its assumed privileges ridiculous. So, I rationalised taking the oath as not so much a pledge to the Queen as, instead, a simple promise to serve my country as best I could. As for the monarchy, I couldn't care less!

In early 2002, I boarded the train for the journey to Army Training Regiment (ATR) Winchester. Looking out of the window at the passing countryside, I let my mind drift back to my first day as a recruit, almost exactly eight years before. So much had happened since then, and a lot of water had passed under the bridge. During the depths of my despair in 1994, if you had said I would be repeating my journey at the age of 30, I would have laughed in your face. I only hoped that this adventure would have a happier ending.

2

THE EVENTUAL SOLDIER

When the train reached Winchester, a gaggle of pasty-faced recruits were huddled around the waiting area, each one looking unsure and jittery in his new circumstances. I cannot say I felt any better as I sidled up to them and leant against the cold concrete wall. We looked like an awkward collection of lost souls, which is exactly what we were, and communication was restricted to brief nods and studied shrugs. Despite there being a dozen or more of us, nobody felt confident enough to break the ice or ask the obvious question: 'Are you here for the Green Jackets?'

Suddenly, a battered-looking Transit van pulled up, honking its horn loudly and exuberantly. Out of it bounded an insanely cheerful corporal wearing a blue beret, which apparently meant he was Army Air Corp, and a thoroughly miserable-looking Royal Military Police (RMP) officer. The cheerful man strode over and beamed at us manically.

'All right now lads? I take it you're here for the Green Jackets. Fuck me, you're in for some fun!' We didn't know what to make of him or whether he was playing some kind of game with us, so rather than rush to the van, we just stood rooted to the spot.

A split second later, we got the message in a clearer fashion when we heard the van door slam shut. The RMP strolled over and looked like steam was about to come from his ears. 'Well, you heard the man, get in the fuckin' van you cretins!'

We didn't need telling twice and flung ourselves into it like demented lunatics. Suitcases and sports bags were squashed on laps and stuck in people's faces as the van roared away.

Mr 'Cheerful' was driving and sped round corners like he was on a racetrack. As we slid about in the back and bounced around like pinballs he laughed like a manic clown. He peppered us with ridiculous questions and not very funny jokes as we careered about the road.

In contrast, his RMP colleague was deathly silent, apart from hissing and muttering under his breath about 'scrote-bags' and 'worms'. It was pretty obvious it was to us that he was referring, and from his highly polished 'bad-guy' act, we could see he didn't like recruits. As we sped down the road, it was a relief to see ATR Winchester loom into view. Turning into camp, the van bounced noisily over speed ramps, and our heads struck the ceiling. We exchanged nervous glances as the armed guard raised the barrier and waved us through.

So this was it. There was no turning back now; we were army property on an army camp. Not only that but recruits to boot: the lowest of the low on the food chain. The expression on the faces of the younger lads said that they were already having second thoughts. I was grateful for my brief time with the Marines, because at least I knew what was coming next. God only knows what some of the doubters were expecting, but I think they were regretting having watched so many Hollywood war films.

When the van stopped, the RMP held the door open for us and kindly volunteered to unload our bags for us. This consisted of us standing to attention and having our luggage thrown at us full force. Most of us ended up in an undignified heap on the floor as a shower of canvas grips and leather cases landed on our heads. Once the RMP had slung the last bag at us, we had to dust ourselves down and thank him for his kind gesture.

'What a complete fucking tosser,' someone with a deep Scottish accent mumbled over my shoulder. A muffled laughter greeted his comments, and I took the opportunity to glance behind me to see who had said it. I got quite a shock.

Half expecting to see a grinning teenage boy, I was surprised to be staring at the chest of one of the biggest men I had ever seen. Looking up to meet his gaze, I found a tough-looking face that seemed only a few years younger than mine. He had very wide shoulders and a decidedly cheeky grin that suggested he had been around the block a few times. I knew instantly that we would get on and was about to say hello when a sharp cry pierced the air.

'You there, face the front and stand fucking still. Stop fidgeting about or you'll be straight out of the fucking gate!' I didn't need to be told twice and stood rigidly to attention. 'Fucking Green Jackets! I might have known! Now pick up your kit and follow me. Thank fuck you're not my problem.'

With that we picked up our luggage and half dragged, half marched our way over to the Green Jackets' accommodation wing. The grumpy sergeant-major figure told us to wait outside until we were formally met by our training team. No noise, no movement, just wait. After a few tense minutes that felt like an eternity, a stocky figure emerged from the building. He was about 33 years old, rough looking and spoke with a broad Birmingham accent. He was clearly anxious to make an impression, so he took the opportunity to walk down the line and personally stare each one of us out. When he had finished eyeballing us, he introduced himself as Sgt. Rickson: in his own words, our 'best friend and master' for the next 12 weeks.

Sgt. Rickson proceeded to give us a lecture on what he expected us to achieve over the coming months, and how it was now his solemn mission in life to transform our pathetically weak bodies into those of fighting men. Much of his speech was liberally spattered with threats of dire bodily harm if we let him or his men down. I don't think anybody was too bothered by his welcoming talk as it was what we had expected, but a few of the lads had begun to shiver noticeably in the winter air.

Just in case our minds were drifting, and to reinforce his point, the sergeant suddenly screamed, 'Get to the fence line and back – go, go, go!' It took a few seconds for what he was saying to sink in to our numbed skulls, but once it hit home, we took off like startled rabbits across the nearby muddy field. The route across the grass was clearly well trodden, and we slipped and collided with one another in the filthy mud. Every man was frantic not to be the last back, and elbows and fists lashed out wildly.

As I staggered back on wobbly legs, it was a struggle to keep my lunch down. A few of the lads weren't so lucky, and the remnants of Mars bars and Coke stained their shirts.

I had a feeling we would become very familiar with the backfield – and not for kicking a ball around. Conveniently, it was right next to our accommodation block, and I had no doubt that the sergeant would consider it a handy punishment for us.

Once the last man had run in, the sergeant stood impassively observing us, his hands on his hips and his face betraying no emotions. As we gulped in lungfuls of cold air like quivering fish, the sergeant tutted to himself about poor fitness standards, before cheerfully announcing, 'What's the matter lads? Feeling tired? Lets go again!'

The second run was even slower than the first, and as we clumsily galloped off, a few lads were already talking of quitting, in between wheezing and gasping for air. To make matters worse, the sergeant had pulled out a whistle, and every time he blew it, we had to dive down and crawl in the mud. It was a ritual called 'Billy the Whistle' that we would come to loathe.

'All right, lads, lesson number one: never feel sorry for yourself in my platoon because it just doesn't fucking work. Now get your kit in the block and stand by your beds.' There was a collective sigh of relief as we realised he wasn't going to make us run again. We wearily trudged inside, shaking our heads at one another and wondering what other treats lay in store for us. The sergeant had rammed his point home that he was king of the castle, and we had better bloody well get used to it or else.

I was shocked and disturbed by how hard the mad dash across the backfield had been. When all was said and done, it was only a few hundred metres, and I shouldn't have been so tired. I turned it over in my mind, before concluding that it must have been the shock of unexpected exertion on the human body – after all, everyone had been pretty fucked after it. If that was the kind of treatment we could expect, I reasoned that I had better switch on pretty quickly.

After an hour of hanging around our accommodation block, we were introduced to our section commanders. These were young corporals in their mid-20s who were tasked with controlling our every move. We were split down into four sections, each section comprising an eight-man team controlled by a corporal.

My section commander would be a Corporal (Cpl.) Rowley. I was pleased about this as I got a good vibe off him and sensed that he would be a fair man. He was a big bloke and had a stern countenance, but I had seen how he interacted with some of the lads, and I felt he would be a good teacher. In contrast, some of the other corporals looked positively psychotic, and I felt we had had a lucky escape.

The platoon sergeant would be in command of the corporals, and he in turn would answer to the platoon commander – in our case a Lieutenant (Lt.) Mercer. We didn't meet the officer until late in the day, when he called us into the corridor to give us our platoon details.

Lt. Mercer began his chat by telling us a little of his own story and how it served as an example of what we could achieve if we buckled down. He was a native of New Zealand and had joined the RGJ seven years previously. He had joined up as a private soldier, just like us, and after passing out from this very same camp, he had served as a rifleman in the ranks for two years. And now here he was five years later back as an officer. Approach the course with an open mind seemed to be his message.

I was impressed by his story, even if I did feel he over-egged it a little. Looking around me, I thought there were only a couple of blokes capable of replicating his feat in our platoon, but I suppose it is better to give hope to soldiers than nothing at all. At least he wasn't born with a silver spoon in his mouth and would be able to understand the problems we faced.

The course we were about to begin was known as the Combat Infantryman's Course (CIC). The first phase at Winchester would last for 12 weeks and would teach us the basic skills of infantry soldiering. The second phase would be delivered at Catterick Garrison, where we would learn more advanced tactics over another 12-week period. Lt. Mercer cautioned us that we were facing 24 weeks of the hardest basic training the army had to offer, and we were to be under no illusions, it was a fucking tough course to pass.

We were christened Peninsula Platoon after a famous Green Jacket victory. It was a custom that all RGJ platoons were named after a famous battle. The barracks were called the Sir John Moore Barracks, after the great general who founded the regiment. Other regiments and corps shared the barracks' training facilities with us, but we were instructed to look down on them and strut about as if we owned the place. Winchester was celebrated as the spiritual home of the Green Jackets, and Lt. Mercer told us to revel in the honour of being the barracks' finest recruits. We also enjoyed an enhanced status on camp as we were the only infantry troops based there. The only exception to this was the Light Infantry recruits from our sister regiment. We actually trained alongside each other and were encouraged to get along – but as for the rest, the general consensus was 'fuck 'em'. I was happy to go along with this, and it did help instil a sense of pride in us, but I could also see that it was the first step in the 'brain-washing' process.

The first week of the CIC was treated as an induction week. We didn't get to do any soldiering but instead endured an endless stream of health and safety lectures, regimental history lessons and mind-numbingly boring talks on military law. I have to admit, it was a bit of an anticlimax. I had been expecting to get off to a fast and furious start, just as I had with the Marines all those years ago. Apart from our muddy introduction to the backfield, we had done virtually nothing physical.

The induction week was a real puzzle, and none of us could understand why we were having it so easy. Even the sergeant was uneasy about how much slack we had, and the corporals were positively champing at the bit to thrash us. But apart from frequent threats and the occasional shove, nothing happened. We felt confused: weren't we supposed to be training to become Green Jackets?

Finally, after one fuck-up too many from our excessively relaxed platoon, the sergeant explained to us how things would soon be changing. The army had recently conducted a review of how it delivered its training packages, and several major changes had been brought in – changes he didn't approve of.

It seemed that the army had been concerned about the huge number of recruits who dropped out or started preparing to leave within the first week of training. It seemed that an unacceptably high number also picked up injuries in the first week, which accelerated the drop-out rate further. Apparently, the powers that be felt that a gentler, more gradual introduction to army discipline was better suited to these modern times.

Sgt. Rickson summed it up more succinctly: 'The army's gone fucking soft, and I can't discipline you cunts properly until you've passed the first week's training – if you can call it that, because so far all you have done is sit in a fucking classroom! But don't worry lads, we'll make up for it next week, when I intend to run you into the fucking ground!'

As much as it pained me to do so, I found myself agreeing with the sergeant's opinion, even though I knew I would feel differently when I found myself on the end of his boot. The sergeant took great pride in telling us that he had passed the CIC in the '80s, when it was a 'proper fucking course run by old-school screws, with none of this health and safety bollocks'.

It seemed that the '70s and '80s were viewed as a golden age of recruit training by anyone who was a product of that time. During those decades, instructors could afford to be a lot more brutal with recruits. There were no business-style target rates for passing out soldiers and no pressure from above to 'make the numbers up'. If a recruit wasn't performing, he could be swiftly kicked out. However, thanks to modern employment laws, that was no longer the case. In the past, if a recruit was struggling physically, he could be made to perform nightmarish PT routines – even if injured or unwilling – until he reached the required standard, but not any more. A modern-day instructor had to be able to justify any physical punishments handed out as a 'legal-beasting'. If he couldn't justify it or it was felt that his treatment was excessive, he could be severely punished himself.

The culture of violence had changed as well. Whereas in the past it was considered fairly routine to hit a failing recruit – or at the least to rough him up a bit – that too was out of date. If an instructor was caught hitting a recruit, it could end up in criminal charges and discharge from the army. Times had changed, but that didn't stop instructors of a certain age and era becoming misty eyed about the 'good old days'.

I had worked out much of this for myself as I struggled to stay awake during the various lectures. Most of it was politically correct garbage: rules and regulations that might have been fine for Civvy Street but were completely useless for training professional soldiers. As we endured lecture after lecture on 'workplace equality', 'spotting abusive behaviour' and other such tripe, I began to wonder if I was in the army or social services. The corporals joked that by the end of the week we would be awarded meaningless National Vocational Qualifications on 'how to sit down in a non-offensive manner'.

The first week ended with the dreaded 'kit issue'. It was a laborious process and culminated in each man finding that he had a mountain of kit that he had no idea what to do with. We were assured that by the end of 12 weeks we would know this kit better than our own bodies, but as I stood looking at the jumbled green mountain, I had my doubts. Wearily I began sifting through the many items, trying and failing to jam them into my locker in some kind of military fashion. Suddenly, a loud cry reverberated through the block: 'McLaughlin. Office. Now!'

I rushed to the office like a madman, wondering what I had done to incur the sergeant's wrath. When I got there, I found the entire training team looking at me with puzzled expressions on their faces. I hadn't the faintest idea what they were peeved about – but perhaps I should have guessed.

'McLaughlin, I have just been looking at your file, and it says you're 30 fucking years old. How can that be? Not only that but I've also checked out your background – you've got exams coming out of your fucking ears. What's going on?'

I stood stock still, not knowing what to say and feeling acutely embarrassed. In truth, I was surprised that the sergeant hadn't questioned me about this earlier. 'I'm not sure what you mean, Sgt. Yes, I am 30. I managed to get special permission to join.'

'Not sure what I mean? Well, fuck me, McLaughlin, you're nearly as old as me! How do you feel about running around with a bunch of teenagers or having a 25-year-old corporal tell you what to do?'

'I don't have a problem with it, Sgt. It was my decision to join, and I am just a recruit the same as anyone else.'

A few of the corporals eyed me suspiciously and muttered amongst themselves. I could see they were concerned about me altering the group dynamics and felt uneasy about my presence. For my part, I felt about as welcome as a dose of clap. I had been careful to address the sergeant with the correct respect, and I was anxious for him to accept me as just another 'crowbag'. Despite his hot temper and sullen demeanour, I sensed that he was a fair-minded man. He sighed and put his head in his hands as if he wasn't sure what to do with me. Finally, he sat up and said, 'Right McLaughlin, understand this: you might like to think of yourself as a young man in Civvy Street. You might like to think of yourself as a fit bloke amongst your mates. But let me tell you something. For a soldier you are middle aged. Most blokes your age have got ten years in. For a recruit you are absolutely fucking ancient! I have never, ever, come across a crow as old as you. That said, you're in my fucking platoon now. Don't fuck up, don't fall behind and don't expect any special treatment.'

As I trudged back to my chaotic bed-space, I breathed a sigh of relief. At least my age was out in the open, and at least I knew where I stood. Looking around me at some of the disorganised and scruffy recruits, I began to feel that my maturity would give me a big advantage.

We had been warned that the course didn't really start until the second week, and I knew that it was going to get very hard, very quickly. There had been a lot of laughter during the first week, and it didn't sit well with the instructors. My instincts told me that before the end of the second there would be more than a few tears. Some of these lads had never been away from home before, and I doubted many took the sergeant's threats of coming hardships seriously. The sergeant might not be able to thrash us to within an inch of our lives anymore, but there were still plenty of perfectly legal and exhausting punishments he could devise for us. And I didn't doubt for a second that he would.

Most of the lads in Peninsula Platoon seemed a capable bunch. The average age was about 18, with a few 'oldies' in their 20s thrown in. I wasn't considered an oldie – I had my own special category that was off the scale! The one common factor amongst the recruits was a veneer of toughness. By and large, they were streetwise kids from poor or working-class backgrounds. They might not have had much upstairs academically, but most were quick and motivated learners, in possession of a different kind of brightness than is found in the classroom.

In other words, just the kind of lads that have been serving the infantry for hundreds of years. Lads who had failed at school and were looking for a second chance. Lads who preferred to let their actions speak louder than words. Lads with chips on their shoulders and something to prove. Lads who had been forced into the army by parents. Lads who felt they couldn't succeed at anything else. Lads trying to escape from abusive backgrounds. Lads like me whose motivations defied description and all common sense. Lads who should have known better.

So, on the whole, a good bunch of blokes with some solid potential. But, even in those early stages, I could already see different strengths and weaknesses emerging. There were certain characters I hoped I'd get the chance to work with, but, equally, there were certain lads whom I avoided like the plague. Burtle was one such lad.

I first noticed Burtle when we did our gut-busting sprints on the backfield. I had been doing my very best to stay in front, going so far as to shoulder barge and elbow rivals out of the way. Amid all the swearing and spitting, I could hear a loud cackle. It sounded like a mad hyena and seemed completely out of place. My gaze fell on a round-shouldered, dwarf-like figure who didn't so much run as lope like an overgrown chimp.

Aside from his shocking appearance, the thing that amazed me was his fitness. Despite his awkward gait, he shot past us like a bullet and easily finished first. Not only that, he didn't even appear tired. While we were all puking up and quivering like jelly, Burtle just stood there with a manic grin on his face, saliva glistening on his cheeks. The guy looked like an inbred hillbilly. After working with Burtle for a week, I was glad that he hadn't ended up in my section. I think the whole platoon was thinking the same.

Dougie was another character from the platoon whom I shall never forget, but this time for positive reasons. We hit it off straight away and had much in common. Dougie was a fanatical body builder who had worked as a bouncer on the Glasgow doors. Like me, he had grown tired of the game and gone back to college, graduating in business studies. He was 26 years old and had been marked down as a potential future officer in his application. Like me, he was looking for a challenge and felt the RGJ would be a good testing ground.

One of his great strengths was that he had a quietness and calmness about him, giving an impression of a sharp intelligence and understanding. But he was in a strange place – as was I – and I wondered if the army would value his qualities. It seemed to me that many of the NCOs I met had a very aggressive, 'live for the moment' attitude. I know a lot of it was put on for show to frighten recruits, but I got the impression some really believed in it. The NCOs would accept intellectual qualities in an officer, but I imagined they would not tolerate them in a recruit.

A problem I shared with Dougie was that we both displayed the personality traits of officers – which is fine if you're an officer but a problem if you're not. From a purely soldiering perspective, we were no better than any of our fellow 'crowbags'. But because of our ages and backgrounds, we had a bit too much maturity, education and confidence for the NCOs' liking.

A 'depot-screw', as a corporal instructor is known, likes to completely dominate his charges. One of his most effective teaching tools is to physically intimidate younger and weaker recruits. It is not bullying but rather a proven system of training rough and ready lads that has been used for decades. Problems can occur when the recruit being taught is too big or too mature to let himself be intimidated. The recruit respectfully does as he is told, but there can be an awful tension in the air and often resentment from the NCO, too.

Both Dougie and I were worried about our positions in the

platoon. It felt like a catch-22 situation – we were not quite qualified enough to be officers but were a bit over-educated for recruits. We felt like we were in a weird kind of limbo, and it was an uncomfortable place to be.

The mood in the platoon was lightened by a contingent of lads from Fiji. They were all beefy types and rugby fanatics, as well as incessant practical jokers. The Fijians made good recruits and had a team spirit that could not be broken. For a Fijian to join the British Army was considered a great honour, and many of them carried the hopes and dreams of their entire village on their backs. To fail would be considered both a personal and a family disgrace – not to mention letting down your fellow Fijian recruits.

The Fijians came from a warrior culture that prized physical performance above all other virtues. They weren't treated any differently to the rest of us, but if one of them had a problem, the instructors often let the senior Fijians sort it out. This was an effective tool, because a Fijian recruit could often go further in disciplining a fellow Fijian than an NCO could. There would be no comebacks, no complaints and the underperforming recruit was certain to pull his socks up. If it required a blind eye being turned to a bit of rough and tumble, then so be it – everybody was happy.

In our platoon, the senior Fijian was a beanpole-like figure named Tabuk. Most of the Fijians had the squat powerful physiques typical of Polynesian genes, but somehow Tabuk had sprouted to well over 6 ft and had the lean build of a marathon runner. He held the tribal rank of 'Chief' which meant all the other Fijians had to follow his example and come to him with any problems.

Tabuk took his role very seriously; in everything he did he gave 100 per cent and did his very best. If he made a mistake, he wore a fearsome scowl that told you to keep away, but, equally, you knew when he was happy, as his infectious laughter would boom around the accommodation block.

If the Fijians were the champions of team spirit, then hot on their heals were the South Africans. Every platoon on camp seemed to have a gang of Afrikaners in it. When it came down to pure soldiering skills, the Afrikaners enjoyed the reputation of being the best around. It puzzled and infuriated us Brits whenever we saw yet another Afrikaner claiming the best recruit or best marksman prize. They seemed to have a permanent lock on the trophies.

I think the secret of the Afrikaners was their backgrounds, as most of them had grown up in rugged surroundings where hunting, shooting and fishing were regular weekend pastimes. Like the Fijians, they had also grown up playing rugby, and they had the same national pride that many of us Brits lacked. They also had great adaptability of mind – many of them had grown up in admittedly racist backgrounds, yet here in Britain they put it behind them and made good friends with everyone.

You often hear it said that the army is a racist institution that doesn't attract enough minority recruits. Well I could see for myself after just one week in the army that that argument was bullshit. I don't know from what or where the detractors compile their statistics, but they do give the wrong impression. As much as a third of my platoon was of ethnic minority origin. A huge number came from Commonwealth states, so perhaps the statisticians don't include them in their figures. But whatever the truth, there was an abundance of different races at ATR Winchester.

We never had any problem or issues with racial tension the whole time I was there. If a recruit fucked up, he was treated like a piece of shit whatever his colour. In the words of one instructor, we were all 'equally shit' – that sounds fair enough to me.

The only tensions we did have to be wary of were occasional disputes with the Jamaican recruits. The Jamaicans were far more individualistic and proud than any of the other Commonwealth lads. They had a big thing about 'personal respect' and giving them their 'personal space'. You didn't really join in with their conversations unless they explicitly invited you to. It wasn't that they were hostile, but more that they came from a community where you have to earn one another's trust to be fully accepted. Whereas the Fijians were warm and open, the Jamaicans could be surly and aggressive if you barged in uninvited. You just had to be a bit more wary and sensitive to their moods.

Week two began with a bang. We were woken up at 5 a.m. with shouts and screams of 'No more Mr Fucking Nice Guy' from the sergeant and his screws. It was made crystal clear that from now on the real training would begin. Still half asleep and reeling from shock, we ran through the showers and shaved at face-ripping speed. The whole time we were getting washed, the screws were manically screaming 'Faster, faster' and banging on the wall with someone's boot. The intention was to disorientate and panic us – it certainly worked.

Each section was assigned a 'block job', which roughly translated to cleaning the whole block as if the Queen was paying us a personal visit. Of course, it was never good enough, and every time a solitary pube was discovered in the bogs, or a smudge on the wall, the manic shouting would begin again. It took us two hours to get it so the instructors were at least half happy, and then we were marched to the scoff house to wolf down our breakfasts.

Scoff was always a ludicrously hurried affair. We were supposed to have half an hour to finish our meals but were lucky if we got ten minutes. Meals would be gulped down in an animal-like fashion, and then we would run outside and form up to be marched back to the block. It was bloody awful because you always felt sick and had to constantly swallow to stop your meals from coming back up.

The second week was one of intensive rifle drills and fitness tests. We were introduced to the SA80 assault rifle and began lessons on how to operate it, strip it down and clean it. I was shocked at how complex the thing was – it broke down into more parts than a kid's jigsaw. I had presumed the rifle split into two like a shotgun and would just have a few simple mechanisms to clean. Boy was I wrong on that one. The rifle was more like a small engine than a gun – springs, bolts and screws fell out of it like confetti. It was a seriously complex weapon.

I had a hard time keeping up with the rifle-training lessons, and it seemed there was a huge amount of technical information to remember in a short time. Each lesson would get progressively more difficult until we could perform the weapon-handling drills with speed and confidence. One aspect of it that pleased me was how rigidly safety drills, known as normal safety procedures (NSP), were enforced. If you made a mistake, you could expect a hefty boot in the arse or a 100 press-ups. I didn't mind that, because I didn't want some gung-ho kid stupidly shooting me in the back. I had already spotted a few Rambo wannabes who viewed the rifle as a big toy, and I didn't fancy popping up in their sights.

The fitness tests threw up some surprises. I had desperately wanted to come first in the runs but had to concede that some of the other recruits were better than me. I was undoubtedly one of the best, but it galled me that some teenager could outpace me when I had ten years of hard training in my legs. One lad in particular stunned even the PTIs with his brilliant running. Cross was a burly 19 year old from Newcastle who resembled a prop-forward more than an athlete. When he began training, he had a puffy face and round belly, and as soon as I saw him, I pegged him down as one who would struggle physically.

We had an endurance run most mornings and were advised to watch what we ate – lest it end up on the pavement. Cross ignored this and made a ritual of consuming a massive breakfast. Nothing was spared from his plate – fried bread, a greasy fry-up, a mountain of porridge. All of this bloating scoff just 20 minutes before a hard run. The first time I saw him do it, I asked him if he was mad. With porridge dribbling down his chin he spat out his reply in his Geordie accent: 'Wahey man – ya need scoff to run. It's you that's daft!'

It appeared he was right. The man was like a steam train. Chunky legs pumped up and down like powerful pistons as he steamed off into the distance at a machine-like pace. Nobody in the platoon could get close to him, not even the PTIs, who were pissed off at his antics. Normally, the PTIs enjoyed setting a ferocious pace that stretched us to our limits. They liked to see us struggle and fight to catch up with them. When we did catch them they would berate us mercilessly about how unfit we were and how easily they could leave us behind.

The problem Cross presented was that he turned the normal order on its head. As a PTI bolted off into the distance he would stick to him like glue. Subconsciously, the offended PTI would raise the pace to 'teach him a lesson', not realising he was getting into a race he couldn't win. At the end of it, we would suffer as a red-faced, wheezing PTI made us pay for his embarrassment with hundreds of press-ups and sit-ups. After a week of Cross thrashing every PTI foolish enough to challenge him, they conceded defeat. Cross was ordered to run at the back and assist the stragglers, but everybody knew it was so the PTIs could save face.

I was fascinated how a chubby youngster like Cross could run so phenomenally, especially as he had received no specialist training. He was mystified about it himself. He told me that when he was a schoolboy his PE teacher had taken him along to a track meet for nationally ranked junior runners. His teacher managed to get him a slot in a spare lane. He came second in the race, being narrowly beaten by the British champion who had five years' professional coaching to his name. Cross said the winner looked pissed off that an overweight novice had almost come first.

The frustrating thing about Cross was that when he told me this story he didn't seem to see anything unusual in it – he knew in his heart that nobody could run like he could, so what was the big deal? I told him that he had a rare and unique gift and should lose some weight and get serious with himself while he still had time. Cross grinned and fobbed me off – he liked his food and beer too much to waste time chasing medals on a racetrack.

During the first few weeks of basic training, we also had our first introduction to the drill square. Learning to march is no easy task and many a grudge began whilst we were marching. Before we even took a step, we had to pass a uniform inspection in which we were expected to be immaculate. The inspections always ended in a predictable display of calculated hysteria from Sgt. Rickson or one of his screws. The slightest crease or speck of muck would trigger a raging torrent of abuse. The offender would be accused of every crime under the sun and marched off to the guardroom for an hour to reflect on his inadequacy.

I learned early on that the secret to getting in the instructors' good books was to never show emotion when you were being bollocked. No matter how unpleasant the punishment, and even if you were innocent of the 'crime', the best way to cope was to stare straight ahead and say, 'Yes Sir, no Sir.'

Occasionally, a recruit would try and argue back, and this would result in some hilarious confrontations. It was hard not to laugh sometimes at the ridiculousness of it all. The sergeant would put his nose about one inch from the offender's and scream in his face like a madman. He would tremble with rage and issue threats about tearing the recruit's face off or rearranging his brain tissue. Even though he had no intention of carrying out his threats, he was very convincing, and it made great theatre. Unfortunately, some of the younger guys took him at his word and were genuinely terrified.

The marching itself was often an ordeal, too. I actually felt sorry for the instructors, as I can think of few tasks harder than teaching recruits to march. Unfortunately, there were no shortcuts; the only way to learn was from endless repetition. It is a skill that you have to get wrong before you can get it right. Although we all struggled and had our fair share of beastings, the one man who stood out as impossible to teach was Burtle.

It is said that in any random batch of recruits you will always get at least one person who is incredibly slow. Burtle was one such person. Whatever task he was set, he would distinguish himself by failing spectacularly. He particularly shone on the parade ground. At first, Sgt. Rickson tried his usual tactics of blood and thunder. But even these did not work as there are only so many press-ups a man can do and only so many times he can bunny-hop around the drill square.

After exhausting his voice and patience with the traditional approach, the sergeant switched to a Mr Nice Guy routine. When we saw him trying to coax and soothe Burtle through the motions, we knew the sergeant was desperate. It didn't last long. The problem was Burtle could barely walk normally, never mind march smartly. Inevitably, the sergeant would throw his pace stick up into the air and begin screaming and shouting.

For Burtle, who was actually quite a nice kid at heart, the drill lessons dissolved into a never-ending nightmare. While the rest of us were marching off the square to our next lesson or looking forward to the day's end, poor old Burtle would be putting in hours of extra drill practice. The tragedy was that he simply couldn't get any better. It was like asking an average person to fly a space shuttle: it was beyond him.

The sergeant even arranged lessons for him with a different instructor, feeling that perhaps his methods had spooked Burtle into terminal decline. But nothing worked, no matter what was tried.

And it wasn't just marching – Burtle was falling behind in every area except physical fitness. Sgt. Rickson told him that unless there was a dramatic improvement in his performance, he was out of the platoon. But the sergeant was a fair man and wanted him to succeed, so he told Burtle that he would be assigning him a 'helper' to watch over him. He hadn't decided who the helper would be, but he assured Burtle that he would soon have one of the best recruits looking after him. He also added that the helper would be held equally responsible for any of Burtle's fuck-ups, so he would have a good incentive to help him out.

A chill spread through the platoon, because nobody wanted to put their head on the block next to Burtle's. The truth was we were all starting to find it a struggle – even the so-called strong recruits. We were working like dogs as it was, often ironing kit, studying maps, revising lessons and preparing lockers into the early hours of the morning. We looked like the walking dead and were dropping weight like candidates for a Weight Watchers' 'slimmer of the year' award. Whichever poor bastard took on Burtle's load might as well not bother sleeping at all.

As the days sped by, we speculated on who might get the dreaded call to baby-sit him. I knew that on account of our ages and maturity, it would be either Dougie or me. Selfishly, neither of us wanted it, and whenever we encountered the sergeant, we did our best to disappear from view.

A short while after, we were ironing kit when a gruff voice yelled down the corridor,

'Dougie, office, now, and bring Burtle with you.' As was the custom when called, the pair of them dashed down the corridor at top speed, bouncing frantically off the narrow walls. I glanced at Tabuk; we exchanged relieved looks, and I resignedly resumed my ironing. Dougie's life had just got immeasurably harder.

There is a myth that is endlessly perpetuated by army recruiters about basic training being all about teamwork. That is bullshit. While there is obviously a teamwork element to everything you do, and it is encouraged, the cold reality of recruit life is that you are on your own. It is a highly competitive wolf-pack atmosphere, where the survival of the fittest is the order of the day. You are frequently pitted against each other, and while you do hear the words 'teamwork' spoken occasionally, you hear a hell of a lot more about 'individual responsibility'. The reality is that most of the time you are struggling to control your own body and emotions. People get tense and irritable, and when a member of the team isn't performing, the likelihood is that the pack will turn on him and cast him out. Recruits tend to be a selfish and miserable lot, because the pressures of training make them so.

Any team member who requires constant coaching and supervision, who frequently gets the platoon into trouble or is forever whining and complaining, isn't going to get help. More than likely, a gang of disgruntled and resentful recruits will drag him into the laundry room and beat the shit out of him. Or they will tip him out of bed while he is sleeping and, with the mattress on top of him, use him as a trampoline. Great care will be taken that no NCOs are about – and even if they are, a blind eye can always be turned.

So you can imagine how Dougie felt when he got the news he was now Burtle's official minder. To say he was pissed off would be an understatement. To his credit, I knew Dougie would do his very best to help Burtle, but I also knew it was a hopeless task. Things got off to the worst possible start.

The sergeant called us altogether and informed us that at 5 a.m. the next morning we would be having a locker inspection. All our kit had to be sparkling clean and utterly spotless, with no exceptions or excuses. Before he left us for the night, he made a point of telling Dougie to make sure Burtle's locker was immaculate.

We knew we would be up all night, but none of us was unduly bothered, as we were used to it by that point. In fact, those long nights preparing kit were often fun-packed affairs, despite the grinding tedium of the task at hand. Ghetto-blasters would come out, and blazing house music would rumble through the block. Frequently, arm-wrestling contests or wrestling matches would spontaneously occur, and everyone would gather round and cheer. If we had time, we would rush across to the NAAFI (Navy, Army and Air Force Institutes) shop and load up on treats or raid the burger bar and stuff ourselves sick.

So, despite the mountain of hard work to be done, we made it bearable by having great camaraderie and a good laugh as we went along. Although we were having a riotous time, we were also working at a ferocious pace and getting the task done. All of us that is except Burtle.

Dougie made the fatal mistake of trusting Burtle and taking him at his word. Early in the evening, Dougie had approached Burtle and made sure that he understood what he had to do. He even went so far as to demonstrate how to prepare the locker for inspection, and, to help his charge along, he ironed some of his kit for him – even before the older man had touched his own. Satisfied that Burtle was off to a good start, Dougie left him alone, with explicit instructions to find him if he got stuck on anything or was falling behind. Burtle waved him off enthusiastically and told him not to worry – he wouldn't let him down. Looking uneasy, Dougie went off and started on his own kit.

I couldn't help but notice that whenever a joke was being played or a story being told, Burtle was always at the centre of it. I could hear his manic laughter above all others, but, unlike the rest of us, I never saw him actually doing any work. He would be sat on his bed scoffing burgers or running about like a kid in playschool. Whenever Dougie popped his head in and asked if he was all right, Burtle would make a show of fussing over his locker and tell him it was going fine. We should have guessed it was all a bluff.

The next morning we were standing by our beds in immaculately pressed uniforms, boots shining and eyes ringed with dark circles. To try and catch us out, the sergeant had appeared 15 minutes early and ordered us to stand by our beds with our lockers open. All of us did as we were told – all except for Burtle. For some reason, his locker remained firmly closed. The sergeant had decreed total silence, so other than threatening him with our eyes, we couldn't make him open it up.

The sergeant's team of screws were with him, and Lt. Mercer stood impassively alongside him. 'Stand by your fucking beds,' hissed the sergeant. He turned sharply to his left to begin his inspection, but suddenly took a step back and swivelled towards Burtle. Swiftly, and with considerable menace, he strode towards him, stopping barely an inch from Burtle's face. In a calm voice, but one clearly tight with fury, the sergeant asked Burtle why his locker wasn't open. Burtle's response was to stare mutely at the floor and look ashamed. 'Dougie, get your fucking arse in here. Take the key from Burtle and open his locker. He seems to have gone deaf as well as dumb.'

Dougie took the key from Burtle's palm and started to open the locker. All eyes strained toward it – we knew this would be too good to miss. As Dougie opened it, a pair of muddy boots fell onto his face, swiftly followed by an overflowing canvas wash bag. A stunned silence filled the room; even the sergeant was temporarily lost for words.

The locker was a complete disgrace and a glowing testament to Burtle's appalling hygiene and complete lack of understanding. Crumpled clothes hung off bent wire hangers. Wet towels and open toothpaste tubes were stuffed on cluttered shelves. Soiled underwear and odd socks battled for primacy in the chaotic space. A solitary bottle of half-drunk Coke stood proudly alongside mess tins. But best of all, and utterly unbelievable, were the half-eaten sandwiches and burger wrappers that littered his shelves.

As he waited for the inevitable explosion, Dougie just had time to let out a short gasp and mutter, 'Fucking hell.'

'Get outside, get outside, you two, get fucking outside!' The guilty pair bolted outside and the sergeant ran after them without so much as a glance in our direction.

As they came to a stop on the grass opposite our window, we strained to see what was going on. Both recruits were in the press-up position, and the sergeant stood over them. On his count, they had to go all the way down – in this instance, all the way meaning nose into the mud – and spring back up again. This was followed by a round of burpees and leg raises, all designed to cause maximum discomfort and pain. To finish off, they had to sprint across the field and back a dozen times, and every time the sergeant shouted 'grenade', they had to hit the dirt and crawl forward. What must have been doubly galling for Dougie, who was innocent in all this, was that Burtle was much fitter than he was and seemed to cope with it better.

While this torture was going on, an NCO began to rearrange Burtle's locker. Every single piece of equipment he found was systematically thrown out of the window. All of Burtle's shirts and trousers were put under the NCO's heels and ground into the floor – first inside, then outside in the mud. Toothpaste and soap were smeared on his shelves, and Coke was poured all over his bedding. The NCO was so engrossed in the destruction of the locker that he didn't even bother to inspect ours.

Eventually things calmed down, and the offenders marched back into the lines, still spitting out grass and wiping mud from their eyes. If we thought the whole episode was over, we were sorely mistaken.

The sergeant coolly strode into our room and surveyed the chaos. 'OK, fellas, no dramas. Obviously you misunderstood me when I said I wanted an immaculate inspection. Obviously Dougie is too stupid to follow basic instructions. We will have a special inspection of Burtle's locker in one hour – and this time it had better be right.'

For the next hour, the entire platoon frantically rushed around Burtle's locker in a desperate effort to straighten it out. We knew that we would all be beasted if it wasn't sorted, and having seen the sergeant's mood, none of us wanted to take the chance. As one person scrubbed the dirt out of Burtle's shirts another would hastily iron the still dripping wet garment. We set about polishing his boots and shining his brass, all the while cursing him under our breath.

We were severely pissed off at Burtle, so much so that whenever he offered to help he would be flung out of the way and told to fuck off. We couldn't trust him to do anything and made it clear he wasn't welcome. Out of sheer spite and anger, we threw his filthy underwear in the bin, rather than give it to him to wash. We were especially pissed off for Dougie's sake, and when he offered to help, we told him to relax and sit on his bed – he deserved the rest.

The repeat inspection passed off without incident, but the sergeant made it publicly known to Burtle that if he didn't buck up his ideas, he would be out of the platoon. I doubted his warning would make much difference.

The sergeant's threat wasn't an idle one, and it was something we all lived in fear of. Once a fortnight, a recruit's performance would be reviewed, and if it wasn't up to scratch, he would be 'back-squadded'.

Back-squadding meant a recruit was ejected from his platoon and placed in a more junior one. The idea was that he would pick up the skills he was lacking by being taught them a second time. The process carried a huge stigma with it, and no matter how the army dressed it up, the reality was it was considered to be a major sign of weakness and failing.

As each week of the course sped by, we were stretched further. The physical fitness side became almost unbearable. Often we would have a double dose of PT: gym work in the mornings followed by a cross-country run in the afternoon. The worst aspect of it was that PT always seemed to come straight after a meal, so you would be fighting nausea as well as fatigue.

After two weeks at ATR Winchester, we had our first proper exercise in the field, known as 'first night'. It was really just an introduction to sleeping out under the stars, but it marked the beginning of a more serious phase in the training. All of a sudden, we had to learn how to build shelters, how to keep clean and dry in the wet, how to patrol in the classic 'four-man-brick' formation, as well as various other survival skills.

I loved getting out into the field and learning about field craft – at long last, it felt like we were becoming soldiers. It was also good to see the skills that the instructors possessed and how seriously they took their jobs. Despite all of the shouting, threats and punishments that we had to endure as part of our daily lives, when we were out in the woods, there was a pleasant feeling of the torch being passed on to the next generation of soldiers.

Sometimes the sergeant would gather us round him for an in-depth explanation of the finer points of soldiering. It would be midnight under a glorious full moon, with a chill breeze blowing through the trees and no sound other than the sergeant's whisper. All our eyes would be on him, our attention held rapt, as he talked us through a planned attack or demonstrated how to move silently through the bushes. His professionalism and pride in his work made us want to please him, to become like him, and it made us forget about the endless bullshit of inspections and parades. This was what being a soldier was all about: being out in the field and learning how to do the business.

As I clumsily clattered about the forest, getting entangled in bushes and tripping over roots, I couldn't help but notice how naturally the instructors blended into their environment. They seemed so cool, calm and utterly at ease with themselves, like creatures of the night. I wondered if I would ever reach the same standard.

If going out on exercise symbolised the high point of our training, then there is no doubt what symbolised the low point – training for the threats of Nuclear, Biological and Chemical Warfare (NBC) was an experience loathed by recruits and instructors in equal measure.

Basically, all it boiled down to was learning how to put on an S10 Respirator (gas mask) in ten seconds flat, in the event of an NBC strike. Preceding this we had numerous lectures about the horrible effects of deadly toxins and how quickly we could expect to die if exposed to them. If we suspected an NBC threat was present, we had to put on a cumbersome 'over suit' and waddle around like ducks. The effect of the suit was like being cooked inside an oven, and sweat would pour off our heavily laden bodies – we looked like Michelin men.

The culmination of our NBC training was the dreaded gas-chamber drill, in which we would be submitted to a live CS gas exposure. The purpose of it was to familiarise us with how it felt and also to make us take the threat seriously. Anyone who has been in the CS chamber will testify to it being an unforgettable experience.

We split up into groups of five and lined up outside the chamber. The chamber was an innocent-looking little place, not unlike a small garden shed; it was made of grey stone and had a large window in the door. You entered the chamber as a group, already wearing your mask and suit. Once you were in there, an NCO would release CS gas and close the door. After a while, he would order you to take your mask off and tell him your name, rank and number – then he would let you go.

It all sounded pretty easy to me: at the most you would only be exposed to the gas for a few seconds, so I didn't anticipate a problem. I remembered seeing CS gas being fired on rowdy crowds at demonstrations, and it didn't seem to bother the civilians too much. I knew some lads were shitting it, but I felt quietly confident. I volunteered to be amongst the first in as I felt it would be a piece of cake and wanted to set an example for the rest of the boys.

An NCO led us into the chamber, and as the door was bolted behind us, wispy gas was already filling the room. We had to walk around in a circle and swing our arms and nod our heads in answer to a series of stupid questions. It was a complete doddle and all of us in the chamber had a confident swagger and appearance of total control. Then we were told to take our masks off.

The NCO stood square in front of the doorway to block any means of escape. Via a series of pre-arranged hand signals and muffled grunts, the first man was ordered to take his mask off. We had formed an orderly queue behind him and were curious what his reaction would be. By then, a thick swirl of gas permeated every inch of the chamber and hung in a menacing cloud.

Tentatively he removed his mask and stood facing the NCO. As instructed, he went to give his name, rank and number – only no sound came out. Instead, his face grew a deep shade of purple, and he bent double, sputtering and retching on the floor. If he had expected sympathy, he was sorely mistaken – the NCO roughly hauled him up and repeated his order. By that point, the instructor was supporting him by his elbows, blocking his exit and still demanding his regimental details.

Somewhere from deep within he dragged the numbers up – spitting out the answer in an anguished rasp. Once he had his information, the instructor opened the door and roughly booted him out. I just caught sight of him collapsing in a heap before the door was slammed shut again.

'Fucking hell! I hope that was just a freak reaction,' I worriedly thought to myself. I had been next in line to go forward, but I managed to slink back a bit, and another lad was dragged up instead.

The unfortunate recruit about to take his mask off next was one of the best in our section and definitely not prone to panicking. His reaction would give me a truer picture of how bad the test really was. I expected him to sail it, just as he sailed most things we did. I was wrong.

'Please, Cpl., get me out of here; I can't handle this.' The voice was that of a frightened little child, pleading desperately to be spared. It was completely at odds with the big body from which it came.

'Fucking hell', I mumbled to myself in my respirator.

He had only just taken his mask off and already he was begging to be let out. He wasn't convulsing and retching wildly like the first man, but in its own way, his reaction was more disturbing. There was genuine fear and despair in his voice, whereas the other lad's reaction had been more instinctive and biological. Somehow he found the words and was unceremoniously flung out of the door. Then it was my turn.

I hesitated before taking my mask off, as I knew it was going to be bad. But I did feel a glimmer of hope, and I reasoned with myself that I was at an advantage compared to the others. I told myself that they had been caught off guard, whereas I had had time to prepare myself mentally. As ridiculous as it may sound, my main worry was about embarrassing myself in front of the corporal. I didn't want him to see any fear or weakness in me – I didn't want to give him that pleasure. But I also knew that the gas could play tricks on you and turn you into a blubbering coward. I would need a strategy if I was to pass the test without looking a complete prick.

I decided that no matter what happened I would concentrate purely on blurting out my regimental details as quickly as possible. Any other questions put to me I would simply ignore, and I would also hold my breath until after I had gotten the words out.

A sharp slap to the head woke me up and reminded me that it was time to take off the mask. In one swift motion, I removed it and faced the corporal. I paused and stared at him, neither breathing in nor out.

Instantly, my eyes began to run and sting as if handfuls of sand were being poured into them. It was a struggle to stay upright, and I had to fight the urge to rub them wildly. An unstoppable wave of nausea and claustrophobia came rushing upwards from my feet. All this and I hadn't even taken a breath!

I realised that I had better get the words out quickly before I began to lose it completely: 'Rifleman McLaughlin, 25146756 Royal Green Jackets, Cpl.!'

The words raced out of my mouth, but were more of a whimper

than a bark. I turned to walk past the corporal and get out of the chamber, but he sidestepped in front of me and gripped my elbows hard. I could see the bastard's eyes grinning behind his mask as he guided me to the centre of the room. I still hadn't drawn breath by that point, and I was fit to burst. The corporal felt that I was cheating and wagged his finger reproachfully. A few seconds more and I had no choice but to take in a lungful of the choking gas.

It is hard to describe how a large inhalation of CS feels, but its effects are devastating. My skin felt boiling hot and itchy, almost like it was about to burst. My throat felt like a hot poker had just been rammed down it. My belly felt as if it had taken a shot from Mike Tyson, and all of the air completely drained out of me. My mouth gaped open like a fish, and my eyes felt like they were falling out of their sockets. And all of this at the same time.

But the corporal wasn't finished yet – he made me repeat my details once more. Somehow I got the words out, but he still wasn't finished. Before I could leave, he wanted me to draw in one last deep breath. I considered shoulder barging past him but decided against it. He would only have dragged me back in anyway. Fuck it. Abandoning my body to his will, I forced myself to take one last drag. That seemed to satisfy him, and he patted me on the back to leave. But I couldn't.

I tried to move to the doorway but felt my knees starting to buckle, my head dipping crazily towards the floor. I reached out for the handle and fumbled thin air. In what seemed like slow motion, I began to fall to the floor. Quick as a flash, the corporal was onto me, holding me up as my body slackened like a rag doll's. And then, in his usual sympathetic style, he roughly shoved me out of the door.

I landed face first in a heap on the sandy gravel. After a short pause, I struggled to my feet. The shock of the cold wind hitting me was almost as bad as the gas. I was instructed to hold my arms out like a scarecrow and head for the debriefing area. As I staggered off, the wind blew the CS particles from my eyes and caused them to sting painfully. As the CS lifted from my lungs, I had an uncontrollable urge to be sick – but nothing but saliva would come out. In common army parlance, I was in 'shit state'.

The NBC course had been a very steep learning curve for all of us, and we had learned a lot about ourselves. Namely that we weren't as tough as we thought we were. The NCOs said we hadn't done badly, and we weren't to be too hard on ourselves. The test was designed to hurt your body, but the effects of it weren't permanent or damaging.

However, the potency and disabling power of the gas, and the speed with which it overcomes you, had given us all a shock. If you're in a crowd and gas is fired, it is easy to run away from it and gulp down some fresh air. That is why it doesn't seem so bad when seen in action on TV. But when you are in a tiny airtight chamber, and the gas is given time to pollute the atmosphere, it is a different story. It is in that environment that you can feel the true power of the gas and its paralysing effect on the body. A few mouthfuls and that's you out of the game, unconscious in a heap in the corner. It is frighteningly powerful stuff.

Despite assurances from the instructors that the gas couldn't harm us, most of us were sick over the following week. I couldn't stop coughing and felt like I had torn my chest muscles. The taste of CS gas also lingered in my throat. Different people had different complaints, and I had no doubts what caused them.

During the training process, the only relief we had from physical trials came in the form of regimental history lessons. I didn't mind these as it was a chance to rest weary bones and reflect on why we were there in the first place. We learned that the Green Jackets was a regiment with many historical firsts to its name:

- We were the first true Special Forces soldiers (although this is a distinction long since lost), in that each man was specially selected for his marksmanship and soldiering skills – hence the title 'Rifleman' and the regimental nickname 'The Chosen Men'.

- We were the first soldiers to wear green camouflaged uniforms, in order to blend into the surroundings – as opposed to red-jacketed Guards regiments.
- We were the first soldiers to use tactical fire and manoeuvring, to take cover when being shot at and to work in small skirmishing teams behind enemy lines. All this at a time when the regular army was still forming up in squares and lines on the battlefield.
- We marched at a faster pace than the regular army (140 paces a minute as opposed to 120) and carried no regimental colours with us – every action we took was only concerned with travelling light and fast, with confusing and defeating the enemy.
- We had also won 57 Victoria Crosses, more than any other regiment in history.

And on and on the list of distinctions went – all constantly being drilled into us to add to our sense of superiority.

The training followed a predictable path. We were ground down and pushed to breaking point on a regular basis; then, just as we were about to hit rock bottom, we'd be picked up again and remoulded to the instructors' specifications. And they would time their respites remarkably well. After a particularly hard exercise or learning period, they would briefly ease the pressure by laying on the regimental history lessons or bringing someone special in for an inspirational chat. One platoon had Andy McNab pay them a visit, and we got to talk with the Falklands veteran Simon Weston. Another time you might be driven to Winchester to visit the regimental museum or travel to Belgium for a battlefield tour.

However, these little 'treats' weren't just mindless days out but rather integral parts of the training designed to make you want to be a part of the army even more. A cynic might say it was good old-fashioned brainwashing, but I prefer to think of it as 'carrot and stick' psychology.

By the halfway point in our training, things had gone remarkably well. As predicted, we had already lost many recruits to injuries, back-squadding and voluntary discharge. But the core that remained was pretty strong, and we moved forward with a philosophy that those who had left us had never really belonged anyway. In any case, we had no time or room for sentiment, as the pace of events meant it would have been a pointless indulgence.

The lads in my section felt particularly lucky because our section commander was one of the best around. Cpl. Rowley was an undoubtedly hard man, but, at the same time, he was scrupulously fair and even handed. If we fucked up, we suffered accordingly, but if we did well, he would generally leave us alone. He wasn't the sort to dish out praise, because that wasn't in his job description or nature, but what he did provide was crystal-clear, first-class instruction.

I actually had a good relationship with the instructors, and because of my age, they would occasionally include me in their jokes. By not asking for any special treatment, by visibly working my socks off and by being a bit of a 'grey man' (someone who quietly gets on with it), I had earned their respect.

The instructors gave me two nicknames: the first was 'Thespian', on account of my time as a drama graduate, and the second was 'Sergeant-Major', on account of my precise and crisp manner. If ever the instructors were bored, they would call me into the office and demand I recite Shakespearian text. They mercilessly took the piss out of me and did their best to embarrass me, but, at the same time, I detected a sneaking admiration that a 'crow-bag recruit' could speak such language.

Another favourite wind-up was to half-jokingly accuse me of being a 'training-wing plant' who had been sent to spy on them. Whenever we had just completed a nasty punishment, an instructor would joke about the Sergeant-Major writing secret reports and assessments on the training team.

The crazy thing was that when this Sergeant-Major routine started, they really suspected me of being an army spy. My age and military bearing caused them to be suspicious of me. At the time, there were rumblings around camp about the growing scandal at Deepcut Barracks, where several recruits had died. It was well known that, in the past, army investigations had used false recruits to catch out bullies.

Daily life got a lot harder for us when we lost Cpl. Rowley to a broken shoulder. He had gone into town to get drunk and ended up falling down a flight of stairs. This was a major loss to our section, because we had developed a good rapport with him, and in his absence, we would have to gain the respect of a totally new screw.

Before he left, Cpl. Rowley paid a visit to wish us good luck. He said he was sorry he wouldn't be around to see us pass out, but we weren't to worry as we were getting 'an absolute nutter' as a replacement. We asked him if he was joking, and he cryptically replied, 'Wait and see.' As he was about to leave, he called me aside for a private chat. I wondered what could be on his mind as it was highly unusual for an NCO to address a recruit as anything but an underling. The news he gave me was yet another of those strange coincidences that seemed to predetermine my destiny as a Green Jacket.

'McLaughlin, I wasn't going to say anything until you passed out as I don't believe in doing crows special favours. Stick with it and don't give up, you'll get there in the end. I was in basic training at Catterick with your brother seven years ago – we passed out together, and I knew him well. Best of luck to you.' And with that he was gone. I couldn't believe he had kept it to himself, but it only confirmed in my mind what a totally professional soldier he was. There were a million miles between the standing of an instructor and a recruit, and Cpl. Rowley had got it spot on by keeping it that way.

I was even more sorry to see him go when I set eyes on his replacement, a ginger-haired Welshman with a beetroot face and volcanic temper. They say that a new brush sweeps clean, and he wasted no time in imposing himself and his personality on the platoon.

Drill lessons became a particular nightmare as he made the sergeant look like Father Christmas. He liked to get in your face and stare you down. If he didn't like the look he got back, he would grab you roughly by the jaw or apply a painful nipple twister. Basically, anything he could get away with without leaving marks on you or getting himself in trouble. His method of instruction was built around fear and intimidation. As he often said to us, 'I don't want you to like me; I want you to fucking hate me.' He certainly succeeded.

One area where I incurred his wrath was on the rifle range. My shooting was by some margin the worst in the platoon. It was a skill with which I struggled greatly and had no natural affinity. Contrary to what is portrayed in popular films, accurate fire from a rifle is a difficult skill to master, and it takes months of training to learn how to use the SA80 effectively.

My ability to fire the weapon and operate it safely wasn't in doubt – it was just that I couldn't hit the bloody target! I did make some improvements, but they were slow in coming. My instructors were just as worried as I was, because if I couldn't pass the Annual Personal Weapons Test (APWT) before the 12 weeks were up, I couldn't pass out of basic training.

My poor marksmanship remained a constant source of tension with the new corporal, and he delighted in telling me I would be history if it didn't improve. It took every ounce of self-control I had not to react when he sprayed my face with spittle and jabbed his finger in my throat, screaming about how fucking useless I was.

The worrying thing was that he was right about my prospects, no matter how harshly he delivered the message. A Green Jacket that can't shoot is about as much use as a tank driver that can't drive. But if I thought I had problems, they were minor worries compared to Burtle's. He had been living on borrowed time for weeks, and all it would take was one more fuck-up to see him booted out of the platoon. He was about to make it.

In basic training you will be forgiven a lot of sins (even poor marksmanship) so long as you employ good safety procedures with your rifle. Every year, a small number of soldiers get shot during training or active operations, and all for no other reason than poor adherence to the safety drills. No mistakes or compromises are allowed when it comes to safety.

We had just finished firing some single shots down the range and were applying our safety catches. As we were laying the weapons down and preparing to unload there was a sharp burst of automatic fire. An NCO shouted, 'Cease fire, cease fire!' and the shooting stopped. All eyes turned to Burtle, as we knew it could only be him. The NCO stormed towards him with a face like thunder; he clearly intended to give Burtle a major bollocking, and we were looking forward to seeing it. Spotting the rapidly approaching NCO, Burtle jumped up and began to stammer out an apology in his infuriating Frank Spencer-style voice. As he was sputtering 'I'm sorry Cpl., I'm sorry Cpl.', another sharp burst of automatic fire ripped down the range. Burtle had been resting his finger on the trigger and had forgotten to apply his safety catch. He had also somehow managed to knock his fire-control change lever from single-shot repetition to full automatic.

The first skill you are taught when handling weapons is never to rest your finger on the trigger, no matter what the circumstances. The only time a soldier's finger should be on the trigger is when he is firing the weapon; otherwise it should be straightened out and rested above it – even in wartime. The reason for this is simple: if you ignore the safety rules, then sooner or later you will have what is known as a negligent discharge (ND) and probably kill someone on your own side. Any self-respecting soldier who is caught walking around with his finger on the trigger can at the very least expect a swift boot up the arse and a heavy dose of extra guard duty – and that would be considered a lenient punishment.

It was a typical Burtle-style mistake, but one that could have had fatal consequences. Fortunately for the corporal, Burtle's weapon wasn't pointing at him, otherwise we would have been scraping him up off the floor. Unfortunately for Burtle, he was now in the deepest shit imaginable. His rifle was snatched from him and made safe, and he was ordered to hand back his ammunition. He was then flung in the back of the wagon like a bag of spanners and driven back to camp.

For Burtle, this latest fuck-up on the rifle range was one too many, and by the time we got back to camp, he was packing his kit ready to be back-squadded. He was put back four weeks in the training programme, and that would be the last our platoon ever saw of him. As unkind as it sounds, we were all enormously relieved to see the back of him. Burtle had been like a noose around our necks and a dangerous liability.

I had been so wrapped up in my struggles on the rifle range that I hadn't considered the possibility of anything else going wrong. Everybody had at least one weakness, and for me it was shooting. I would get over it. Where I shone was in the physical arena, and although my body was covered in cuts and bruises and constantly ached, I never for one second thought it would let me down. How could it if I was one of the fittest and strongest recruits? I was about to find out.

'Tabbing' – a corruption of the term 'Tactical Advance to Battle' – is an activity I was becoming uncomfortably familiar with. Basically, it was a forced speed march during which we would double along at a ridiculous pace until told to stop. At first, we did just a couple of miles, but as our abilities increased so did the distances and the weight of the backpacks we carried.

I actually enjoyed the tabs and often found myself being ordered to the back of the group to help with the stragglers. Tabbing really separates the men from the boys and measures a soldier's true combat fitness. You often find that the skinny snake who laps you on the racetrack collapses when a heavy bergen backpack is placed on his back and he is ordered to 'get tabbing'.

On one occasion, we had only been tabbing for a couple of miles when I suddenly felt a sharp pain in my foot. It felt like I had stepped on a drawing pin or had a stone in my shoe that wouldn't go away. The more I tabbed, the more it hurt. I hadn't a clue what was wrong with me but resolved to check it out once the march was over. In any case, when I was moving it didn't feel too bad, so perhaps it was just a pinched nerve or ligament strain. I put it to the back of my mind and ignored it.

We came to a halt and began to stretch off. My foot felt red hot, almost as if it was on fire, but, strangely, I could walk on it fine. The PTI asked if there were any injuries he ought to know about before he dismissed us. I kept quiet and hoped the pain would wear off after an hour or two. Big mistake.

Within two hours I couldn't walk and had to be supported by my colleagues. Once the adrenalin had left my body and my blood returned to normal, my foot had swollen up like a turnip, and I could do nothing but lie on my bed. The sergeant came to take a look at me and sent me straight to the medical centre. I kept up a cool appearance on the outside, but inwardly I was seething. I could not believe I was injured when I had come so far without incident.

To be seriously injured is the nightmare that keeps recruits awake at night. It is the one thing that can stop your progress dead in its tracks and make an already hard life infinitely harder. You put your body under such huge stress that it is inevitable injuries will occur – but hopefully not to you. You look around camp and see groups of recruits on crutches or in plaster, and you pray you won't join them. You avoid them like the plague in case they bring you bad luck. Was I going to be one of them?

The doctor took one look at me and ordered me to be driven to a specialist clinic for a bone scan. I did a double take when I saw the address of the clinic as it gave me a sickening sense of déjà vu. It was the Royal Naval Hospital at Portsmouth: the hospital where my earlier dreams of becoming a Marine had come crashing down, the hospital that had recommended my medical discharge from the corps. Could history be repeating itself? Would this be the hospital where my hopes of becoming an infantry soldier were destroyed, too? I had felt certain about becoming a Green Jacket, but, then again, I had felt certain about becoming a Royal Marine – maybe I would become neither? Was this the end of the dream for me – once and for all?

Limping along the hospital corridors brought all of the old memories back. I told myself that if I failed again, nobody would ever be able to say I hadn't tried. But such thoughts were no consolation, and I didn't kid myself that a second medical discharge would be anything less than a devastating blow. One of my faults has always been an inflated sense of pride and self-satisfaction, and if I failed this one, I doubted I would recover from it.

The bone scan revealed a stress fracture of the foot. The doctor said it would take three months to heal and would need to be treated with great care. There was no question of me remaining in training, so as of that moment on I was 'on the sick'. The good news was that I had every chance of making a full recovery. The bad news was that if my foot didn't repair itself properly, I would be discharged from the army. I breathed a cautious sigh of relief as I realised I was being given a second chance.

However, my relief was tinged with fear as the doctor expanded on the problems I might face: my foot had broken down without reason or warning, so there might be a genetic weakness. If there was an inbuilt problem, nothing could be done to remedy it, as it was a bone deficiency, not a muscular one. If my family had a history of foot problems, it would be a good indicator of trouble ahead. I cast my mind back to Damian's gruelling struggle with injury when he was in basic training. His foot had broken twice and taken him to the brink of medical discharge. I hoped that history wasn't repeating itself.

I returned to camp and bade farewell to Peninsula Platoon. I was sorry to be saying goodbye as these were my boys, and this was my team. But I was out of it now, and soon I would be forgotten. The training routine ground on remorselessly and nobody had the time or energy for sentiment. I was particularly sorry to be leaving Tabuk and Dougie behind and told them I would meet up with them again when we made it to the battalion. I said this more for my benefit than theirs as I was trying to reassure myself that I would get there. Inside, the doubts were already forming.

3

THE CATTERICK EXPERIENCE

My time in the rehabilitation platoon was the most depressing experience of my army career. Its official title was Java Platoon, but it was universally known as 'Mong Platoon', on account of the quality of recruits passing through its doors. It had a curious mix of characters in its ranks: some were determined individuals suffering from genuine injuries, others were out-and-out charlatans looking for an easy ride.

The daily routine was fairly relaxed as it was accepted that the vast majority of recruits in Java would end up being discharged. There was a distinct lack of discipline and team spirit within the platoon – and that included the instructors, most of whom had simply given up on the recruits. I have to say that having seen some of them, it was easy to understand why they had been abandoned.

Most of the recruits in Java had about as much chance of becoming soldiers as they did Prime Minister. The vast majority were grossly unfit and hated army life, having only joined to please unhappy parents or because they had completely underestimated how tough basic training was going to be. I was pleased to note there were very few Green Jackets amongst their number, which confirmed we were made of sterner stuff. Instead, the platoon was filled with disillusioned trainee clerks, medics and airmen.

Many of the patients seemed to be suffering from phantom injuries that never healed or couldn't be properly diagnosed. A typical recruit would drop out of training with a twisted ankle and be glad to find himself in rehab. After a while, he would get so used to the easy routine that he wouldn't want to leave – so the bad ankle would evolve into a bad back or persistent migraine. After a few months of this, the army would get fed up of the reluctant recruit, and he would find himself being medically discharged.

Everybody would be happy with this result, especially the failed recruit who could tell his parents he had given it 100 per cent and live off their sympathy. Privately, he would be pleased to be out and consider it a lucky escape. So it was not hard to see why we were labelled as 'mongs' and ridiculed by the instructors.

It took a long time for me to come to terms with being in Java Platoon – with being one of the mongs. Inwardly, I was absolutely seething, and I would deliberately provoke arguments with some of the lazier recruits. It made my blood boil that we were all tarred with the same brush and made to feel like lepers – and all because of the actions of some spineless, work-shy, poor excuses for soldiers. What irritated me the most was that the good recruits were lumped in with the bad. You might have some young lad with a broken leg or dislocated shoulder who was keen as mustard, and he would be expected to share a room with some 'no-mark' suffering from a chipped fingernail.

It was a constant battle to maintain morale, and some of the genuine lads became clinically depressed. It took an enormous amount of self-control not to lash out when a squad of healthy recruits would march past you, shouting out taunts of 'Lazy bastards' or 'Bluffing cunts'. For a Green Jacket it was particularly shaming, and my former instructors would look at me sadly and shake their heads. I felt like screaming back at them, 'Do you think I chose to have a broken foot?' but I knew it would just land me in more trouble. Instead, I reserved my ire for the fakers and bluffers in Java Platoon who attracted this abuse to us. Some of them even revelled in it and seemed to view it as a big game. They saw skipping training as getting one over on the army and considered it a victory.

The culture in Java Platoon was an unfortunate result of the slackening standards in the British Army. The wave of health and safety legislation, along with the human rights culture, meant that many unsuitable recruits were simply kept on. Couple this with the phasing out of the 'old-school' instructors, and you ended up with a farcical situation like Java Platoon. Recruits who 20 years earlier wouldn't have passed selection for the army were now getting in on a regular basis. Most of them were only let in to allow the forces to reach their recruitment targets, but once in the system, they were hard to get rid of. They would arrive at Winchester out of shape and unmotivated, struggle through a few weeks' training and then transfer to Java Platoon where they would languish for months.

Java Platoon lost a lot of good lads to voluntary withdrawals from training. The pressure and stigma of being amongst the mongs was simply too much for some to bear. I myself came close to quitting on many occasions, and only a stubborn pride and angry attitude got me through.

As part of our recovery we had to go to the gym twice a day and put ourselves through a series of exercises. This was the one part of rehab training I found enjoyable, as I felt I was doing something useful. I pushed my body as far as I could, while being careful to work around my injured foot, in a mission to get out of Java and rejoin training as soon as possible. Everyday I would do two hours on the weights, hundreds of sit-ups and press-ups, followed by intensive stretching and a long swim. The intensity of my workouts was such that I could feel myself getting fitter and stronger everyday – despite the fact that I couldn't run and was confined to the gym. Whereas most recruits had to be told to speed up by the PTIs, I was constantly being told to slow down.

The only relief we got from the gloomy atmosphere of rehab was on a Saturday. Unlike the rest of camp who had to work seven days a week, we were allowed a day off to go into town. Not surprisingly, many of the lads seized this as an opportunity to go and get pissed up. This was another source of tension between the genuinely injured recruits and the fakers, because it was remarkable how someone with 'a bad knee' would be dancing on tables after a few drinks.

As much as I disliked being in Java Platoon, I had to admit it was a refreshing change to be working under the command of non-infantry instructors. It gave me a chance to see the other side of the coin, but it also made me question where my talents would be best employed. Physically I was up to the challenge of being an infantryman, but I wondered if the non-stop 'army barmy' discipline would eventually wear me out.

The infantry has always been a refuge for hard-core, 'streetwise' types, and I began to wonder if I could ever fit into such a world. Eight years previously, when I had joined the Marines as a rowdy twenty-two year old, I was a different person. I was at the peak of my 'yobbo years', having just finished two years as a bouncer on the doors of some of Blackpool's roughest clubs. At that time, I would have fitted into the violent environment required for infantry soldiering perfectly. But that might as well have been a lifetime ago, because I was now 30 years old and had grown up considerably.

Perhaps I had spent too much time in college, read too many books or grown soft from managing a shop and dealing with 'business problems'. I didn't know what the answer was, but I did know that I was questioning a lot of the things I had seen – and questioning them in a way that I wouldn't have done previously. Things came to a head when I received an offer from a most unexpected source – an offer that was very hard to turn down.

As part of our military history lessons, we were tasked to put together a presentation on the Falklands War. As usual, I ended up being the team captain, not because of any leadership qualities I had, but because I wasn't a lazy bastard and could be relied upon not to embarrass the platoon in front of the watching dignitaries. Most of the Winchester top brass would be there, including the camp regimental sergeant major (RSM) and commanding officer (CO).

I had read quite a few books on the Falklands and spent a lot of time in the library researching the latest conclusions. I decided to base my arguments for the war's success on the famed 'Powell doctrine' and its application in that conflict. A quick summary of the doctrine is that to ensure total and swift victory you should only go to war with the following conditions in place:

- A clear and distinct plan for total victory
- Support and backing from both politicians and the general public must be 100 per cent
- A willingness to strike with overwhelming power from the start
- A clear and distinct exit strategy to end the conflict

(It is interesting to note that in the case of Iraq, General (Gen.) Colin Powell completely ignored his own advice – and look at the mess we are in!)

The presentation went remarkably well, and at the end of it, I was asked to remain behind by the officer commanding (OC) of Java Platoon. I was introduced to the CO and questioned closely on my ambitions within the army. I was astounded when the OC started talking about recommending me for a late entry commission. I have to admit, I got excited at the suggestion and liked the sound of it – but there was a catch.

I had presumed they were planning on commissioning me into the Green Jackets, which would have been a dream result beyond my wildest expectations. What he was offering me was something considerably less but still sorely tempting. The OC was a member of the Adjutant General's Corps (AGC), which is the clerical branch of the army. He wanted to try and get me an AGC commission and for me to forget about becoming an infantryman. My preference was to be commissioned as a Green Jacket, but he said that the age restrictions made that impossible. He reiterated that the AGC was far more flexible about age and qualifications and that I should give it some serious thought. I told him I would get back to him in a few days when I had had time to think about it.

Being as close to full fitness as I was, I knew I would have to return to regular training soon. The prospect of a commission had put me in a dilemma and forced me to question what I hoped to get out of being in the army. The hardest and most dangerous route to take would be continuing as an infantryman. The most comfortable and lucrative would be training as an officer in the AGC. I had to admit that I liked the idea of being called 'Sir' and taking drinks in the officers' mess. Such a move would represent a huge leap in my status and prospects – but at what price to my self-respect? At the end of the day, all I would be was a highly paid clerk, and I wouldn't be the 'proper soldier' that I had set out to be.

I reviewed my motivations for joining the Green Jackets and decided to continue down that route. As tempted as I was, I wasn't going to take the easy option and 'bottle it' by packing it in. The Green Jackets had been good enough for my brother; therefore, it would be good enough for me. I remembered what Sgt. Rickson had said to us on our first day of training: that although being an infantryman was the coldest, shittiest and dirtiest job in the army, it was also the most important. Being an infantryman was the very 'essence of soldiering'.

The OC seemed disappointed when I told him my decision, but, at the end of the day, I had not joined the army to be a pen pusher. He told me that he could guarantee that in the future I would regret turning the opportunity down. I told him I agreed but it was something I would have to find out for myself.

By that point, I had been in Java for three months and was almost ready to leave, when I got another unexpected surprise: Burtle was to be my new room-mate. After a long and drawn-out struggle, he had somehow managed to complete basic training and pass out. I was amazed at this because I had heard that he had been back-squadded several times and had failed a number of key tests and exercises. Also, he still looked like a scruffy new recruit, and he had none of the polish or confidence you would expect from a recent graduate. I asked him what he was doing in Java and found myself very disheartened by his answer – it typified everything that was wrong with the new 'caring and sharing' style of training.

Although Java Platoon was supposed to be for injured recruits only, it had been forced to take Burtle in when there was nothing physically wrong with him. He had been back-squadded so many times and screwed up on such a regular basis that the instructors had hoped he would drop out of training – but he hadn't. Two qualities that Burtle did have were courage and determination; he was one of those characters that never quits no matter how hard it gets. This was actually very admirable but didn't alter the fact that Burtle remained a dangerous liability.

In the old days, Burtle would have been taken aside for a quiet chat and advised to leave the army, or he would have been packed off to the General Service Corps to spend four years painting sheds, but these options no longer existed. Instead, the instructors had been pressurised into pushing him through training and sending him onwards, at which point he would be someone else's problem. This strategy backfired spectacularly towards the end of Burtle's training, and after one mishap on the rifle range too many, it became glaringly apparent that he could not be posted to Catterick to complete his infantry training. His instructors had no idea what to do with him or where to send him next.

When his platoon passed out, to prevent any parade ground cock-ups, Burtle was given a pair of crutches and told to fake injury. He had to watch the parade from a chair in the stands, and when it was over, instead of celebrating he came straight over to Java. The sergeant-major paid him a visit and told him he was to just hang around until they could think what to do with him next.

Months later, Burtle was still languishing there and still getting into all kinds of trouble for the most stupid of offences. I never knew what became of him or where he ended up, but I suspect he must have been discharged in the end.

I left Java Platoon shortly afterwards. As glad as I was to be leaving, there was one particular NCO that I would miss tremendously, because he had been a great source of encouragement to me when I was battling against injury and feeling sorry for myself. Cpl. Gordon Pritchard, a member of the Royal Scots Dragoon Guards, was a firm but fair, gentle giant. In a dreadful twist of fate, he later had the unfortunate distinction of becoming the 100th British soldier to die in Iraq when a roadside bomb hit his vehicle. In life you remember the people who have helped you get through tough times, and I remember Cpl. Pritchard. He was an exceptional man and a true soldier – in every sense of the word.

During my time in Java Platoon, the Royal Green Jackets regiment had decided to uproot their recruits from Winchester, and transfer them en masse to Catterick Garrison. This left me in a difficult position as I was now the only remaining Green Jacket at Winchester, and there was no combat infantry platoon to send me to. The powers that be couldn't send me up to Catterick as I was still only halfway through my basic training, and I was completely out of sync with their training regime.

It was decided to place me in an all-arms platoon for the remaining six weeks of my basic training. Once I had finished that, I would be posted to Catterick and fall in with the next available infantry intake. To be honest, I wasn't too bothered where they sent me – I was just desperate to pass out and make up for lost time.

It was quite an eye opener serving in an all-arms platoon. The term 'all arms' refers to the fact that the platoon is made up of 'mixed cap badge' regiments and corps. In my new home, we had a motley crew of recruits from the RMP, AGC, Royal Tank Regiment and various other units.

The pace of life was nothing compared to the one I had endured on the CIC, and it was reflected in the standards of both the instructors and recruits. There was still a lot of shouting and bawling, and the same old litany of bullshit inspections, but the threat of violence wasn't there, and the atmosphere was nowhere near as intimidating.

On the CIC it was presumed that as a would-be Green Jacket you had a high standard of fitness and determination – and God help you if you didn't. In contrast, my new platoon was a real mixed bag of porky clerks, whiny medics and would-be tank commanders. There were some decent lads who would have made good infantrymen, but the majority had no interest in field soldiering and struggled with even the most basic of its concepts. As before, we were split down into sections, and, this time round, I found myself working with a group of military police recruits.

The actual course we followed was no different to the infantry programme that the Green Jackets followed, except that it wasn't quite as intense, and we didn't do as much PT. The element of extreme punishment was absent, too – there was no sprinting about until you were sick straight after breakfast, no doing push-ups in the dirt for the sake of it. It was still bloody hard work but, on the whole, a lot more relaxed and humane.

Towards the end of training, we were sent off to Devon for a week's adventure training. We were billeted in an old disused army camp that had clearly seen better days. By day, we did all the usual stuff of climbing rocks, orienteering and abseiling down water towers. But by night, the exercise degraded into a 'shag fest'! For the first time during basic training, we were allowed contact with female recruits and encouraged to mix with them socially. Back on camp, we rarely worked together and found ourselves in strictly segregated platoons, but for one week only, this rule went out of the window. I was surprised at this generosity towards us recruits – until I saw that it was mainly for the benefit of the instructors.

The instructors were invariably young, single men who liked a drink and a good party. Very early on in the week, it was made clear to us that if we bought them plenty of drinks in the bar at night, we could expect an easy time of it in the day. It was the only time throughout basic training that they dropped the 'tough instructor' routine and behaved like mates towards us. They were, of course, also extremely attentive to some of the more attractive female recruits.

As the beer flowed and the music got louder, it wasn't unusual to see an instructor slipping away with a young girl on his arm. By the end of the night, they wouldn't even attempt to hide it, and some would be openly canoodling on the dance floor. All this interaction made us blokes insanely jealous, as we couldn't get a look-in or compete with the instructors' stripes.

The girls seemed to have a thing for the PTIs on camp, and when the beer was flowing, they weren't shy in letting it be known. If anything, I would say the girls were keener than the men, and it was they who were doing all the running. One of the PTIs drunkenly confided to us lads that he had never had as many women in his life. He told us that he had shagged three girls from the same platoon in the camp swimming pool and that one had given him a blowjob in the changing rooms.

As much as the men were impressed by such tales, which we had no doubt were true, we were also a bit disheartened and resentful of them. On camp it was an open secret that one way a struggling female recruit could ensure she passed out was by dispensing 'favours' to certain instructors. It was known as the 'sex option', and both parties knew exactly what the agreement was. I knew of one girl who had failed her APWT several times. She had no hope of passing out until she passed the test, which it seemed she was unable to do. All of a sudden, she produced a miraculous score – and everybody knew how she had achieved it.

I couldn't blame the instructors for enjoying sex with a gorgeous young girl when it was so blatantly offered – but, on an emotional level, it really offended my sense of fair play, because it meant shit soldiers who should have been kicked out were making it into the army. For us blokes, the only way we could pass out was to improve our performance and work our socks off. If we were struggling with our marksmanship or physical fitness, there were no sexy female PTIs offering us 'another option'. It sickened me when I saw a good lad being discharged because he couldn't run very fast or had some other weakness, when for the same sins you would see a female recruit passing out who you knew had given favours.

In all fairness, I would say that the majority of females are good soldiers who don't need to resort to knicker dropping in order to pass out, and the idea horrifies them. Honest female recruits will sometimes take offence and complain loudly about the few girls letting the side down, as will offended female instructors.

That's what happened when we returned from adventure training. We found a posse of RMPs waiting for us, and certain individuals were taken aside for questioning. Thankfully, none of our lot were involved, but I know another platoon lost several instructors, and a group of female recruits were given warnings. So, whenever the army says that such things don't go on, or that it is shocked by such allegations, take it for what it is – bullshit!

With the party atmosphere of adventure training behind us, it was back to the usual grind of turning us into soldiers. We spent almost every day crawling through thick mud or firing countless rounds down the ranges. Whenever we weren't doing anything soldierly, we would be flying over the assault course or tabbing round the country lanes of Winchester. All this work was designed to get us fighting fit for our final exercise of phase one basic training. Exercise 'Final Fling' was a three-day affair during which we would be tested on everything we had learned so far, as well as picking up a few new skills along the way.

An atmosphere of dread always descended on us at such times, as we knew we were in for a rough ride. Inevitably, we would always end up wet through and shivering after only a few hours. One ray of hope was that the warm weather would hold out, as it made life a hundred times easier. Any soldier will tell you that working under the sun is a far more appealing prospect than slaving away in a lashing rainstorm.

For once, we were lucky, and the weather was kind to us. When I had begun my training, it had been in the depths of winter, and the exercises had been something to endure, not enjoy. But this was different, and for the first time, I experienced the genuine joy of spending life outdoors. Salisbury Plain is a glorious place in summertime, and as we patrolled for miles and miles over green fields by day and through cool woods by night, it was hard not to break out in a smile.

The platoon had been together for a long time at that point and some strong friendships had been formed. Nobody wanted to be the guy that fucked up and ended things on a sour note. At the back of our minds, we knew this would be the last exercise we did as a platoon and the last time we would all be together. Beneath the deadly serious atmosphere, there was a feeling of nostalgia and mutual respect.

The grand finale of the exercise was an all-out assault on a concealed enemy position. It was a midnight attack and involved us running up a steep hill and showering the trenches with gunfire. The instructors had spent much of the day psyching us up and pacing about nervously, clearly anxious that their individual sections perform well and the objective be achieved.

They had worried needlessly as the attack came off like clockwork. In carefully rehearsed movements, we bounded up the hills in pairs, each man covering the other as we made our way to the target. At the top of the hill, we switched to automatic fire and cleared the trench, before diving into the forest to look for more enemy positions. This standard method of overcoming the enemy is referred to as 'pairs fire and manoeuvre', and you are trained to 'pepper pot' either towards or away from the enemy with soldiers always moving in carefully timed 'bounds'. It is a proven system that has been taught to soldiers for decades, and it can be adapted to either a section level or platoon-sized attack.

As we pushed deeper into the woods, branches twanged in our faces and the sweat ran down our panting cheeks. We squinted our eyes and strained our senses trying to locate hidden enemy positions (known as 'depth positions'), but in the overwhelming blackness, we struggled to keep sight of each other, never mind the fleeing troops. Finally, the words came that we had all been waiting for: 'End ex, end ex!' A loud cheer went up in the forest, and we wearily trudged down the hill.

On the coach back to Winchester, a calm and relaxed atmosphere replaced the tension of a few days before. Recruits argued about the highlights of the exercise and what had been the best part. All we had left to do was a week of solid drill practice for the big passing-out parade and that was it – we were out of Winchester and on to phase two training.

I didn't get involved in the chatter or disagreements about what had been the most memorable experience, because for me there was no contest: we had just finished a ten-mile patrol over the rolling expanse of Salisbury Plain. It was early evening and a warm breeze was drifting in the air. The sergeant called a halt, and we collapsed onto our bergens, our bodies dripping with sweat and our bones aching with exertion. The sky was a stunning shade of deep purple, and the setting sun cast a red streak across the clouds. As we rested on the dry grass and caught our breath, a blissfully chilled-out atmosphere settled on the group.

Gazing into the distance we could see the church spire of a

quaint village glinting in the sun. None of us said a word, but I could tell we were all thinking the same thing: 'Life doesn't get much better than this.' We communicated this silent message with nods and smiles, because it was one of those moments when everything becomes clear and words aren't really necessary. That was the high point of my entire time in basic training – a peaceful moment of fleeting beauty that I shall never forget.

A week later, I found myself staring into the hooded eyes and craggy face of Gen. Sir Mike Jackson. He had come to review our passing out parade and made a point of speaking to me as I was the only Green Jacket there. We exchanged a few brief words and then he was gone. I drew quite a bit of attention that day as I was making my own piece of regimental history: at the age of 31, I was the oldest and the last-ever Royal Green Jacket to pass out of Sir John Moore Barracks at Winchester. The regiment had an unbroken bond with Winchester going back 30 years, and I was being given the honour of being the last of the RGJ recruits to graduate from that barracks.

It made what was already a special day for me even more so, and I felt very proud to be representing the regiment that day. After the immense struggles I had had with injury at Winchester, I was just glad to be finally passing out. Finishing phase one training gave me a level of protection and security that I hadn't enjoyed before. I was now classed as a trained soldier, and if I got injured again, I couldn't be kicked out of the army on a medical discharge. If the worst happened, the army would have to retain me and train me to do an alternative job – but I would still be a soldier. This meant that I could attack phase two with a lot of passion and commitment but with no worries about 'what ifs?'

Not that I was complacent about what lay ahead. For my phase two training I would be rejoining the CIC at Catterick Garrison. Although I wore the uniform of a Green Jacket, I was still only halfway there, and I faced another three months of training before I could call myself the genuine article. I knew I had been lucky to finish phase one with an all-arms platoon at Winchester, but I didn't expect such an easy ride at Catterick.

Catterick Infantry Training Centre (ITC) is the largest recruit depot in Europe. It is situated on the North Yorkshire moors, and it is infamous for its cold weather and harsh treatment of recruits. The only soldiers trained there are infantry soldiers, and the only courses offered are the CIC, P Company for the Paras and Gurkha selection. It is an all-male camp with an aggressive culture, and it has a reputation for being a tough place to train. Whereas my former colleagues were now off to sunnier climes with the Military Police and the Medical Corps, I was under no illusion that for me the hard work was just about to begin.

I passed out of Winchester on a Friday, and I arrived at Catterick on the following Monday. Stepping off the train, I felt the cold snap of the wind hit me in the face. It was supposed to be summer, but the place was bloody freezing! I got a taxi and sat quietly in the back of it, looking out of the window at civilians scurrying about, envying them their freedom. I felt like I was surrounded by invisible bars. The novelty of being the last Green Jacket out of Winchester was wearing off fast.

As much as I was looking forward to the Catterick experience, I was also wary of it. I had heard so many stories about recruits getting hurt and about the savage beastings dished out, it was hard to separate fact from fiction. More often than not, these stories turned out to be gross exaggerations, but sometimes they were true.

I paid the taxi driver and approached the miserable-looking corporal guarding the gate. Five minutes later, I was being marched to my new platoon lines, where I would find out what lay in store for me. In comparison to Winchester, the camp was absolutely huge – it was so big it straddled two sites linked together by an underground tunnel. Everywhere I looked there were groups of soldiers being marched about – some in PT kit, some in immaculate smart dress 'Number Twos' and others lugging huge bergens and machine guns on their backs. It was like something out of a film.

The Green Jackets had their own separate platoons at Catterick, and they generally kept themselves to themselves. As at Winchester, an atmosphere of 'them and us' prevailed, and a competitive attitude towards other regiments was encouraged. I was looking forward to joining in with this, as I had missed the *esprit de corps* feeling it gave you.

My new home would be in 15 Platoon of Wellington Company. I wasn't too bothered where they sent me, just so long as I was back amongst the Jackets. Imagine my dismay when I opened the door to be confronted by a sea of multicoloured berets. Out of about 40 blokes I didn't see a single green one. I was absolutely gutted and plucked up the courage to ask the corporal what was going on.

He explained that as I was out of sync with the training programme the only available slot was in a mixed cap badge platoon. The next batch of Green Jackets was six weeks behind us in the course, so joining them was out of the question. I think my face told the story of how pissed off I was, and the corporal told me not to worry, as the regime they followed was exactly the same. I considered making a fuss but realised it would be pointless: the last thing I wanted was to alienate my new platoon and piss off the instructors.

I was introduced to my new training team. The sergeant was a gruffly spoken Scot, the captain an unbelievably laid-back Scouser and my new section commander a blunt Yorkshireman. They all belonged to different regiments and had very different personalities. The sergeant and corporal were exactly what you would expect experienced NCOs to be – their whole manner spoke of discipline, efficiency and tradition – but the officer was a bit of a shock.

Captain (Capt.) West was the first working-class officer I had come across. Up until then, every officer I had met spoke as though he had an orchard full of plums in his mouth, but 'Westie', as we called him behind his back, positively wallowed in his Scouse dialect. God only knows what they must have made of him at Sandhurst, because he came across as more of a corporal type than a captain. The irony of it was that he was actually a high-flyer and had achieved his rank while still in his late 20s.

As he interviewed me in his friendly manner, I was careful to give him his due respect, because I didn't doubt for one second that he would be a capable soldier. His appearance may have bordered on the scruffy, and his manner might have been eccentric and unconventional, but these types are often the best soldiers. He was the archetypal working-class lad made good, and I knew it would be impossible to bullshit him, as he must have been bright to have got to where he had.

When the sergeant spoke to me, his manner couldn't have been more different. He was all brisk and 'let's get down to business'. He made it very clear that he was the king, and that if I wanted to succeed, I had better start impressing him. This didn't surprise me, as it is the same in any infantry platoon – the sergeant is always the man you need to worry about: he is always the top dog.

Before I was dismissed, they all expressed amazement at my age and questioned my fitness levels. I was used to this by now and told them to wait and see before writing me off. It turned out that in a company of 100 soldiers the only people older than me were the sergeant-major and the OC. This time round, I was actually a couple of years older than the platoon sergeant!

The 12 weeks I was at Catterick were probably the hardest I have ever had. From the very first day it didn't disappoint, and the pace of life was relentless. Whereas phase one had been all about bringing us up to the level of a basic soldier, this was all about turning us into advanced infantrymen. We spent hours out in the field and in the classroom, studying what is referred to as 'skill at arms'.

We were introduced to the advanced weapons' systems that would make us 'masters of our profession', and we were taught how to fire, clean and repair them all. At Winchester we hadn't gone beyond the basic SA80 rifle, but now we were playing with the belt-fed general purpose machine gun (GPMG), the LAW 94 rocket launcher and live hand grenades.

Everything we did was notched up a level, and we were expected to reach a perfect standard. If we didn't, we could expect a swift boot up the arse and a trip to the assault course. We could joke around all we liked in the lines (accommodation block), so long as they were clean and tidy, but any pissing about when handling weapons and we could expect instant and painful retaliation, and rightly so. Some of the kit we had our hands on now made the SA80 look like a peashooter.

The GPMG ('gimpy' in squaddie speak, pronounced 'jim') was an awesome weapon that fired 7.62 mm rounds with enough force to punch through a brick wall – any accidents with that and you would be lucky to lose only an arm. I used to wonder how a tiny bullet, which is only a sliver of steel when fired, could manage to kill a grown man when it struck him. I used to think that as the entry wound was only like a small stab, the victim would surely be able to walk away. A few days on the ranges cured me of that notion.

Even with the SA80, which is only a lightweight assault rifle, the power is unbelievable when the round comes out of the muzzle. You grip it tightly and pull it into your shoulder, but when the bullet leaves the barrel, you can actually feel an incredible power pulling you forward and then kicking you back. When you feel this power for the first time, it comes as a shock. You get a sense of the speed and heat that the tiny round must carry, and then you realise how it can kill so easily. With the GPMG the feeling is magnified a hundred times, and you understand how easily it could blow an elephant apart, never mind a human being.

I made it a personal rule never to fuck about on the ranges when

I was handling live ammunition. To me it was basic common sense and wasn't something I needed to be taught. Amazingly, some of our more immature recruits disagreed, disregarding safety rules and treating them as a joke. I won't go into the punishments they received here, but it is safe to say that they learned their lesson in the hardest and most painful way possible.

Another weapon that we learned how to use effectively was the SA80 bayonet. Scarecrow-like figures would be strung up in a field, and we had to charge and scream at them, wildly slashing and stabbing the targets with our bayonets. The instructors thought it was hilarious and would instigate competitions based around who had the best 'war-face' or the most aggressive style.

If they were feeling particularly generous, they would place the scarecrows on the banks of a winding stream. At their command, we would have to charge down a hill, dive into the freezing water and half wade, half swim towards the enemy scarecrows. Once we reached them, we were supposed to spring out of the water and cut them to ribbons. The only problem was that by the time we reached them we were so completely fucked our 'attacks' resembled those of drunken tramps and were distinctly unimpressive – much to the fury of our instructors.

I had always imagined a bayonet to be a slim and pointy dagger that was as light and flimsy as a kitchen knife. I was completely wrong. The SA80 bayonet is a thick slab of solid steel that is designed to punch through bones like they are made of papier mâché. It has anti-suction holes and rivets down the side of it so that when it stabs, it doesn't get stuck. The blade itself is so heavy and strong you could stab it into a tree trunk and it wouldn't break. If I was given the choice of a bullet or the blade, I think I'd take the bullet – because one stab of the bayonet and your guts would be in a steaming pile on the floor. It is a truly frightening weapon.

The most important lesson I took away from Catterick was what an awesome and heavy responsibility it is to be in charge of any weapons' system. When placed in your hands, they are quite literally deadly, and the only way to treat them is with a solemn and dutiful respect. The weapons are issued to you on the basis of trust, and to treat them in a light-hearted manner would be an unforgivable sin.

The one lesson in phase two that I had been dreading above all others was the hand grenade instruction. We were introduced to their use gradually, first with dummy versions, then with smoke-generating ones and finally with the real thing. I wasn't looking forward to using them because I could barely chuck a tennis ball 20 metres – and they don't blow up.

The grenade range consisted of a reinforced concrete shed, in which the waiting recruits stood, and a tall brick wall over which you threw the grenade. The idea was to try and hit a target in the distance, scream 'grenade' then dive down quickly. The way the range was constructed it would have been hard to have an accident, although they had occurred in the past. The biggest danger was if the grenade failed to clear the wall or you dropped it before you threw it. If that happened, you would have about three seconds to dive behind a reinforced safety wall. If you didn't make it, they would be scraping you off the floor.

On the day of the dreaded live hand grenade tests, we were herded into the shed and each made to nervously await our turn. Every few seconds, you would hear the cry 'grenade' followed by the most incredible whoosh. When the grenades detonated, the shock wave that hit the shed shook it to its core – it was almost like a sonic boom. I shuddered to think what the blast would do to a human body; it would probably just vaporise you.

The instructors at Catterick wouldn't tolerate any signs of nervousness or bad technique when it came to handling weapons. You had to display confidence and certainty at all times, and if you didn't, you could expect no mercy. Despite our best efforts, and the threats of the instructors, quite a few of us were judged to have performed badly with the grenades. I have to admit that I was amongst the worst offenders, and I was made to throw three grenades in a row before I was considered competent.

Weapon handling was never my strongest point as a recruit, and although I was never a safety risk and took great care, I was never what you would call 'smooth and slick'.

I think this was because to be really good requires a degree of manual dexterity and confidence that I just didn't have. By the end of the course, I was as slick and fast with an SA80 as anybody else, but when it came to the GPMG and LAW 94, I was embarrassingly slow and clumsy. The instructors pressured us to constantly improve our skills, but they were more concerned with us being safe and competent than super fast, as we could gain speed with experience.

Where I did shine was on the PT side. I found that my older and stronger legs were an enormous benefit on the tabs, and my powerful upper body served me well in the gym. The tabs we did at Catterick were brutally hard compared to the ones we had performed at Winchester. Miles of dusty hills and dirt tracks surrounded the camp, and some of them were unbelievably steep. We would load up our bergens with up to 60 lb of weight and be expected to fly over the hills like mountain goats. We would have a PTI in front of us setting the pace, one alongside us shouting abuse and one at the rear to push up the stragglers. At the very back we would have a military ambulance and a spare Land-Rover, known as the 'Jack Wagon', following us. Both vehicles were put to good use.

The Jack Wagon was for those lads who decided to quit or for those who simply couldn't stand the pace. To end a tab in the Jack Wagon was considered a huge disgrace, and anybody that did would find themselves in front of the sergeant-major, pleading not to be back-squadded. The ambulance saw plenty of action, too, and at the end of a tab, there was always someone who had passed out through dehydration, or perhaps fallen head over heels down a hill. Nobody ever thought of getting in it for a minor injury like a twisted ankle or a torn muscle – and if they did, they would be met with a mouthful of abuse and told to 'fuck off and sort themselves out'. The medics were usually infantry medics attached to our platoon, and tea and sympathy wasn't their style.

The funny thing about tabbing is that, just like weapon handling, some people are naturally good at it and some aren't. We had some very fit lads who struggled horrendously on the tabs no matter how hard they tried. I was extremely thankful that I wasn't one of them. Life was hell for them, and everyday they would find themselves at the back of the pack, retching their guts out and stumbling along blindly in a world of pain. Their only encouragement would be a sneering PTI cursing them for their lack of effort and pathetic weaknesses. It was a grim predicament to be in, and I don't know if I could have hacked it in their shoes.

I think the fact that I had done a lot of heavy squats over the years somehow insulated my legs against the shocks of tabbing. In a perverse way, when I found out I was good at it, I actually began to enjoy it. I say it was perverse because daily tabbing wreaks havoc on your body – it literally wrecks it. You would find yourself getting fitter and fitter, but, at the same time, you were becoming more and more injured. Aches, pains, scrapes and bruises all seemed to build up on top of one another. For example, any sane person would stop and rest if they badly twisted an ankle, or tripped heavily onto a knee, but when you were tabbing, you wouldn't even consider it. You would just jump up, dust yourself down and jump back into the pack. You would worry about any pain or injuries once the tab was over – then you would find your foot was so swollen you couldn't get your boot off.

Judging it by civilian standards, you would have to say it was a mad activity, but when you apply infantry standards, you realise its worth. Tabbing is all about building a strong body and robust mindset, and fostering a 'can do' spirit. The irony is that the lads at the back who suffered such heartbreaking hardship, got more out of it than those at the front who found it easier. To get the most from it you really had to struggle.

Whenever we weren't tabbing or learning how to use weapons' systems we would be out on exercise. In phase one our exercises had been classed as introductory; in phase two they were referred to as tactical or 'Tac-ex'. The emphasis was on reconnaissance patrolling and launching aggressive attacks on fortified positions – things we hadn't touched on at Winchester.

We would load up our bergens with a week's worth of supplies and disappear into the woods. When we came out, we had usually lost a stone in weight and our faces would look gaunt. The learning curve on these exercises was incredibly steep, and there was a great deal of pressure. Every possible aspect of field craft and soldiering was covered, and nothing was left to chance. We learned how to plan an ambush, defend against one, navigate with compasses, construct defences, build shelters and apply first aid – everything a soldier could possibly be asked to do.

Sometimes you would be given so much information that your brain would be ringing, struggling to take it all in and remember everything. At other times, you would be lying in wet grass or snow for hours at a time (known as a LUP, for lying up point), waiting to spring an ambush on passing troops. It could be incredibly boring, feeling like it would never end. On those occasions, the silence would only be broken by a recruit's unmistakable snores, followed swiftly by a corporal's sharp dig in the ribs to wake him.

The worst exercise Catterick had to offer was the infamous Tac-ex 3. This came towards the end of training, but such a legend had grown around it that I worried about it from day one. It didn't help that recruits who had just completed it gleefully stoked my fears with exaggerated tales of their own experiences. Passing Tac-ex 3 is a significant milestone in a recruit's training and a good indicator of whether he will pass the whole course.

The structure of the exercise never changes and has been the same for years. Quite simply put, it is a 'digging in' exercise. A lorry drops you off in the middle of nowhere, usually on the moors surrounding Catterick. Once the lorry disappears, you begin a very long tab that stretches for miles and miles, covering very boggy and difficult ground. The tab will last for most of the first day, only breaking off occasionally to allow for a tactical sweep through nearby woods, or a quick recce (reconnaissance) on a deserted farmhouse. By the time you come to an eventual stop, you are already tired, hungry and ready for sleep. And then you start digging.

For the next 48 hours, all you do is dig trenches non-stop. There are no stops, no breaks and no let-up. You scoff chocolate bars and flapjacks on the move, and nobody stops until the last trench is dug. The ground you dig in is a combination of wet clay and heavy soil – the worst kind of terrain possible to build a trench in. The objective is to construct a company-size trench system that can support 100 men. The trenches must be 5-ft deep and fortified with corrugated iron sheets. They have to be big enough for you to eat in, sleep in and fight in, because that is what you will be doing for an entire week.

After 12 hours' straight digging, you can see men getting irritable and snappy with one another. The tiredness really starts to kick in, and it becomes a huge mental chore just to stay awake. Inevitably, some work harder and faster than others, but some seem to switch off and become lazy, and so the occasional scuffle breaks out. The instructors are quick to jump in and split them up, but the digging never stops.

After 48 hours, a halt is called, and you are ordered into your trench. For the next few days, you live in it and conduct patrols and guard duties from it. Anybody caught sleeping is back-squadded a few weeks and has to repeat the exercise. There are always a few who get caught out, and there are always desperate pleas not to have to go through it all again. At the end of the exercise, you defend the trenches against a full-scale attack, and then you spend all day filling them in for the next batch of unfortunates. Finally, there is a long tab back to camp for weapons cleaning, before 'End ex' is mercifully called.

The tiredness I felt after I completed the Tac-ex 3 was beyond description: every fibre of energy was wrung from my body. My hands were covered in blisters, and my wrists felt like they had been rapped with a baseball bat. It had pissed down with rain the whole week, and after a few days, the trench walls had collapsed and caved in. To say I had been in 'shit state' would be putting it mildly, but I didn't mind because everyone else had been, too, and at least the ordeal was behind us.

When I visited the shop to stock up on chocolate bars, I made a point of pulling some new recruits aside and telling them how bad Tac-ex 3 had been. Their hushed reaction and worried faces brought a smile to my cheeks and cheered me up no end! I suspect the same conversations are being had to this day, and so the legend grows.

We only had a few weeks left of training, and as much as we continued to give it 100 per cent, there was also an increasing anxiety to protect our bodies from injury. I knew from my own experiences how devastating and morale sapping an injury could be, and perhaps the worst part of it was how unexpectedly they sprang up. By the latter stages of the course, most recruits were carrying some form of niggling injury or, like me, recovering from a serious one. It was just an unpleasant fact of daily life that you learned to live with. You never got used to it, but you had to accept it. After a while, it became normal to ask yourself, 'Will I break a leg today? Will I break an arm?'

Most of the injuries came from falls on the assault course or tabbing accidents. Some came from previous weaknesses and overuse. Each one had a shattering emotional impact on the recruit concerned – many of whom had nowhere else to go if they didn't make it as a soldier. The rehabilitation platoon at Catterick was always full to the brim, often with well over a 100 soldiers. It was called Williams Platoon, and it was the one place none of us wanted to end up – because once you were there, you were halfway out of the army.

The rate of attrition on the CIC was enormous, and 15 Platoon in Wellington Company was a typical example. In the first week, a total of 45 hopefuls had formed the basis of the platoon. By the final week, only 30 of these were passing out as qualified infantrymen. Out of the successful 30, almost half were back-squadders or transfers from other platoons. Indeed, I was one, having been forced out of my original intake due to injury. So, that means a typical platoon can expect to lose up to two thirds of its members to injuries, unsuitable discharges, transfers and police troubles. These grim statistics demonstrate that passing the CIC is quite an achievement – an achievement that not only depends on grit and determination but also on sheer good luck.

Passing out of Catterick ITC is a day I shall never forget, as aside from the parade, I had another honour to be proud of as well: at 31 years old, I became the oldest ever recruit to pass out of Catterick, having completed the entire modern CIC from scratch. When the parade was over, we all went for a few drinks in the bar, and I was touched that several senior NCOs approached me and shook my hand. It meant a lot to me because only days before these men had been cursing me to the heavens.

I found a quiet corner in the bar and sipped my beer, reflecting on all that had happened to me since joining the army. It felt deeply appropriate that I had passed out as a Green Jacket, and the process had seemed almost driven by fate. When I had broken my foot and been left behind at Winchester, I had been wallowing in self-pity, but now I was almost glad that it had happened. The broken foot had granted me the distinction of being the oldest and last-ever Green Jacket to pass out of Winchester – and now I was the oldest out of Catterick, too.

A large part of my joining up was to replicate my brother's

service in a sentimental journey, and now we shared an eerie parallel: we had suffered the exact same injury and had both taken over nine months to pass out. I now knew how he had felt in the depths of his despair and in the triumph of his success, and I knew what it had taken for him to achieve what he had.

Before I left the camp for the last time, I gave Capt. West and the sergeant a bottle of whisky each. I knew they liked a drink, and when the sergeant clapped eyes on my gift, his eyes almost popped out of their sockets. His gruff exterior melted away, and he insisted I share a glass with him before I left. A few other recruits joined us, and now that he was no longer our sergeant, he addressed us as equals. He seemed genuinely proud that we had made it and treated us like long-lost friends. It was nice to be seeing the real him at last, and as we parted with a handshake, I surprised myself by getting a bit teary eyed.

The train ride home took five hours, and I found myself reliving and mulling over all the experiences of the CIC and basic training. I had a feeling that a pivotal moment had just passed in my life's journey, and that the experience would often colour how I viewed the world from then on. The training had been difficult and intense, and it had wrought some permanent changes in my physique. Whereas before I had been stocky and bulky, now I was leaner and harder. I had developed what you call a 'squaddie body', and I was fitter, more agile and more robust than I had ever been. But I had expected this, and the physical nature of the course hadn't surprised me.

There had been a lot of talk in the media around that time about bullying of recruits, and the words 'Deepcut deaths' were becoming known to all soldiers. I thought back to the violent and aggressive culture that surrounded Catterick – the constant threats, the extreme punishments. Did that constitute bullying? I didn't think so. In all my time in basic training, both at Winchester and Catterick, I didn't see one incident that I would categorise as bullying. What I did see, and what I fully supported and understood, was recruits being severely punished for fucking up. It happened to me, it happened to everybody else and none of us had a problem with it.

At the end of the day, we were training to be professional soldiers, a very serious and potentially deadly job. We weren't training to work on the checkout at Tesco – it was something far more important than that, and the training and discipline had to reflect this. I think if the attitudes and punishments had been slacker and less severe, I would have been hugely disappointed. Ultimately, we were striving to be good soldiers; wasn't that supposed to be hard?

I couldn't understand the mindset of recruits who whined or complained about being bullied. If a recruit cannot cope with a robust bollocking from a sergeant-major, how will he cope if he comes under enemy attack? Most of my intake would be serving in Iraq or Afghanistan within weeks – we were glad we had received hard training. I think a lot of complaints about bullying are from recruits who should never have joined the army in the first place or who are confused about the difference between being pushed and being picked on.

If you examined most of the bullying allegations in the British Army, you would find that the majority of them are made by non-infantry recruits and they are against non-infantry instructors. I don't think this is coincidental. As a general rule, infantry recruits tend to be more robust than other recruits, and the instructors seem to have a different attitude. Some of the recruits that turned up at Winchester would have struggled to pass a Cub Scout course: they were grossly unfit and prime candidates for bullying. It was hard to feel sorry for such types, even if they only aspired to be a clerk or a driver. By setting themselves such low standards, they became easy targets for predatory instructors and suffered accordingly. Because of our better attitude, the infantry recruits avoided these problems.

All of the infantry instructors I met, including even the very strictest, seemed to have an inbuilt sense of fair play. All that they were concerned about was how well you performed as a soldier, and nothing else mattered. If you fucked up, you received a tough punishment, but, at the same time, no grudges were borne, and you were soon forgiven.

At Winchester, there was a sharp contrast between the infantry and non-infantry instructors – most of whom were AGC, Royal Logistics Corp (RLC) or Air Corps. They weren't held in the same esteem as the 'infanteers', and some of them were overweight and badly out of shape. As a consequence, they would try and overcompensate by being 'ultra-hard' or ridiculously loud and threatening. I knew that the Green Jacket instructors considered many of them to be a joke, and the recruits picked up on that vibe. After all, it is hard not to laugh when you see a grossly unfit instructor trying to beast recruits or an obese drill sergeant waddling along the parade ground trying to look scary. It just doesn't work.

As I stared out of the train window, lost in a private reverie about the highs and lows of basic training, a broad smile broke out on my face, as I realised that it was something I would never have to worry about again. I had done it, and it was behind me – my next challenge would be daily battalion life and operational tours.

4

SENIOR BODS AND STAG BITCHES

I arrived at the 1st Battalion of the Royal Green Jackets (1RGJ) regiment shortly after Christmas. The barracks was based just outside Preston, and when I compared it to the sprawling giant that was Catterick, it seemed tiny in comparison. The relative smallness of the camp pleased me, as I had been hoping it would have the cosy and intimate atmosphere that Catterick sorely lacked.

The camp was practically deserted when I got there, as most of the regiment were covering the fire-brigade strikes in Scotland. I was shown to my new room and spent most of the first day lazing about on my bed. After the constant tension and pressure of Catterick, my new home felt like a holiday camp. My slumber was only broken by the occasional arrival of another new recruit or some other soldier passing through. I learned a valuable lesson that first day about how the regular army operates: when there is work to be done, you work very hard, but if you can avoid it, lie peacefully on your bed and do fuck all!

After a week of doing nothing, I was collared by a sergeant-major and told to make my way to the Motherwell Territorial

Army (TA) barracks in Scotland. I was going to meet my new platoon and help out with the fire strikes. As I hadn't done any fireman's training, I would be standing guard on a gate for most of the time ('stagging on' in squaddie speak). My face dropped at this, and the sergeant-major said I had better get used to the concept of stagging on, because I would be doing a lot of it in the Green Jackets. He wasn't kidding.

I arrived in Motherwell and was led into the makeshift fire station. Thick snow carpeted the ground and ancient Green Goddesses were parked up in rows. There was a group of frustrated-looking mechanics gathered around them, and my guide told me they had dreadful problems getting them to work. The station was pleasantly warm and jam-packed with soldiers in various states of undress. One group sat around in full kit waiting for a turn out, another was watching a porno film and another was sleeping peacefully on tiny camp beds.

The atmosphere was cheery and informal, and amid the card playing and loud banter, it seemed like the soldiers were happy enough. I sat down and began to relax, thinking I could enjoy a few more weeks of this, when I felt a tapping on my shoulder. 'Are you the new lad?'

'Yes, Cpl.,' I replied.

'Right then, get your kit on. It's your turn on stag.'

Great. Five minutes later, I found myself shivering in the snow and guarding a rusty old gate. I stood shifting from foot to foot for the next four hours. The only time I moved was to let cars in or out. This would be my new routine for the next fortnight – four on and four off. It was explained to me that as I was the newest guy I would do the most stag – until such time as an even newer guy arrived. Apparently, it was a Green Jacket tradition: for now, I was the 'Stag Bitch'.

My new home was in 15 Platoon of F Company. I had a brief chat with the sergeant, and he told me to keep a low profile and do a good job: no more, no less. I was just to do as I was told, and he would be happy. I met the other NCOs, and they seemed like a friendly bunch, even going so far as to insist I call them by their first names. That came as a big shock and took some getting used to. If I had done that at Catterick, I would have got a punch in the guts. So, apart from being the resident Stag Bitch, I was feeling pleased about where I was.

I got my first inkling that there could be trouble ahead when I met my fellow soldiers. It was ironic that I was most worried about making a good impression with the NCOs, when I should have been more concerned with the junior ranks. I introduced myself as cheerfully as I could and was astonished to be given the cold shoulder by a couple of cockneys. They weren't all hostile, but there was definitely a bad vibe coming off a few of them. I asked one of the friendlier lads what the problem was, and he explained to me why I was being ignored.

Apparently, the lads giving me the brush off were what is referred to as 'senior bods' or 'senior riflemen'. They were given this unofficial title because they had served in the ranks for a couple of years and were considered senior to the other riflemen in the platoon. If I wanted to gain their respect and friendship, I would have to earn it over the coming months – but for now I was *persona non grata*. Not only that but I was a 'nig' too, which is the term used to describe a new arrival.

I didn't complain or protest, because I was the new boy, but, privately, I thought it was all bullshit. I was all for respecting rank and experience, but to me a senior man was somebody wearing stripes. I suspected the real story about this seniority fuss was to do with preserving power and status within the platoon. As far as I was concerned, we all wore the same rank of rifleman, and the argument ended there. I would follow the sergeant's advice and keep a low profile, but if some 21-year-old 'senior bod' tried to pull any tricks on me, he would get a nasty surprise.

Apart from the few awkward sods in my platoon, the rest of the company seemed reassuringly friendly and welcoming. I got a lot of good-natured ribbing on account of my age, and a few blokes spoke well of my brother. It turned out that my old mate Tabuk was in F Company too, and I was pleased to see the big Fijian again. We swapped a few tales about Catterick, and I caught up on the gossip about what had happened to my friends in Peninsula Platoon. The first person he asked me about was the one-man disaster zone Burtle, and he roared with laughter when I told him he was still at Winchester because the army didn't know what to do with him.

A faint warning light went off in my head when I asked Tabuk which platoon Dougie was in. He shifted uncomfortably in his seat as he told me that Dougie was AWOL and had been missing for months. I couldn't believe Dougie would disappear like that as I had him down as an outstanding soldier. Tabuk explained that Dougie had found it hard to fit into his platoon and ran into some trouble with his sergeant. He didn't elaborate further, but he left me with the clear impression that I would have to watch my back, especially as I was the new guy. It would turn out to be good advice.

One consequence of the fire strikes was that it turned many soldiers on to the idea of becoming a fireman. In comparison to the life of a squaddie, the job was a doddle. We had a retired fireman who was now employed by the MOD drop by the station and give us tips and guidance on how to fight fires. He told us that after two days' training, he had the Green Jackets doing stuff it would take Fire College recruits a month to learn. He reckoned that with our extra fitness and commitment we could give the real firemen a run for their money. Quite a few of the lads became openly scornful of the fire strikers, as they couldn't see what they were complaining about. The firemen did seventeen weeks of relatively easy training, worked a four-day week, slept half the time and earned almost twice what a versatile infantryman did – it sounded like a good deal to us.

Once the strikes wound down, we returned to camp and a more

usual routine. A typical day consisted of fitness training in the mornings, followed by weapons training in the afternoons. And, of course, a platoon would also have to do their fair share of stagging on at the gate. Now that we were back on camp, I also had a chance to make some friends and get a good look at the battalion.

One man who made a lasting impression on me was the OC of F Company, Major (Maj.) Squibb. Despite being just a year older than me, he was considerably more accomplished and had already racked up ten years' service in the army. He had joined the Green Jackets straight from university, and he had what you could only describe as a perfect 'officer's pedigree' – public school, a top university, Sandhurst Academy. But, despite his privileged background, he had that rare ability of being able to speak to you as an equal, even though you patently weren't. He would address the roughest of riflemen in the same relaxed and confident manner in which he would speak to the CO or a visiting general.

But what really made Maj. Squibb stand out, and the reason why he was treated with such respect, was that he was a member of the SAS. Although he had begun his career in the Jackets, he had spent the previous four years down at Hereford. The reason he was back with us was because he was newly promoted, and it was felt that he needed more experience of commanding regular troops. He was only with us on a temporary basis, and it gave F Company a lot of kudos to have him as an OC. His obvious joy at being back amongst the Jackets had also won him the respect and admiration of the lads. As proud as he was of being in the SAS, he was always quick to point out that he was a Green Jacket, too, and that this is where it had all begun for him.

I had been told that the best way to get to know what life in the Jackets was really like was to have a few beers in the NAAFI; speak to a senior bod when he is pissed and you will get the true picture. At Catterick, the atmosphere had been positive and enthusiastic, and despite the hardship, everyone was as keen as mustard to progress and achieve. I had hoped it would be the same when I reached my company, but what I found when I visited the NAAFI bar for the first time was profoundly depressing and disappointing.

The general morale of the average soldier was absolutely rock bottom. I had been expecting to receive advice on how to achieve promotion, what the most interesting courses were and which were the best companies to be in. But the only topics of conversation were about how quickly you could get out, when you could sign off and how to dodge courses. I was astounded that out of a large group of random soldiers, not a single one was interested in getting on. Time and again I heard the words 'dog shit' and whenever I asked why, I would get a knowing nod and a wink and an assurance that I would soon find out.

I left the NAAFI feeling angry and downhearted at what I had discovered. I hadn't just done six months at Catterick, up to my eyeballs in mud and shit, to come and do a job that was described as 'total pants' or 'completely fucking anal'. Thinking that perhaps it had been a mistake to listen to a gang of pissed-up squaddies, I decided to approach some more sober types. The reaction I got was exactly the same. Although the men were proud to be Green Jackets, worked extremely hard and loved the regiment, the vast majority were very unhappy in their jobs and couldn't wait to leave. The main reasons were that the regiment was undermanned and overstretched, and they were constantly abroad on operations or exercise. These problems never seemed to get any better, and now that the Middle East was going up in flames, it seemed the situation was permanent.

The turnover rate at 1RGJ was high as far as I could see – every week a newly minted batch of soldiers would arrive from depot, and every week a gang of old hands would leave. I now had a theory why so much pressure was applied to depot instructors to keep recruit numbers up – it appeared more were leaving the battalion than were arriving. A by-product of this that caused problems within the regiment, in my opinion, was that some unfit recruits arrived who shouldn't really have passed out but had managed to slip through the net. A lot of time then had to be wasted on retraining them within the battalion and bringing their basic skills up to scratch.

The regimental make-up was about 75 per cent white working-class, and the remaining 25 per cent were soldiers from Commonwealth nations. Most of the Brits were exactly how you imagined infantry soldiers to be. They conformed to the squaddie stereotype, and the bulk of them were cockneys, Brummies and Scousers. They were a rough but likeable bunch, very quick to fight but, at the same time, quick to forgive, fair and open-minded.

I had friends in both groups, but I found I had more in common with the foreigners than my own countrymen. The Commonwealth soldiers tended to be older and more mature, and they had a wider spectrum of interests. I admired them for having the guts and determination to travel to a strange country and join a foreign army. I felt it showed a lot of ambition and imagination, and their actions spoke highly of them. We also shared the bond of being outsiders in a strictly regimented place, and I think that always brings people together.

Despite the vast majority of the regiment being typical squaddie types, there was a surprising number who were the polar opposite. For the life of me I couldn't understand why some of them hadn't been commissioned, because they were clearly as bright as any officer. We had Rifleman Spamer, a tall South African with a business degree and thoughtful manner. Then there was Rifleman Chege, a quiet and serious soldier, and the son of a Kenyan coffee merchant. Chege was descended from a Masai tribe, which was an honour he was rightly very proud of. I grew close to these guys, and I liked hearing their stories about life in a different culture.

The issue of race within the battalion wasn't really an issue at all, because we were all dealt with fairly, and we all knew where we stood. How it worked in the Green Jackets was scrupulously honest and upfront. If you fucked up and made a serious mistake, you would receive a 'gobful' of abuse or possibly 'a dig'. If your mistake was considered exceptionally bad, parts of that verbal abuse would relate to your physical characteristics. Whenever I fucked up I was a 'bald-headed short-arse cunt'; a tall, blond person would be a 'lanky streak of piss'; a tubby, ginger-haired lad would be a 'fat, ginger bastard'; and a black man might be a 'stupid black twat'.

It wasn't racism, and it wasn't personal; the insults were soon forgotten, and we would all have a laugh at the offender's expense. You could call it good old-fashioned British humour, but I prefer to call it equality of treatment. This kind of humour brought soldiers together and put them on the same level – you were being bollocked for your mistake, not your race, and everybody understood that.

The friendships and bonds of trust that developed within a platoon crossed all racial and class boundaries. It would be impossible for racism to take hold, because if it did, none of us would be able to trust one another, and we would end up fighting amongst ourselves, instead of against the enemy. The social engineers and do-gooders that point the finger of blame at the army have no understanding of the culture in which it exists. It is not like working for the DSS in some air-conditioned office. The pressures are enormous, and a thick skin and over-the-top sense of humour are the only ways to survive the experience. That is the way it has been for soldiers since time began, and it will never change.

Of all the 'racial' groups on camp the ones who got the most abuse were white Liverpudlians! If a Scouser so much as opened his mouth, he would be hit with an avalanche of jokes about 'thieving scallies' and 'robbing old ladies'. They got an unbelievable amount of stick – even the Jamaicans would join in and try to mimic their accents. When it came to winding Scousers up, the whole battalion joined in – including the officers. But none of it stuck, and the quick-witted Liverpudlians often came out on top.

Because of my age and background, I was always going to stand out amongst the riflemen. When you consider that most of them were teenagers, I was almost old enough to be their dad and most of the time older than the platoon sergeants. I still made a big effort to fit in and be accepted, although I would always be an outsider within the main group. This was most apparent at weekends when the entire company descended on Blackpool, with the sole intention of getting legless. I always received an invite, but I only went along a couple of times, because I had outgrown that scene. This did cause some friction with the wilder party animals, who couldn't understand why I didn't want to get drunk and have a tear-up. Without wanting to sound like too much of an old fart, I had to explain to them that I had done my carousing and scrapping back in the early '90s, and I was now more interested in curling up with a good book.

I was actually flattered that they tried to drag me out with them, because it showed that they were looking at me as one of the team, but I had to reluctantly accept that we were of a different generation. In recognition of my 'Mr Boring' persona, I was given the nickname 'Grandad' and became the butt of endless jokes about pipes and slippers. It was all done in good humour, but, I have to admit, I wished they could have met the old me of a decade before. They would have been stunned to learn that I was once one of the most recognised doormen in Blackpool, or that I had partied harder in the rave era than any of them could have imagined. But that guy was gone, so I kept my little secret to myself.

Daily life in the platoon lines wasn't too bad really. It resembled living in shared college dorms, with all the music and laughter you could handle, but with an added element of tension and aggression. We slept four to a room and were allowed to plaster the walls with pornographic posters and set up gigantic speaker systems. The only stipulation was that our sleeping quarters were kept tidy for an occasional inspection.

It was quite rare for a fight to break out in your own accommodation block – that pastime was generally reserved for civilian bashing at weekends – but heated disagreements did occur. The most sickening and disappointing of these arose from allegations of stealing. We all hoped to avoid such arguments, but we all got sucked into them anyway. Whenever the issue was raised, you could guarantee that a lot of misguided venom, false accusations and a kangaroo court atmosphere would occur.

One of the lads would foolishly leave his wallet lying around, and when he went to retrieve it, he would be shocked to find it had gone. Usually, he had mislaid it or drunkenly forgotten where he had put it. After about five minutes of calm discussion, the accusations would fly around, and chaos would ensue. Inevitably, it would turn up somewhere and peace would be restored – but the bad feeling would remain. What pissed me off was how some lads never learned, and despite repeated warnings, they would leave crumpled up tenners lying around and then fight like hell when they disappeared. At times like those, I felt like I was living in a madhouse and couldn't wait to leave.

While most of the riflemen got on well together, there was no escaping the fact that the battalion did have a smattering of nasty bastards who would try the patience of a saint. The relationships you had with such individuals often led to feelings of claustrophobia and suffocation, because living on an army camp you couldn't just walk away from them. There might be someone you detested but had to stick to like glue – you could be in the same section, share the same room or be paired up as 'battle buddies'. The problems would begin whenever you tried to reason with them or suggest a different way of doing things, because your comments were invariably taken as unfair criticism, no matter how carefully phrased. With these types everything was about playing to the crowd and 'giving it large'. It was wiser to just let them get on with it, otherwise you would end up fighting like two ferrets in a sack.

What quality of life you had in the battalion was a bit of a lottery. If you were fortunate, you went to somewhere like F Company, where Maj. Squibb ran a tight ship, and the NCOs were a reasonable bunch. If you were unfortunate, you could find yourself in a platoon with an extreme old-school sergeant who ruled with an iron fist. Working for that type of sergeant was fine when things were going well, but if you made a mistake, God help you. I thanked my lucky stars that we didn't have any such sergeants in our company, but my heart bled for those that did.

There were two particular sergeants who were well known for using their fists on young soldiers. As soon as I arrived in Scotland for fire duty, I had been taken aside and warned about them, and when I had learned I wouldn't be in their platoon, I was over the moon. I was curious to meet them, as stories often get exaggerated, and I wondered if that was the case in this instance.

The first time I encountered them was on a live firing exercise in the Brecon Beacons. I had completely fucked up an attack by firing at non-existent targets, and I had gotten separated from my section. The fuck-up was down to me, but, to be fair, the NCO giving directions had got in a muddle too, which had made it worse. I made my weapon safe and wearily stood up. In the distance, I saw two bulky figures approaching, their faces deadly serious. I prepared myself for a bollocking.

My heart leapt as they stomped towards me, because, for a split second, I didn't think they were going to stop and would plough right through me. They were big fuckers too and must have weighed at least 16 st. apiece. They were neither 'steroid bloaters' nor fat men but looked extremely fit and strong. I was given the tongue lashing of a lifetime and threatened with all kinds of harm if I ever screwed up like that again. That in itself didn't bother me, because it was par for the course, but what did worry me was that one of them looked like he really wanted to hit me. He kept on looking over his shoulder, as if he was checking for witnesses.

I antagonised him by stepping back out of his range and tilting my body to the side in anticipation of a strike. He seemed greatly offended that I had the effrontery to make myself less of a target, as if he expected me to just stand there like a dummy. An NCO came running over, and the moment passed. The two sergeants then moved on to bollock somebody else, and I breathed a nervous sigh of relief.

Most platoon sergeants wouldn't dream of striking a soldier, unless it is for the worst offence possible, in which case it is fair enough. But there is another type, of which those two were the worst examples, who take a great pride in their ability to give someone a dig or 'a jab'. The problem is, the jabs are often for the most minor misdemeanours. Certain individuals in the regiment deliberately cultivated and revelled in this hard-man image. As a grown man of a similar age and background, I found it pathetic and disturbing – to me it had the whiff of the playground bully about it. By that stage of my life I was too old to fall for such childish mind games, but a skinny teenager fresh out of school would have found it terrifying.

After that little episode, I realised that the only way to make life bearable was to keep an ultra-low profile and avoid trouble. I also began to understand why so many lads wanted to leave the regiment and why so many were happy to melt into the background. Living in a pressure-cooker-type atmosphere, having to watch your back all the time and never being able to escape, began to feel like being in prison. No wonder squaddies go berserk when they are let out at weekends!

But it wasn't all doom and gloom, and life in 15 Platoon had its funny moments. I was no longer the new guy as we had nigs turning up from Catterick every week. By that point, the so-called senior bods had at least acknowledged my presence, albeit grudgingly. Because of my age and attitude, they knew they couldn't bully me, so they tried to punish me with silence instead. I was more than happy to oblige them, and rather than sulking, as they were hoping I would do, I made an all-out effort to befriend the new arrivals – which, of course, annoyed them further.

One of the platoon ringleaders was an extremely loud and obnoxious big mouth. He rated himself very highly, as these types always do, and he went out of his way to make the new guys feel uncomfortable. The truth of the matter was that he himself was a shambles who couldn't even get up in time for breakfast and was forever in trouble, which is why he would always be a senior bod and never an NCO.

Whenever a new recruit turned up who appeared very young or a bit weak, this particular senior bod made a point of turning the more junior man into his 'platoon bitch'. However, he grossly misjudged the baby-faced Rifleman Devlin, for beneath the meek exterior of the new recruit beat the heart of a crafty and cunning trickster. Every day for weeks on end, Devlin had been going to the scoff house and bringing back a bacon sandwich for his tormenter, just as he had been ordered to. What he forgot to mention was that every day he had been adding a thick glob of snot and spit to the sandwich – free of charge, of course.

I had established a reputation in the company as a quiet and serious type: not army barmy or terribly ambitious, but I could be relied upon to do a good job. However, it was around about that time, when I was posted at Weeton Barracks and had already decided to just do my three years, that I had to do my first serious case of course dodging.

There were certain positions in the regiment that were always undermanned and nobody wanted. I was happy being a simple rifleman in a rifle company – it might have been the dirtiest job on camp, but it was straightforward soldiering, and that was what I had joined up to do.

Unfortunately, the sergeant-major had other ideas and told me I had been selected to attend the Assault Engineer Course run by the Royal Engineers (RE). This entailed spending six weeks under their command learning how to use explosives, detect and mark out landmines, and construct razor-wire defences. As soon as I heard the word 'landmines' my antenna shot up. I had absolutely zero interest in going anywhere near landmines or explosives. If I had wanted to be an engineer, I would have joined the RE and done it for real, and, in any case, I still had a lot to learn as a basic soldier. When it came to dealing with landmines, my motto was 'leave it to the experts'.

As soon as word spread I was on the course, I had a seemingly never-ending stream of junior ranks advising me to get off it. I was told that if I did the training, I would spend the remaining two years of my service in the Assault Engineer Platoon. I told the sergeant-major how I felt, and he said the only way I could avoid it would be if I could persuade the sergeant who had recommended me to change his mind. 'Brilliant,' I thought to myself. 'Now I will probably make an enemy of the platoon sergeant.'

I went to see him anyway and pleaded my case. He knew I had spoken to the sergeant-major about it, and I felt like an absolute Judas as I asked him to be taken off the list. I felt bad because he loved assault engineering and was a qualified specialist. He made a real effort to convince me what a great job it was and how I would love it. As I respectfully disagreed, I could see he was upset. There was a palpable tension in the air, made worse by the fact that everyone selected had tried to get off the course.

However, the assault engineer sergeant wasn't like the aggressive pair I had encountered at Brecon; he was a genuinely nice and fair-minded man. He was in an awkward position because nobody wanted to go on his course, and I could see it worried him. Standing there in open disagreement with him I felt like a disrespectful pain in the arse. He dismissed me without an answer, but the hurt and betrayal in his eyes told their own story.

It was at times like those that I hated the army and the lack of freedom that I had to make my own decisions or manage my own career. I hadn't realised as a civilian just how much of themselves soldiers gave up when they signed on the dotted line, but I was certainly beginning to. I was starting to understand why my brother, and so many of the current crop of squaddies, couldn't wait to get out. Being a private soldier at the very bottom of the food chain was an emotionally draining experience and something I hadn't prepared myself for.

As a private soldier, the feelings of powerlessness and drift that accompanied my life were difficult to deal with. Every second of my time on duty, and a good deal of off time too, was dictated and controlled by an unseen hand. The only way out of it was to get promoted and work my way up the ranks. This was a fair system but like the emotional impact of service, it was one I had underestimated.

When I had been a civilian, and later a recruit, I imagined that to achieve promotion all you had to do was gain experience and perform well in your job. I thought that after a couple of years in a certain rank, you would automatically move up to the next one, provided you had put the work in. I realised there might be a short promotion course to attend, but I didn't think it would be anything too hard. In my naivety, I assumed that once you had passed the CIC at Catterick, most of the hard work was behind you. I had got it completely wrong.

The reason the British Army is the best in the world is because of how hard it trains and how difficult the courses are. In the infantry, the promotional cadres are referred to as 'dirty courses', and if you want to progress, there are three of them you must pass. Each course is harder than the previous one, and they are all run in the Brecon Beacons region of Wales, on the same hills that the SAS conducts its selection process. The Brecon hills and surrounding terrain are amongst the most dangerous and inhospitable training grounds in the world, and their bleakness has to be seen to be believed.

To become a lance corporal a soldier normally has to serve at least two years, and then he will be off to Brecon for six weeks to complete the junior NCO cadre. It is an exhausting course to pass, and you can tell when someone has done it because they are covered in bruises and limp like cripples. The next rank in line is that of corporal, which requires a 12-week stay at Brecon, this time doing 'Juniors' – or 'Junior Brecon' as it is also known. In order to move on to sergeant, you then have to be recommended for 'Senior Brecon' and face another 12 weeks in the hills.

Each of these courses carries a high failure rate, and there are always lots of injuries. It is like being back at depot (basic training), but it is even harder. Most blokes that make platoon sergeant have been in the army for about eight years, so it is not a quick process either. And the physical toll that these courses take on the body is great: most career soldiers suffer from persistent knee and hip problems in later life. For this reason, the army likes you to get the dirty courses out of the way while you are still in your 20s. If you do them when you are any older, you will suffer tremendously in middle age.

It is ironic that I had pushed so hard to join the army at the age of 30, still believing that I was young and fresh enough to serve for many more years, when, in fact, I was already considered too old to attend the promotion cadres. I had to wake up to the fact that the army really is a young man's game, and that the age limits are in place for a very good reason – so that you can have a full career and retire in good health at 40. At 31, I was still one of the fittest riflemen in my company, and I was way ahead of men a dozen years younger. But what would happen in another couple of years when I was leaving my prime behind and theirs' was only beginning? Would it be worth wrecking my body trying to keep up and ending up like an ageing footballer who has played too many games and done himself permanent harm? These were difficult questions that I would have to answer and problems that I hadn't banked on facing.

The demands of being a professional soldier are similar to those of being a professional athlete. It is an intensely physical existence, and by starting at the age of 30, as opposed to 20, I had turned the natural order of things completely on its head. The best I could hope for, and the most sensible thing, would be to maintain the highest standard of fitness I could and try to avoid injury. I would leave after my three years were up, and, until that point, I would do my very best to make the most of the time I had left. The cold and brutal fact was that I had arrived in the Green Jackets ten years too late.

As my time in the regiment would be short, I decided to push myself forward more. If it was possible, I wanted to pick up some skills that would be useful to me when I went back to Civvy Street. My refusal to budge about the Assault Engineer Course had left a bad taste in my mouth, and I knew that the sergeant-major was pissed off. I didn't want to get on the wrong side of him, or to get a reputation as a coaster, so I asked him if I could train to be a Combat Medic and a Land-Rover driver. It turned out to be a shrewd move, and he complimented me on my 'change in attitude'. The funny thing was that nothing had changed about my attitude, because I had always wanted to do those courses – just not the Assault Engineer one.

One of the bonuses about being on a course was that it broke up the daily routine and got you out of camp. The Land-Rover course was run out of Catterick, so it meant a return to my old stomping ground. We had an absolute blast, learning how to drive across steep hills and through flooded ditches. At night-time, we would have a barbecue on the backfields and shout abuse at passing recruits, safe in the knowledge there wasn't a thing they could do about it. Courses like these were an opportunity to relax, as well as work hard.

My next course was the Combat Medic cadre, which meant a

three-week stay at Aldershot Barracks. The camp was also a training facility for tri-service medical recruits, and we spent our nights chatting up girls from the RAF and the navy. As we were trained soldiers, we could come and go as we pleased and didn't have to march about everywhere. It gave us a certain status with the young recruits who hadn't yet passed out, and it was particularly useful in securing a shag!

I couldn't help comparing the lives of the medical recruits at Aldershot and the course they were on, to the infantry recruits at Catterick on the CIC. The difference was unbelievable. Aldershot was like a holiday camp, and the recruits still complained. The NAAFI bar was turned into a disco every night, and the recruits openly fraternised with the instructors. At Catterick we had to ask permission to buy a newspaper, but here there wasn't much difference between an instructor and a recruit. There was none of the aggression or physicality that characterised an infantry battalion, and it showed in the condition of the instructors.

My time at Aldershot also made me realise that being in the support arms is like being in a separate army to the infantry, because much of the hardship and danger is removed. Whilst the infantry does all the frontline work, such as security patrolling or quelling riots, the support arms are often 'at the rear with the gear'. If you look at the army as a spear, the Special Forces are the spear tip, the infantry the spearhead and the supporting arms the spear shaft.

The medical course was something I enjoyed immensely, as I felt I was learning something that could benefit me for life, and it was also a chance to get away from the daily grind of battalion life. However, when I returned to Weeton I got a nasty shock: the compulsory drug testing (CDT) team had booted out several of our soldiers. The CDT guys visited us three or four times a year on a random basis, and they had a habit of appearing when you least expected them to. They had even been known to swoop in on combat operations or overseas exercises with foreign armies. Their sole purpose in life was weeding out druggies, and every time they came, they caught about ten guys.

Most of the positives came from cannabis, cocaine and Ecstasy, and it was surprising how many soldiers dabbled, particularly the younger lads. Whenever we returned to camp from leave there would always be a smattering of soldiers bragging about getting 'whizzed up' or 'hoovering up the Charlie'. I think a lot of it was just childish boasting and probably made up, but there were undoubtedly a few hard-core users in the battalion.

Life in Weeton Barracks was like living in an enclosed bubble – it was our own little universe cut off from the rest of the army and the outside world. But while we continued with our daily routines of exercising and maintaining military skills, the rest of the army was involved in a far more serious venture. The Iraq War had been raging for a number of weeks, and there was a feeling of disgruntlement that the Green Jackets hadn't got involved. Whatever the rights and wrongs of it, there was no denying it was a major conflict, and it didn't sit well with us that we were stuck at home, while other soldiers were fighting their hearts out in the desert. Just like the rest of the country, we would watch the nightly reports on the evening news and wonder what it must be like to be a participant in that deadly conflict.

Over our evening meals or in the NAAFI bar, frequent squabbles and intense discussions would break out about what the army was doing wrong in Iraq or how it could be done differently. Some were in favour of the war and some were against it, but, without exception, everybody had a strong opinion on it and plenty to say.

The general public and the media like to portray soldiers as having a neutral opinion on matters of war and peace, but I found that assumption to be completely wrong. It might be comforting and fashionable to imagine soldiers as unflinching and devoted patriots, ever ready to sacrifice their lives without hesitation, but the reality is rather less romantic. You can be sure that if a soldier suspects he might have to go to war, he wants to know all of the reasons why and whether there is any way an alternative can be found.

With the Iraq conflict looming ever larger on the horizon, everybody wanted to become an expert on the Middle East. I saw barely literate soldiers that only ever watched soap operas or cartoons transformed into avid newshounds, watching Sky News in hushed silence and devouring broadsheet newspapers. Books on the history of Iraq started appearing and were passed from soldier to soldier like over-used porn mags.

Amidst all this learning and endless debate, there was an uncomfortable question being asked that wouldn't go away: were we being lied too and taken for fools? We were by no means bleeding heart liberals, but neither were we thick-headed squaddies, and all the talk of massive oil reserves and missing WMDs wasn't lost on us. It was recognised that Saddam Hussein was as bent as a snake in a jam jar, but some people were feeling equally uncertain about George Bush and Tony Blair. We were feeling a little bit doubtful about the whole thing, because the more we read and learned, the more we suspected we weren't being told the whole truth.

For my own part, I began to feel very ambiguous about the Iraq War and was confused about the moral issues. I had begun to study the conflict, hoping to find reasons to support it – but the more I studied, the more I began to feel it was fundamentally flawed. I decided to trust the Prime Minister and the government for the time being, but I couldn't shake the feeling that this was the wrong war, at the wrong time and place, for the wrong reasons, and being fought with the wrong strategy.

At any rate, as it seemed that for the moment we weren't going to be taking part, I decided to push it to the back of my mind and pray that my suspicions were wrong.

A few weeks later, we received the news that 1RGJ had been selected as the nation's 'Spearhead Battalion'. This meant that we would have to complete an intensive training package, at the conclusion of which we would be placed on 48 hours' notice to deploy to any trouble spot in the world. Of course, everybody assumed we were being primed for Iraq, but the officers told us that it was an unlikely destination as other regiments had been lined up for that duty already. Apparently, the troop numbers in Iraq were more than sufficient, and it was anticipated that the conflict would soon be over.

The CO said that we would only go out there if there was a sudden and massive deterioration, so we would be wise to forget about it and put it out of our minds. We would be more likely to go to the Democratic Republic of the Congo, because recently it had been experiencing problems, or perhaps some other region of Africa. I breathed a sigh of relief and focused my mind on the training ahead.

The nature of a Spearhead deployment means you normally only go in when a situation has broken down or is spiralling out of control. With that in mind, the long and arduous training package is designed to bring you to a peak of fitness. For those of us in F Company under the command of Maj. Squibb, it promised to be even more so, as his SAS background meant he was a hard taskmaster.

The first skill we had to master was that of riot control: how to use batons and shields against petrol bombers. We all peeled onto the backfield training area and formed into groups of attackers and defenders. Each group would get a chance to play both roles, and the order of the day was to be hard and aggressive. This was a new area of soldiering that hadn't been covered at Catterick, and I was looking forward to learning something different.

The man conducting the training was a real character by the name of Cpl. Tradusca. I was pleased we had Cpl. Tradusca in charge as he was a very capable soldier. He was popular, had a likeable and friendly manner, and had been in the regiment since the early '80s. He had been around the block a few times and knew what he was talking about. If he thought an order was wrong, he wouldn't hesitate to describe it as shit, and if he felt someone had fucked up, he wouldn't hesitate to get physical. But he wasn't a bully either; he was a fair man who genuinely believed his style of discipline was the best. I hadn't fucked up yet so I hadn't attracted his attention. I just hoped it stayed that way.

I hadn't done riot training before, but one of the NCOs warned me to watch my back as it could degenerate into a mass brawl if it wasn't tightly controlled. Generally speaking, all of F Company got on well together, but once we split down into platoons, all friendships went out of the window. 16 Platoon had been detailed to attack us and push us back, and we had been ordered to stand our ground and push them back. We all wore arm and leg pads, and as defenders had rubber batons and shields to protect ourselves. The NCOs in 16 Platoon were winding their lads up and telling them to rip into us and make us 'look like cunts'. We weren't supposed to strike them with our batons, but we all agreed that if they took the piss and tried to kill us, they would get a good fucking lashing back. I noticed a group of senior officers watching us and rubbing their hands with glee, and I had a sickening feeling that things were going to get out of hand.

Suddenly, the cry went up, and they charged down the field towards us. It had been agreed that they would start with verbal abuse and then make an effort to grab a couple of shields from us. It didn't quite work out that way. They hit us with boots and fists in a wave of snarling aggression. We managed to withstand the first attack and even dragged a few of them into our rear lines – where they were rewarded with a good kicking. The second wave was a bit more organised, although it must have been comical to watch as they launched flying kicks against our shields that would have done Eric Cantona proud. This time we retaliated, and as they got closer, we lashed out with the batons. The batons were a very effective defence, and as both sides parted, there were a lot of cut lips and bruised faces.

By the time of the third attack, both sides were so pumped up that the violence was getting out of control, and the instructors struggled to part us. One of the Fijians was going wild with his baton and had to be rugby tackled by the sergeant, while various others became involved in private wars. I was faced with Anthony and Jameson, two best friends who were intent on caving my head in. The pair of them wrestled me and my shield to the floor, but I wouldn't let go of it and ended up being pulled along as if on a sled. I was dimly aware of the two sides running back to their positions, but Ant and I were locked in a duel over the shield and rolling around in the mud, neither one of us willing to give in to the other.

All of a sudden, Cpl. Tradusca came running towards us, screaming at us to break it up. Ant jumped up and scarpered back to his own side, and I went to do the same, but the shield and baton meant I was a bit slower. I was halfway up when I felt a heavy boot slam into my exposed ribs, knocking me back down again. The pain was immediate and intense, and I felt as though I couldn't breathe – all of the wind had been knocked out of me. Cpl. Tradusca had kicked me full force in the ribs and was now screaming at me to reform the line. Inwardly seething and reeling from the shock of his actions, I staggered back to the line. I considered dumping the shield and attacking him on the spot, but the line was already being primed for another attack, and he was off barking orders to someone else. If I went for him immediately, I would just look like a twat and ruin the day's training, so I would have to bide my time before making a decision.

How I got through the rest of the day I shall never know, but I think it was only adrenalin and pride that kept me on my feet. I was hurt and angry that I had received my first jab from an NCO when as far as I was concerned I had only been defending myself. When time was called and the kit handed in, I went and sat alone on my bed and had a long think. My ribs were absolutely throbbing, and I suspected they were broken: every time I inhaled, it felt like a knife was stuck in my sides. More importantly, my pride was wounded. I had always told myself that if any NCO ever struck me, I would immediately strike him back. The army didn't pay me enough to be a punch bag, and I wouldn't put up with it in Civvy Street, so why should I put up with it here?

But it wasn't that simple – other factors were involved. The right time to have struck back would have been instantly – if I did it later, I would look like a cunt and be treated like one by the other men, too. Cpl. Tradusca was also extremely popular (even I liked and respected him). I also had to consider that he himself never bore a grudge, and as far as he was concerned, the incident was over – he had even said I had done well as we were washing the kit down.

As much as it hurt my pride and made me feel like a coward, I decided not to retaliate. In the end, it simply wasn't worth opening up a can of worms I couldn't control. I reluctantly swallowed my pride and made a promise that the next time a soldier took a liberty with me he would pay for it on the spot.

Later, I drove to the local hospital and was diagnosed with a hairline fracture of the ribs. The doctor said it would take six weeks to heal and wouldn't give me any lasting problems. I didn't report it because I didn't want to be accused of stirring up trouble or making a big deal. In any case, every one had seen Cpl. Tradusca stick the boot in, and everybody knew what the score was. For the next few weeks, I could only sleep on my back and felt like passing out whenever we did PT or went on a tab, but I did it all anyway because I didn't want to draw attention to myself. Sometimes in the Green Jackets you just had to grit your teeth and smile, no matter how shit the reality.

* * *

The preparation for Spearhead was exhausting and intensive. The regiment had to prove it was fit for overseas operations by completing a series of physical tests and military exercises. Of all these, the most feared was the fit-for-role tab, or FFR as it was known. The FFR involved completing a twenty-six-mile tab in six-hours' marching time spread over a twenty-four-hour period, concluding with a battalion attack on an enemy position that lasted for several hours. You tabbed the first thirteen miles in three hours straight, then went into a 'harbour area' (wooded area) to sort your feet out and devise a battle plan. Once that was sorted out, you then tabbed the remaining thirteen miles in another three hours before launching the big attack.

The FFR took place in the hills of Scotland and was a nightmarish ordeal for some. While it proved to be a tough test for us all, and every man finished with bleeding blisters and swollen ankles, for a few unfit unfortunates it was a trip into hell. We had done a lot of pre-training and preparation back at Weeton, so by the time the exercise came round, we were good and ready. If you had half a brain, you also did extra gym work in your spare time, because nobody wanted to be struggling on a 26-miler.

Nonetheless, a few of our more unwise members felt they didn't need to put in any extra work as they were good enough already. Such individuals contrived to go on the sick ('on the biff' in army slang), or claimed to be doing their own training, when, in fact, they were trying to improve their scores on PlayStation games. What they failed to understand was that on the FFR there would be no Jack Wagon following us around, and every man that started the tab had to finish it, otherwise his whole company would be classified as having failed its task. And just to make sure there wasn't any cheating, we had an independent troop of observers marking our performances and times. So, on this occasion, there would be no dropping out or coming in at your own pace – you had to keep up with the pack no matter what.

For the first five miles everyone was together and in good order, but soon after, the weaker lads began to fall behind. At first, they were motivated with words of encouragement and slaps on the back. That strategy worked for a few miles. Once they began falling behind again, the motivations were kicks up the arse and thumps in the kidneys, as well as some 'strong language'. Again, this special encouragement worked for a short while, but soon afterwards, the stragglers fell apart altogether. They had now become a pitiful sight, drooling and vomiting down their shirts, staggering along like drunks, their bodies refusing to obey their minds. Thankfully, there were only a few of them, but they were slowing us down to such an extent that the entire company was being put at risk.

One lad collapsed altogether and was spread-eagled in the dirt, his platoon sergeant frantically dragging him to his feet. By that point, he was in such a shit state that his kit had been pulled off him and distributed amongst the company. But even without his kit weighing him down, he could still barely walk, and the sergeant had to drag him round and prop him up for the entire distance. Towards the end, we were all struggling so much that we had no pity for the stragglers, only a vicious contempt, because we were carrying their kit and being punished for their sins. Thanks to the dead weight slowing us down, we were forced to run the last few miles and only made it in with minutes to spare.

Once we came to a halt, a cloud of steam rose from the company and hung in the night air. We had a short break to catch our breath and sort our kit out, and then we launched into the battalion attack. Just to make our lives that little bit harder, we had to complete an 'insertion tab' of two miles before we could launch our attack. It came as no surprise to find ourselves wading through streams chest deep in water and clumping through thick forests – and all before a shot was fired.

With the FFR out of the way, Maj. Squibb organised a special treat for the lads in F Company. We travelled down to Brecon with him to complete the 'SAS 8-miler' selection tab. This was the tab that all would-be SAS troopers had to pass before being allowed onto the hills phase of selection. He felt that as we had just successfully cracked the FFR, the time would be ripe for us to test ourselves with this new challenge. On paper, it sounded easier than the FFR, but, in reality, it was a lot harder because of the lie of the land. We had just two hours to cross a series of incredibly steep valleys and hills, and the ground was atrociously boggy and wet.

Carrying the full range of platoon weapons hampered us further, including several Gimpys and bulky LAW 94 rocket launchers. These heavy weapons would be passed around the platoon like a parcel nobody wanted to receive. When it was your turn, you carried it until you were fit to drop and then passed it on to the next man. It was a tough test, and we lost a couple of blokes along the way – most notably an exhausted soldier who had to be carted away in an ambulance because of dehydration. Unlike the FFR, it was no disgrace to fail this tab because it really was approaching the premier league of soldiering, and for many of us, it was the toughest test we would ever face.

For the final phase of Spearhead preparation, we returned to the Scottish hills for an escape and evasion exercise called 'Green Muscle', followed by an exercise in Dartford. In Scotland, the battalion split down into two halves – if you were lucky, you were on the hunter force; if you were unlucky, you were on the escapee side. The blokes on the run had to spend three nights in the most awful flea-ridden forest imaginable – the place was awash with the kind of aggressive midges and flies that were more common in the Mediterranean. If you prepared well, you had a 'mozze net' to put over your face and some repellent spray; if you didn't, you suffered horrendously. Even with all the proper kit, I almost went mad, and I honestly think a week in those hills would break anyone.

We then moved down south for the fortnight's exercise at

Dartford camp, where we were pitted against the Royal Irish Regiment. For the first week, we would act as defending troops and for the second as rioters. It was similar to what we had done on the backfield area at Weeton but on a much bigger scale. We were tasked to occupy a purpose-built village area, and we had to defend the buildings and local population (soldiers in civvies) against ambush attacks, petrol bombers and rioters. The Royal Irish were a tough bunch thanks to their participation in the Troubles, and they attacked us with all they had. Green Jacket pride meant we more than held our own, but, as before, it dissolved into a mass brawl, and many soldiers on both sides used it as an excuse to take gross liberties. It wasn't unusual to see soldiers wandering around with broken noses or split lips, and by the end of the first week, it had got very personal.

We had our revenge in week two when it was our turn to play the bad guys. This time the attacking force was designed to simulate rioters and terrorists, as opposed to enemy troops. We wore tracksuits and jeans and were referred to as 'Acting Civ. Pop.' or the civilian population. However, having a 4x4 licence meant that while my pals were getting battered and bloody, I bagged myself another cushy job. I was given the keys to an old Range-Rover and linked up with a group of Small Arms School specialists. We played the part of enemy terrorists and drove round setting up ambushes for the patrolling troops. The idea was that we would lie in wait in a field or farm barn, and when the troops got within range, we'd jump out and spray them with fire. I'd then start the car, and we'd crash off through the forest, across fields or down the nearest dirt track. It was great fun because we always had the upper hand and got to play with some 'Gucci' kit.

Strictly speaking, we weren't supposed to leave the confines of the camp when we were tooled up for an attack, but occasionally we did. We got some funny looks when the sergeant nipped to a nearby garage for a paper. Sitting in the big Range-Rover and wearing blue boiler suits, we tried to look as inconspicuous as possible – which was pretty hard when you have a couple of Gimpys, an AK47 and M16 spilling over the back seats. A truck driver pulled up alongside us, and when he looked down, his eyes nearly popped out of his head.

That was the first time I ever handled an M16, and I could instantly see why it was rated as a better weapon than the SA80. The M16 was significantly lighter, much simpler to use and a hell of a lot easier to clean and maintain. It had taken me weeks to become competent with an SA80, but within half a day, I knew how to strip and assemble the M16 and managed to pass my weapons' handling test first time. Whereas the SA80 broke down into dozens of fiddly parts, the M16 snapped in two like a shotgun, and you simply slid the guts out and gave them a quick scrub. I was in heaven! Ask any infantry soldier and he will tell you that the bane of his life is cleaning weapons – it is a tedious process of scraping away carbon residue that can take hours. We all love firing them, but we bloody well hate cleaning them!

Squaddies argue endlessly about the comparative benefits of the SA80 and the M16. A case could be argued for the SA80 having greater killing power and a superior sighting system, but the ultimate decider of a general assault rifle is its ease of use and reliability – and on that count the M16 wins hands down.

As Spearhead troops we were issued with the updated SA80 A2 rifle, and while it was a significant improvement on the older version, it still carried the fatal flaws of excessive weight and complexity of construction. The modern day M16 is a 40-year-old weapon that has undergone several major upgrades to keep it ahead of the field, and it has an impressive track record in urban, desert and jungle warfare that the SA80 cannot match. Other nations have recognised its superior qualities, and it has consequently been sold to virtually every nation on earth. Compare this to the SA80, which is used by no nation other than the British and is scoffed at by our own Special Forces.

From my perspective, I was just grateful that the Spearhead training package gave me an opportunity to become familiar with such an iconic weapon, because unless you're involved with the Special Forces, the SA80 is always your primary weapon.

Before we left Dartford, a few of the lads decided to give the Royal Irish boys a leaving present, as a way of saying thank you for their rough treatment. They snuck into an unoccupied area of the bar and smeared it with their own shit. What they didn't know was that the whole episode had been captured on CCTV and was shown to the camp regimental sergeant-major. A minor scandal ensued, and a senior officer was forced into making a grovelling public apology on behalf of the battalion. As a punishment, the lads who turned the bar into a toilet were mercilessly beasted and hammered into the ground by a PTI. When the officer made his apology, even the Royal Irish boys raised a laugh when he described the culprits as 'crazed apes' in his incredibly posh accent. It might have been disgusting, but it did end the exercise on a high note.

And that was that, the end of our Spearhead training regime. We were officially ready to deploy anywhere in the world at two days' notice. This meant we could never stray too far from camp as we had to be able to return there within six hours. We also had to have our mobile phones switched on 24 hours a day, just in case a shout went out. There were no exceptions to these rules, even if we went on holiday, and unless we were deployed somewhere, we would have to live like this for four months.

The CO recognised how depressing and restrictive this lifestyle was, and so he made sure we got plenty of leave and had a relatively easy time of it on camp. So long as we maintained our physical fitness and personal kit to the highest standard, we were allowed to come and go as we pleased. We were also spared the usual bullshit routine of doing jobs just for the sake of it and making ourselves look busy.

Although the days of painting grass greener had long since

gone, there still remained plenty of paths to sweep free of leaves and lots of walls to scrub, so we were glad of the break. My brother had told me of an amusing incident when he was stationed in Bulford. He had been leaning on a Land-Rover when he spotted the CO coming over. Damian began taking the wheel off, and when the CO asked him why, he replied, 'Because you're here, Sir.' A perfect illustration of army bullshit at work.

The leave was much appreciated and an aspect of my army service that pleasantly surprised me. No other job could compare to it when it came to having time off work – not even being a teacher. I had heard all of the horror stories about soldiers being deprived of their holidays, but in the Green Jackets that was never the case. I soon learned the reason behind it: quite simply, you were worked like dogs for a couple of months and were then rewarded with two to four weeks' leave. By the time your leave period came round, you would be in bits psychologically and crying out for a break – but when it was over, you were raring to get stuck in again.

It was while we were enjoying our summer leave of 2003 and approaching the end of our Spearhead commitment, that we received the urgent phone calls we had been secretly dreading – we were going to Iraq. I had been half expecting the news because I had seen how the country was falling apart on the TV, but when it came, it was still a shock, and I felt sick to my stomach. All of a sudden this 'army lark' felt frighteningly real. Yes, I had trained long and hard for this moment, and, yes, I had expected it to arrive eventually, but, no, I didn't feel emotionally prepared for what we might have to face.

For many years, I had devoured war books and films, all the time marvelling at how exciting and wonderful it must be to be part of an adventurous military force. The problem was, all of those glorious thoughts and grand ideas had arisen from the comfort of my favourite armchair. But this wasn't just a harmless fantasy and me putting the world to rights over a few pints – this was a real conflict, and I was now a part of it. For a brief moment, I wished I was a civvy again, but I knew I could never go back to that, and I was shitting myself. From the reactions I saw back at camp, I knew I wasn't alone.

5

WELCOME TO BASRA INTERNATIONAL

When I arrived back at camp, the atmosphere was palpably tense. Everywhere you looked was a hive of activity, and soldiers were rushing about wearing grim expressions. Wild rumours about the nature and scope of our deployment were doing the rounds, and groups of riflemen gathered together to gossip and speculate on what might be the outcome. Would we be joining the Americans in Baghdad and the ravaged northern cities, or would we be used to restore order in Basra and the southern deserts? Nobody knew, but everybody had a theory and opinion. We would put questions to the senior officers and sergeant-majors, and we would always receive the same answer: wait until the CO gives his battalion address.

The CO assembled the battalion on the parade square and marched briskly to its centre. As was his style, he came straight to the point. He told us that while we had been enjoying our summer leave, he had been conducting a reconnaissance trip to Iraq. He apologised for not having been able to tell us sooner, but we would be flying to Basra in one week's time, for a deployment entitled 'Op Telic 2' – the original war effort that had ended a few months before had been called 'Op Telic 1'. Our mission was simple – we had to provide security for Basra International airport and force protection for all allied activities in the region. In recent weeks, there had been a huge increase in attacks upon allied troops and signs of a growing terrorist insurgency. He added that terrorist attacks were averaging ten a day, and the death toll was rising – indeed, a policeman who had assisted him on his recce had just been assassinated driving to the airport.

It is normally deathly silent while a CO is speaking, but as he reeled off more sombre statistics and warnings, a few lads muttered 'fucking hell' and sighed loudly. Worried glances were exchanged and heads shook as the enormity of what we might be facing sank in. If the CO was deliberately trying to frighten us into being hyper-vigilant and cautious, he was doing a good job of it. Technically speaking, the Iraq War was officially over, and our mission was being classed as a peacekeeping tour, but we had no doubt that the dangers remained the same.

The CO described for us the kind of welcome we could expect on the dusty streets of Basra: 'The war has ended, but Iraq has dissolved into a state of medium-intensity conflict, terrorist attacks are increasing and civilian unrest is becoming hard to manage. It is on a par with Northern Ireland at its very worst and could well significantly surpass that.'

Admittedly, it wasn't an all-out war that we would be facing, but peacekeeping in a hostile region could present equal or even greater dangers. At least in wartime you could blast away at the enemy whenever you saw them, but as peacekeepers we would have to adhere to strict rules of engagement and have eyes in the back of our heads. The enemies of the peacekeeper weren't uniformed soldiers driving tanks but smiling terrorists wearing jeans and trainers, and we couldn't anticipate raging gun battles with organised enemy troops. Instead, our enemies' tactics would be to detonate roadside bombs and attack us using unseen snipers. I realised that facing an invisible enemy that melts away into the crowd could be as disconcerting, in its own way, as facing a column of enemy tanks.

On the upside, at least we now knew where we were going and what our mission was, and we could mentally prepare for it. I was pleased that we had a full week to get our affairs in order and tie up any loose ends. I chose to go for a long run every day, because I wanted to be as fighting fit as possible. It seemed that I wasn't the only sudden fitness fanatic as former couch potatoes dug out their trainers, too. In reality, a week's training wouldn't make any difference to your fitness levels at all, but it did put your mind at ease to know you had done everything possible.

Another curious phenomenon was the sudden appearance of bibles – even the hard-core atheists stashed one in their kitbags, because 'you never know'. Being the hypocrite that I am, I took one along, too, and I vowed to read it from cover to cover while I was out there. Basically, anything that you felt might give you an edge, be it spiritual, mental or physical, was fair game.

Everybody dealt with the pressure of preparing themselves in a different way: some lads would lock themselves in their rooms and watch endless war movies; others wrote melodramatic love letters to wives and girlfriends; and the usual suspects went into town and partied every night as if it was their last on earth. Some of our loudest and most gregarious characters became quiet and sullen, and a few became aggressive and edgy. Sometimes, I'd be chatting amicably to a mate, and I would see in his eyes that he was weighing me up with a hint of suspicion, wondering how I'd hold up if it all went 'Pete Tong' (rhyming slang). And yet others displayed not a hint of emotion or worry and seemed utterly unaffected by it all. It was fascinating to watch.

Internally, I felt as though I was on an emotional roller-coaster, made all the worse by the fact that I couldn't give voice to my doubts or acknowledge my fears. I felt more awkward than most lads because deep down I was beginning to have serious concerns about the validity of the war. Whenever a critical thought came into my head, I would beat it down and try to erase the question. The reality was that I had voluntarily joined the army, and I couldn't pick and choose the wars I fought in – the fact that I didn't agree with it was an irrelevancy, because as a soldier I was a mere instrument of government policy and not a decision maker.

I wondered how I would react if I was horribly maimed or disfigured fighting for a cause in which I didn't believe – no doubt it would turn me into a bitter and twisted figure consumed by self-hatred. I mulled over possible scenarios in my head – what would be better: to lose my legs to a bomb or to be killed outright? What would happen to my dick if a bullet hit it? It would probably be blown off. I think I'd prefer to be killed. And on and on with such ridiculous questions.

My stomach was doing cartwheels for the entire week, and I practically lived on the toilet. It didn't matter that I wasn't ill or hadn't eaten any food – the shit was pouring out of me. But whenever I felt sorry for myself, I only had to look around to know that I wasn't alone and that for some lads their misery was considerably worse. Perhaps it was because of my age and life experience, I don't really know, but I seemed to be able to disguise my fears quite well. Nobody had a clue about how I was feeling inside, and I even managed to manufacture a fake enthusiasm and cheerfulness.

In contrast, one of my good friends couldn't hide his tears or control his fear, and it took a lot of gentle persuasion to calm him down. There were other lads who also became a bit tearful and morose – usually the teenagers straight from depot – but, again, a bit of encouragement and reassurance seemed to perk them up. To the credit of the regiment, whenever we thought we might have a problem with a lad becoming upset, he was taken aside and treated with respect. There was none of that 'pull yourself together' shit you see in war films, as that only stokes the fear and makes it worse.

The lads I felt most sorry for were our two newest recruits, who both came from Caribbean islands and had joined the British Army in search of a better life, feeling that it was a safer bet than the United States military. The pair of them had passed out of basic training only a week before, and were busy celebrating their achievement with relatives in London when they had received a most unwelcome phone call: 'Pack your kit, you're going to Iraq next week.' Instead of enjoying a nice holiday and looking forward to being eased into battalion life, they were being packed off to Iraq with maximum haste. I asked one of them how he felt about it, and all he could mumble was, 'Stunned.'

Once the first few days were out of the way, the shock began to wear off, and I started to feel better about things. As selfish as it sounds, I was glad to see other lads getting upset, because it told me I wasn't alone. The nerves were still there, but there was also a calmness and acceptance at the same time. At least we were beginning to feel like proper soldiers again and not the war dodgers who had been ducking out on Iraq. There was actually a perverse satisfaction in knowing that we were going out there to do a job, no matter how much we'd rather be staying at home. At least we would be able to say we had been there whenever the question came up, as it frequently did, with family and friends.

We received some bad news when Maj. Squibb was recalled from the battalion in order to attend Staff College. His speed of thought and presence of mind would have been a huge asset on the ground, and a lot of us were sad he wouldn't be in Iraq with us. But aside from that disappointment, we were as well-prepared as we could be, and I felt confident in the men around me.

As soon as they heard we were being deployed, the media descended on the camp like a swarm of locusts. There were dozens of reporters and cameramen roaming about, and it wasn't unusual to see your face on the nightly news. The newspapers chose to take the angle that the Green Jackets were being sent in to 'sort out the mess and kick some behinds'. It might have suited their purposes to put an aggressive spin on it, but inside the regiment, we were hoping for a more sedate experience.

At last, the day of our deployment arrived. At the crack of dawn, a huge armada of Land-Rovers snaked out of Weeton Barracks and headed for Southampton docks. As we drove out of the gates, dozens of cameras flashed and TV cameras filmed our departure. It was actually quite a moving moment, and the fact that we were so newsworthy underlined the significance of the tour. In the past, it had always bothered me that I was only a tiny cog in such a huge machine, but as I took in the sea of green vehicles around me, I realised for the first time how essential each cog was. Here we were, hundreds of anxious and apprehensive cogs, all grinding into life and moving forward together, despite our fears.

It seemed the whole country knew we were going to Iraq, and cars would pause and respectfully wave us past or honk their horns in greeting. Halfway to Southampton, we stopped at a service station for refreshments, and the staff treated us like we were VIPs; they were full of good wishes, excessively polite and urged us to keep safe. I must admit, I revelled in the attention and enjoyed it while it lasted. My philosophy was that whenever the job presented a special moment it was wise to seize it and wring it dry – because you never knew if you would get another one.

We dropped the vehicles off at the docks then headed off to RAF Brize Norton to catch our plane. I tried to sleep on the flight but couldn't: my mind had gone into overdrive and was mulling over worst-case scenarios. I alternated between feeling high and low, and allowed my eyes to wander round the craft, settling on random individuals and wondering if they would be coming home. Each face told its own story, and people were unable to hide their feelings: some were looking thoughtful, others anxious and agitated, while others looked serenely peaceful. As I glanced around, I surprised myself by experiencing a sudden rush of comradeship and compassion for my fellow soldiers.

The one thing I didn't want to do – and it did worry me – was to perform badly or let any of those men down. The emotions that I had gone through when preparing myself for the tour had convinced me that I wasn't cut out for fighting wars and that I wasn't the kind of bloke who would perform heroically. I had previously entertained foolish fantasies of Victoria Cross-winning heroics, but when I found myself entering a genuine danger zone, I sensibly downgraded my expectations. I would be happy if I could merely perform well and not let anybody down – fuck winning medals.

The plane touched down on the bumpy runway, and a sarcastic cheer went up. Looking out of the window at the surrounding desert and burning oil wells was a sobering moment – we were now on Iraqi soil. It was 7 p.m. local time, and the sun was still blazing, its blinding rays glinting on the airport terminal. As we trudged down the steps a hot blast of stifling air immediately hit us. It was like standing in front of a giant hairdryer, and it sucked the breath from your lungs. My first thought was that it was the engines winding down, but as I got further away from them I realised that it was the hot desert breeze.

The incredible heat astounded us all – it felt like we had stepped into a furnace. Even my Kenyan friend Chege said that he had never felt heat like it. A sergeant from the RAF Regiment (air force infantry) led us into the baggage area and gleefully told us that we were lucky it was a cool night for a change!

The baggage area was a gloomy-looking hall that had clearly seen better days, and it was showing signs of the recent war. Gaudy orange tiles, which were decorated with deep cracks and splinters that spread out like spiders' legs, covered the walls. Pictures hung at crazy angles, and bits of random piping peeped out of crumbling plaster. The floor was bare concrete and covered in a thick dust that kicked up whenever you took a step. The sickly orange tiles and outdated decor created the image of an abandoned cheap '70s' hotel.

We waited around for what seemed like hours in the baggage area, each man frantically trying to locate his bergen and black grip bag amongst the hundreds stacked up. This was no easy task as all our kit was virtually identical, save for some small coloured tags that identified the company to which the bags belonged. Thanks to the heat and inevitable difficulties finding kit, tempers were already getting frayed.

Once we secured our luggage, we all piled onto the waiting coaches. Outside, the time-warp theme continued, and giant turquoise squares covered the front of the airport. We then made the short journey to 'Tent City', where we would spend the remainder of the tour. It was situated on the edge of the airport, behind high fences and concrete barriers. It consisted of scores of huge beige tents, all linked together by hard plastic walkways. As well as accommodation tents, there were TV tents, food tents, games tents and a well-equipped gym tent. The Royal Engineers had designed and built the facility, and I got the impression that the tents could easily handle years of occupation – an ominous sign, perhaps. However, Tent City was a surprisingly comfortable place to live, and to a man we were very impressed with it.

Now that we were finally there much of the tension and fear I had been feeling began to leave me, and I think that was the case with most of the lads. Self-preservation and common sense told us that our best chances of surviving and remaining sane were to try and remain positive and confident – although sometimes that is easier said than done.

For the first week of our stay, we didn't actually do any work at all, other than attend some security briefings. This was because the effects of the summer heat were so crippling that they required an acclimatisation period. At first, I thought this was a luxurious indulgence and unnecessary (although I wasn't about to complain), but after only a few days, I realised how important it was. The shock of the unrelenting heat was incredible – we drank gallons of water every day and still felt thirsty. It became a struggle to stay awake, and we slept like exhausted dogs all day and night. I broke out in a nasty sweat rash that covered my balls in an angry, red eruption of sores and chaffed skin. In the end, I had to ditch my underwear and smear myself in antiseptic cream and talcum powder. A few of our dimmer recruits managed to fall asleep in the sun and found themselves being charged by the sergeant-major for wilfully becoming sunburnt – a serious military offence.

Although the first week felt like a bit of a holiday, the intelligence briefings gave us a brisk wake-up call. It was during these that we learned about the exact nature of our deployment and the threat we faced. Most of our time would be spent providing security for the airport (translated into hours of stag – so no surprises there) or escorting diplomatic VIPs into Basra and around southern Iraq. It was also explained to us that the local population would be by and large friendly, though there was a sizable minority that would prove an exception to that rule.

One possible problem we could face was stumbling into an inter-tribal fight that had nothing to do with us. Apparently, there was a myriad of warring tribes that hated one another with a passion, and in the past, patrolling soldiers had wandered into some vicious tribal disagreements only to find that the mob would cease fighting and turn on them instead. These local battles had raged for decades, and it was the best policy to back off if you saw one – otherwise a two-way fight could develop into a three-way one.

I was surprised to learn that Basra played host to about 20 different Muslim sects. Previously, I had thought that if you were a Muslim, then that was that, but my ignorance was being exposed, and I sat up to pay attention. It seemed that, just like the Christian faith, there were different branches and styles of worship, and, worryingly for us, some of them hated one another to a murderous extreme. We were told that we had no idea what religious intolerance was until we saw two opposing Muslim factions fall out – it made the Catholic and Protestant disagreements in Northern Ireland seem like a schoolboy squabble. It was hard not to get confused by the many religious differences in the country, and I was glad to be a simple atheist!

Another group we were told that we would have to watch out for was the Fedayeen. This force was made up of former Saddam loyalists who had infiltrated the Iraqi police. The Fedayeen were responsible for many successful attacks on coalition troops, and British soldiers remained a tempting target. More worryingly for us, the latest intelligence suggested that they were planning to use a Russian made DShK heavy anti-aircraft machine gun to attack Basra airport. The DShK (pronounced 'dushka') was a weapon that could bring down a chopper when fired from a mile away, and it could even cause tanks problems, so the thought of facing that bastard whilst on stag wasn't a prospect we relished. Another possible headache was the upcoming Ramadan festival, because although it was supposed to be a religious time, the local extremist clerics felt it would be a nice symbolic gesture to kill some troops.

We were also instructed to bear in mind that the streets we would be patrolling were the same ones on which British soldiers had been ambushed and killed only a few months previously. A favourite tactic of the terrorists was to use a mob of hostile locals to block or slow down a patrol's progress, and whilst they tried to negotiate a safe passage through, the insurgents would emerge from the crowd and attack. The army had learned its lesson from previous deaths incurred in this way, and if we suspected such a trap was being sprung, we would react swiftly. If we were in vehicles, we would at first nudge, hoot and gently drive through the crowd – but if that didn't work, we would floor it and accelerate through the mob as quickly as possible. If the crowd contained innocent women and children, it would be a tragedy, but after recent British fatalities, we couldn't take any more chances.

There were a few raised eyebrows at this possible course of action, although deep down we knew it to be the only thing we could do. The decision to plough through a crowd would be made by the patrol commander, and only as an extreme last resort, but it would still be an unbelievably tough call to make. Quite a few of the lads grumbled about potentially being placed in that kind of a situation and having to make such a dreadful decision, unsure whether they would be able to live with the consequences afterwards. But if it came down to it, what else could we do? To hesitate could mean being torn apart, but acting rashly could mean killing dozens of innocent demonstrators. For my part, I just prayed that it was not a choice I would ever have to make, because if I had to do it to save me and my comrades, I would. However, it would kill me in spirit, heart and soul, and a part of me would die with the crowd.

In another briefing, an intelligence officer gave us an assessment of the local population and how we were to interact with them. He told us to put aside any preconceptions about our own superiority and prejudices regarding the men of Basra. If we chose to mock and deride them as 'Rag Heads' and 'Flip-flops', that would be our choice and he couldn't stop us, but it could well prove to be a fatal mistake. On first impressions, the locals could come across as poor, uneducated and barely literate victims of a cruel regime. The reality was, in fact, very different. Far from being powerless victims and figures of fun, the local men were intelligent, tough, resourceful and cunning survivors – even Saddam hadn't managed to break their spirit and resolve. And many were soldiers, too, some having been trained from childhood. Others had fought in the bloody Iran–Iraq war. The officer concluded his lecture by telling us to treat people with a firm but polite respect, and to be careful not to insult their dignity, because to an Arab loss of face is an intolerable insult. Above all else, we were to remain wary, watchful and alert when we were around the civilian population.

I enjoyed his lecture and took heed of the warnings he gave, but I was disappointed to see a few of the usual suspects sniggering like they knew better. I made a mental note to watch my back and be hyper-vigilant whenever I was dealing with the locals and the idiots on my own side at the same time. My intention was to be as respectful and friendly as I could be, whilst still doing my job and not jeopardising operational security. Ultimately, I wasn't doing this out of the kindness of my heart or because I believed in fair play – I was doing it because it made good military sense and might help to save my own skin.

The lectures invariably led to discussions between us squaddies, and, in particular, our 'rules of engagement' briefing later prompted a heated debate. We were operating under the 'White Card' system, in which you were expected to go through a ritual of checks and balances before you could pull the trigger – by which time you would probably have flirted with death anyway. It was the kind of ludicrous, overly complicated and inflexible waffle that only a pen-pushing UN bureaucrat could come up with. The White Card was a potential recipe for uncertainty, confusion, second-guessing and hesitation on the part of a soldier – and all at the very time when he might need to make critical and decisive decisions. The logic and intentions behind the system are sound enough and based on the idea of a slowly escalating conflict that builds to lethal force, but the application and reality of it can be clumsy and slow.

I think the army knew this, too. As the officer briefed us he sounded almost apologetic and uncertain. Many of the recent deaths of soldiers had been suffered because individuals had hesitated and been slow, or were unwilling to 'let rip' on an aggressive crowd. We were told not to worry or hesitate about opening fire, because no one was going to arrest us afterwards – just as long as we could prove that we had followed the White Card system! Apparently, if we felt that our lives were in danger, we could exercise our own judgement and open fire, but, at the same time, we had to realise that we would be judged by the White Card rules afterwards. Some of the more senior lads said to the officer's face that this was bullshit and an extra headache that we could do without.

Long after the briefing was over, we continued arguing amongst ourselves about the rights and wrongs of the system. Some were envious of the American troops who remained on 'war fighting' rules of engagement, which meant that if they felt at all threatened they could apply firepower. Of course, the downside of the American rules was that nervous and trigger-happy soldiers could cause mayhem on the streets, but the upside was that if they felt genuinely threatened, they could wholeheartedly fight their way out of it. According to our rules, a soldier who made a genuine mistake, or couldn't prove afterwards why he had opened fire, could face a possible jail sentence. He would have to convince anti-war human-rights lawyers and a ravenous media that he had acted in good faith – not to mention a politically correct and guilty-feeling government that would gladly sacrifice him as a convenient way of shifting attention away from an unpopular war, which was widely perceived to be illegal and unnecessary.

The general consensus was that if it came down to it, we would use our weapons as we had been trained to, because there was no contest between being sent to prison or being buried in a coffin. As the saying goes, 'Better to be tried by twelve than carried by six.' All in all, I thought it was an absurd position to put soldiers in – who the hell wants to risk a prison sentence just for doing their job?

Towards the end of the first week, we were introduced to some physical exercise, because the amount of sleep we had been enjoying was bordering on the ridiculous. A PTI roused us from our beds at 6 a.m. and informed us we were going for an introductory run, before the blazing sun appeared and made exercise impossible.

There was a four-mile 'safe route' that took us from the camp gates down a long road to a fortified checkpoint and back again.

The distance itself would normally present no problem, but the oxygen-starved air and hot stillness of the muggy atmosphere turned it into a torturous test of endurance. I could well understand how the best runners in the world came from hot countries, because after only one mile, it felt like you had run ten. Even running at the most gentle jogging pace (which we were) felt like a flat-out sprint in England.

It took us the rest of the day to recover from the run, and we dozed on our beds like over-heating Labradors. Once the sun had gone down, we found ourselves being roused again and marched off to build some Sanger defences. We waited until dark because building Sangers was a backbreaking ordeal that could only be done at night, thanks to the intense heat. We spent hours filling sandbags and then piled them up until we had a safe and secure guard post to stand in. My friend Danny was putting the finishing touches to the Sanger roof when the whole thing collapsed onto his head and knocked him out. It was no laughing matter as he was out cold and had to have stitches in his scalp, but, even so, it broke the tension of a long night, and we were in fits of laughter as we dug his groggy body out. The image of his shocked face staring open mouthed as the roof collapsed on him was the only thing that kept us going till the 2 a.m. finish.

Once the Sangers were built, we only had one night of leisure left before we took over the camp officially and the serious work began. We were feeling tense and apprehensive about what lay ahead, but, at the same time, we were grateful for the easy first week that we had enjoyed. Unspoken, but hanging in the air, was the thought that there would be no more easy weeks and that we would be lucky to all make it back alive.

Normally, the TV room was a place of much laughter and carousing, but that night it had only a sombre and reflective air about it. Perhaps it was because of the subject matter on the TV that we found ourselves exchanging worried glances and raised eyebrows – the programme seemed eerily prescient and apt for the eve of our command in Basra. A ripple of unease and discomfort swept through the room.

A satellite TV channel was screening a vigorous debate about the pros and cons of the Iraq War, and the implication was that it was a colossal miscalculation built upon a tissue of government lies. Various experts on the Middle East – distinguished academics, former generals and intelligence analysts – chipped in with strong opinions and damning allegations that didn't exactly inspire confidence in the legitimacy of our mission. I felt deeply uncomfortable watching the debate, and it struck me that neither the American nor the British government spokespersons seemed able to respond convincingly. A series of devastating claims and accusations were made, and each one of them stuck in my head. For example, it was argued that the war was really about the West satisfying its gigantic oil demands and that George Bush and Tony Blair were well aware that there were no WMDs in Iraq when they chose it as a target.

Listening to such strong arguments being put to members of my own government and seeing them squirm and wriggle out of answering them made me intensely angry. And I wasn't alone – many soldiers exchanged pacts that if any of us were killed in what we thought was a fake and phoney war, the survivors would raise hell in the media. I agreed with my mate Roger that if either one of us was killed, the other would go on the television to slate the Prime Minister and denounce British involvement in Iraq. We could see the point of being killed in a legitimate war like the Bosnian one, where innocent women and children were being slaughtered by marauding gangs, but to die for the greed of some fat Texas oil barons or some grossly vain politicians would be a waste of life.

In the House of Commons, the Prime Minister had described us as the 'new pioneers of twenty-first-century soldiering', in response to awkward and critical remarks about the legitimacy of the invasion. Now, a British soldier can be many different things at many different times (and not all of them nice), but he is seldom a mug. I for one wasn't about to be taken in by such flattering and silky-smooth words, and I recognised them for the bullshit they were.

The first duty of my Iraq tour was providing security for Basra airport, or, in squaddie language, 'stagging on like a bitch'. We were split down into sections and had to provide three days' guard duty at a time, followed by a day off. Three days may not sound like a lot, but when you are doing five hours on and five hours off, it is a mind-numbing ordeal; you never get any quality sleep and are permanently exhausted.

The first two hours were spent on the airport entrance, which was actually quite enjoyable, and the remainder of the time we guarded the back gate or offices. I liked manning the entrance because it was interesting to see all the different nationalities on duty and to have a bit of banter with them. There were Spaniards, Italians, Americans, Aussies and just about every race you could think of involved in the operation. After a while, I got to know certain individuals and would compare weapons, equipment and tactics with them – it passed the time and made me feel good about being part of a truly multi-national force. Meal times at Basra airport were a strange experience because you would often find yourself sitting next to a Polish general or an American colonel, and they would chat and joke with you as if you were old friends. There was a feeling of shared comradeship, and it was a pleasant thing to experience.

In contrast, by far the worst part of stagging on was the shift on the back gate of the airport. It wasn't too bad during the daytime as there was always lots of activity to keep you alert, but the night-time stag was a morale-sapping ordeal of epic proportions.

I can only describe the scene at the back gate as one of utter chaos and surreal madness. During the day, we worked in pairs to police the area and prevent the local workforce from stripping the airport bare – and we certainly had our work cut out. The local Iraqis who were employed at the back gate were known as 'Choggies' and they were the noisiest, craziest and most manic bunch of people I have ever come across. They were mostly young guys who were supposed to cart boxes around in trolleys or shove excess rubbish into huge skips and wheelie bins. The only problem was that they were completely unsupervised and spent most of their time having furious rows, impromptu wrestling matches and wheelie-bin races. For local workers, they were surprisingly well paid, but by the end of the day, the yard was usually in a worse state than when they had arrived in the morning.

From a squaddie's point of view, we couldn't give a shit if they did the work properly or not (and they knew this too), but whenever an authority figure appeared, they became the model of efficiency. Once the boss departed, the place would again descend into something approaching a chimps' tea party. We weren't supposed to speak to them or acknowledge their presence, but after a few days of watching them run about like madmen, it was impossible not to like them, and we would find ourselves chatting to them out of sheer loneliness and boredom. They spoke a barely understandable form of broken English – but the insults and swear words were clear enough. They had nicknames for us, too, the most common being 'Ali Babas', inspired by the famous story *Ali Baba and the Forty Thieves*. I found that quite ironic considering the amount of stealing they got up to and told them so, but I had to concede defeat when they replied that at least they weren't stealing a country.

In truth, I enjoyed the banter with the workers because it made the time pass quicker, and beyond the jokes, I wanted to demonstrate that we weren't all twats who looked down on them. However, as much as I joked along with them, I always kept my physical distance and watched my back, because on the back gate you were vulnerable. If terrorists were ever to launch an attack, the back gate would have been the easiest option – there was an abundance of crates, containers and abandoned machinery lying around that would have provided excellent cover for a sniper or a bomb. Of course, the real danger would come at night-time, when sleepy squaddies battled to stay awake and were preoccupied with trying to ward off the flies that forever buzzed around.

Naturally, not all of the Choggies were the comic lunatics that we had come to expect. Every now and then a particularly serious-looking individual would appear, and it paid to keep an eye on those types. All of the legitimate workers had special passes issued, but sometimes unfamiliar faces would show up without one, and you would be forced to move them on.

It was situations like those that made me always hope I would be paired up with a switched-on soldier, because I had noted that some were slack when they came on the back gate, and they clearly saw it as an opportunity to relax. My attitude was that it was all right to have a laugh and a joke with the locals, but we had to retain our authority and gain their respect at the same time – otherwise they would go home and pass on information that we were shit soldiers to the enemy.

As regards staging on, I just wanted a nice quiet time of it and not to fall out with or antagonise the locals, but it seemed some of our number had other ideas. There was a roaring trade that went on at the back gate between the soldiers and the Choggies. Most of it revolved around Iraqi army insignia and medals, and the now defunct currency of dinars. Our officers had given us strict instructions not to get involved in any trading, but clearly it was just for show, as they themselves would often show up looking to buy some souvenirs. Of particular value were the larger Iraqi banknotes with pictures of Saddam on them, and we would barter for these with American dollars.

Everything was OK as long as you agreed to a price and stuck to it – on the few occasions a soldier tried to pull a fast one, we would find ourselves with a mini-riot on our hands and had to work hard to calm things down. In reality, we were actually getting some good souvenirs on the cheap, so to try and drive too hard a bargain was more hassle than it was worth.

Tennant was a burly lad from Jamaica, and while he was fine if he liked you, if he didn't, you were in for a pretty miserable time of it. When he was feeling down in the dumps, which was often when he was on stag, he would become very surly and aggressive towards the Choggies. I tried to tell him that it wasn't a good idea to piss the locals off as they could make trouble for us, but, not surprisingly, he wasn't willing to listen to any advice. I never managed to get Tennant's life story out of him, but from his manner and attitude, I could tell he came from a pretty rough place.

One of the quieter Choggies was a rather intense-looking middle-aged man. He said very little, and my instincts told me to treat him with respect. He was one of those guys who looked like he had been about a bit, and against my better judgement, Tennant insisted on doing a deal with him. I stayed silent and watched the whole thing. Tennant agreed to pay him $20 for a full set of Iraqi dinars and $5 for some officer's epaulettes. They communicated with the usual sign language and gestures necessary to get their points across and ended the negotiation with a handshake. The bloke seemed happy with the price, and I reckoned that Tennant had got himself a good deal. The chap wandered off with a wave and chatted to his mate in Arabic.

The next day, we were on duty when the serious-looking Iraqi walked over with a few friends. He showed Tennant that he had brought what he had asked for and gestured for his money in return. Tennant examined the goods and began grumbling loudly that they were sub-standard (which they weren't), and he refused to hand over the agreed amount. The Iraqi said nothing but just stood there regarding Tennant with suspicious eyes, looking pissed off. When Tennant offered a solitary $10 bill, instead of the agreed $25, the man's companions began waving their arms around and gibbering loudly. I kept out of it for as long as I could before stepping in and telling Tennant to just do the decent thing and pay up. In reply, Tennant basically told me to fuck off and that I was a soft touch – he also gave full vent to his true feelings about the Iraqis and what fools they were.

I gestured for the Iraqis to back off a little, as I felt they were getting into our personal space, and then I calmly but firmly told Tennant not to behave like a prick and to honour the deal. I told him that to us a few dollars were nothing, but to the Choggies they represented a fortune, so we should be careful how we bandied them about. I also told him that the locals would think we were nasty bastards if we sneered at them and tried to double-cross them. My criticisms weren't getting through, so, in the end, I gave the bloke my money and bought the gear from him myself. I had been planning to get some souvenirs anyway.

Tennant told me not to be a fool and scowled as I handed over the money – but I replied that the money involved was peanuts to us and he should be ashamed of himself. We continued with our own little squabble until a cut-glass English accent interrupted us: 'You have a very honest nature, thank you for your kindness.'

At first, I wondered who it was and looked over my shoulder, half expecting to see an English army officer standing there. It took me a few seconds to realise that the perfect English accent had come from the scruffy-looking figure in front of me. The serious-looking Iraqi handed the money I had given him to his friend and extended his hand. I shook it and told him I had no idea he spoke such perfect English. He told me that many soldiers made the same mistake and that he had understood every word Tennant and I had said about him. As he said this, he looked Tennant in the eye and gave him a warm smile, but Tennant glowered at the floor and cursed him under his breath. The guy was well into his 40s, which meant he was old enough to be Tennant's dad, and I felt a hot sting of shame at the way Tennant had trampled on his dignity for no reason.

As a British soldier on duty one thing I couldn't do was

apologise to him, no matter how much I wanted to, because we had to preserve the balance of power in our favour, and I couldn't go against one of my own. The most I could get away with was to gesture at Tennant and shake my head, and I think I made my disapproval clear.

Before the guy left he told me a bit of his remarkable story, which demonstrated why we shouldn't make assumptions about 'thick Choggies' or our own superiority. In his youth, the man had been a highly educated army officer, even gaining an advanced degree from an English university. Once his military term was over, he had become a history teacher in Baghdad, but he had fallen foul of the ruling Ba'athist party, who didn't like his style of teaching, and had been expelled to the southern deserts. He had hoped to begin a new life in Basra, but the black mark against his name meant that the only work he could get was sweeping streets and emptying bins. Now that Saddam had fallen, he was hoping for a second chance in the classroom. I wished him well, and he replied that so long as he was on duty he would see to it that nobody gave me any trouble.

He was as good as his word, and whenever the young Choggies began to get a bit too energetic, I only had to nod in his direction and they would quieten down. The man seemed to have an unspoken authority with the workers, and it was clear that they respected him as a leader. I had no reason to doubt the man's story, because I had seen a deep sincerity and inner calmness in his eyes. And as much as I disagreed with the Iraq War, if it gave a good man like that a second chance, then at least something worthwhile might come out of it.

I felt humbled by my encounter with him, and I reflected on how cruel fate could be, regretting having met in such tense circumstances. Sometimes I would catch his eye while he was working in his tatty robes and give him a wave – and I would always feel guilty that I had to watch over him while wearing my uniform and carrying a rifle. I hoped that he could see beyond the soldier to the person inside and that he realised I would never look down on him and considered him to be my equal in every way.

The stag rotation continued to drag on in tedious style for several more weeks, and, not surprisingly, the boredom and constant tension began to get to some of the lads. The problem was that the tour was structured in such a way that we were doing a large block of stag duty, followed by a large block of escort duties and ending in a large block of security patrols. The different platoons of the company would rotate through this system so that we all got to perform an equal amount of each duty. From the perspective of the company commanders who devised the system, it was an efficient and fair rotation of duty, but from the perspective of the squaddie on the ground, it condemned you to a long and stressful period of hated stag duty.

Stag duty was considered to be the safest task we performed whilst on the tour, but this welcome bonus came at the price of extreme boredom, especially at nights. Some of the lads took it seriously and adapted to it well, using the tactic of cheerful resignation and black humour to get through the long evening shifts. But other lads treated it as though they were stagging on at the local Tesco and completely switched off. And worse still, some lads started to come apart at the seams. Both reactions were understandable but unforgivable for a professional soldier on an operational tour, where slack attitudes could lead to an early death.

I think that the army needs to review its whole attitude towards stagging on – both in peacetime and at war. Army commanders might think that it is a reasonable expectation for a junior rank to spend hours on a lonely stag post (until he is reduced to a dribbling zombie-like state), because it is in his job description. No doubt they would also say that for a fit and robust soldier it is no great hardship, and indeed they may be right. But to that I would add that this 'fit and robust soldier' is also likely to be a very young, immature, easily bored and overly confident human being.

Most likely he will not see the inherent dangers in his position (because he thinks he is going to live forever) and he will choose to switch off, or 'mong it' as we said in the Green Jackets.

It would be incredibly easy for a determined terrorist to launch a successful attack on a sleepy-headed sentry. With the knowledge and experience I have of 'stagging on', I know with certainty how quickly a supposedly secure stag position could be overwhelmed – I wonder if an officer sleeping in his bed could say the same?

After a fortnight's stagging on at the back gate, many of us were beginning to see things, and the only distractions keeping us awake were the incessant flies and repugnant smell of rotting garbage. Sometimes I would be so fucked that I would squint into the distance at some hazy shadow, imagining it to be someone, and then with a jerk snap awake and almost fall over as I rocked on my heels. Occasionally, I would fall asleep for a few seconds whilst standing up, and I only came to at some far-off sound or a pal hissing my name. But these were genuine mistakes, and afterwards I would curse my weakness and force myself to jog on the spot or hum a favourite tune – anything to stay awake.

During the daytime, because of the boisterous Choggies, we always stagged on in pairs at the back gate. This was good because it gave you someone to talk to, and it meant you kept on your toes a bit more, as no soldier wants to appear to be a lazy bastard in front of his colleagues. But at night-time we were expected to stag on by ourselves, because of the reduced threat level thanks to the absence of the Choggies, and this is when the problems began. The system was run on trust, and it was assumed that you would stay awake and do your job.

The daily grind of stag became so unbearable that at times you almost wished for an incident to occur. The frequent squabbles and shoving matches that broke out between soldiers were a symptom of the underlying tension. Whenever anything kicked off or an argument broke out, I generally tried to keep out of it or calm things down – but I would later learn that this wasn't always possible, particularly if the violence was directed my way.

On one unbearably hot night, the tense tedium was briefly broken when a distraught RAF corporal came running towards me screaming for help. The way she was carrying on I thought she must have been raped, but after five minutes of hysterical babbling, she managed to get the story out: an RAF wing commander was lying injured and bleeding heavily from a deep gash on his left thigh. He had suffered a freak accident when he had tripped and fallen onto an alcoholic hand-washing stand, and one of the spikes on the supporting legs had somehow ended up in his thigh. I was annoyed at the female corporal because we had wasted valuable time getting a simple story out of her, and for a junior NCO, I felt her reaction had been rather pathetic.

I found the man lying on the ground outside the portable toilets on the edge of the airfield. He seemed to be in a bad way and was pale and shaking, although he was making an impressive effort to keep his cool. A thin stream of blood was spraying out of his inner thigh area, and I immediately suspected a femoral bleed. With the help of a passing soldier, I elevated the injured leg and applied pressure to it, to try and slow the bleeding. It didn't work, so I pulled out two field dressings and bandaged them tightly round, one on top of the other. This didn't work either, and I was beginning to feel a bit panicky myself. All I could do, other than provide pressure and elevation to the wound, was give him reassurance and pray that an ambulance arrived soon. In a flash of black humour, I thought how ridiculous it would be if he died in such an undignified manner in a fierce war zone. I could imagine the headline: 'Distinguished officer killed in Iraq washing his hands after a piss'.

At last, help arrived in the form of the duty NCO and the ambulance. The doctor opened his leg up and inserted a clip into it, which immediately stopped the bleeding. There was a collective sigh of relief all round as we realised he was going to be OK. The doctor explained that the officer was incredibly lucky: although he had severed some surrounding veins quite badly, he had just missed his femoral artery. I left the medical team to finish up on the patient and trudged back to my lonely guard post, still drenched in the guy's blood and feeling a bit light headed about it all. I felt pleased with myself because although it could hardly be described as 'a glamorous rescue under enemy fire', at least I had done my job and hadn't fucked it up. Most importantly, the guy was going to be all right and would make a full recovery.

The injured officer had hugely impressed me with his black humour and calm resolve. Despite bleeding like a stuck pig, he was as cool as a cucumber throughout the whole ordeal. While he was lying on his back watching his leg pumping claret out into the night air, listening to his corporal wailing like a banshee and observing me trying and failing to stop the bleeding, all that he kept on saying was, 'Thanks very much, old chap!' I was impressed by how calmly he had coped with the situation when inside he must have been shitting himself, and I had to admit that I didn't think I'd be anywhere near as level-headed in his shoes.

I was sorry for the injuries the officer had received, but for the next few nights, it at least gave us something to talk about on stag. Thanks to the never-ending cycle of guard duty, I didn't get a chance to change my shirt until several hours later, and for the remainder of the shift, flies buzzed around my bloodied uniform like vampires.

Occasional light relief from the boredom and rigours of stag duty came in encounters and conversations with the locals. Most of the time you would exchange jokes or humorous insults, but sometimes a threat would be issued that sent a shiver down your spine. One of the lads had been stagging on at the back gate when a Choggie without a pass had approached him and promised to kill him. When the soldier asked him why he was given the following reply: 'My son was killed by a British soldier during the war. I want vengeance, and I have discussed this with my cleric.

He has told me that I must provide him with five bodies to atone for the death of my son. The five bodies must be British soldiers, and this I promise to do.'

Before the soldier had a chance to arrest the Choggie or radio for help he managed to slip away and evade capture. Incidents like this happened quite regularly, and we were always receiving threats. All you could do was report what had happened to the intelligence corps and hope that the guy was just trying to scare you. Most of the threats did turn out to be empty, but there was a lot of hate out there, and you always worried about the one that might come true. Incidents like this only managed to increase the tension that little bit more.

6

BUTTSTROKING WITH A SA80

Whenever you're on a particularly hard routine or working for long periods without a break, the stress begins to show, and you learn a lot about a person's true character. You often find that people you think are pretty chilled out can transform into raging bullies in the blink of an eye. These transformations are usually brief and temporary, and they are often followed by profuse apologies, but by then it is too late: the damage has been done.

The reasons for these explosive changes are the same ones that have plagued soldiers since time began: homesickness, fear of death and injury, doubts about one's own strengths and abilities, missing loved ones, spending too much time with the same people, lack of sleep, and loss of hope. At one time or another, we all suffered from these worries in Iraq, but while some people found strength in adversity, others cracked like eggshells. One thing you could guarantee was that if a man had a propensity for bullying or a predisposition towards violence, it would show its face on an operational tour.

Rifleman McCray was having a shower one morning before it was his turn to go on stag. A NCO who had been attached to his platoon entered the showers and began mopping the floor. A few of his NCO friends accompanied him and made good-natured jokes about cleaning the toilets and finding his vocation in life. Rifleman McCray kept out of the conversation until the NCOs invited him in and encouraged him to join in the fun. As he continued his shower, he made a few light-hearted comments but, at the same time, was careful not to overstep the mark.

The NCO must have been in a bad mood because he stopped his mopping and began to slowly and methodically unscrew the head of the mop. Once this was done, he picked up the sharp-ended mop handle and stepped into the shower to face McCray, who was dripping wet, naked and vulnerable.

Before McCray even had time to protest, the NCO attacked him with the wooden stick. The nature of his attack was sickening: the end of the handle had a sharp metal base into which the mop head was screwed. As the naked McCray tried to ward him off, the NCO repeatedly rammed the metal end into the soldier's shin until he fell over and was screaming for mercy. The attack only stopped when McCray's shin was pissing blood and his deeply cut skin was hanging open. If it had gone on for much longer, his shin would have snapped like a fishbone.

What made this incident particularly disturbing to me wasn't just the vicious assault itself – it was that two other NCOs had stood there watching without intervening. To my mind, the fact that they just watched with their arms folded was almost worse than the assault itself.

This incident was hushed up, as these things invariably are in the army, although the NCO was forced to issue a feeble apology – which, of course, McCray was obliged to accept. For a month afterwards, the injured soldier could barely walk and limped badly. When he showed me the extent of the wound I was staggered – a deep jagged cut was scabbed over and surrounded by a huge bruise. Rifleman McCray required extensive medical treatment for his injury, and I would not be surprised if it leads to medical complications later in life or he has problems with it when he is older. He was a nice guy and a good soldier who kept himself to himself. What I think about the NCO who made the attack and the NCOs who 'let it go', I think you can guess.

In another similar incident, which was also ignored, one of our smallest and weakest riflemen was battered by an NCO a foot taller and 6-st. heavier. They had been enjoying some good-natured banter about who had the worst haircut, when the unwise teenager pointed out that the much older NCO was losing his hair. Now I can only presume that the NCO must have been very sensitive about his receding hairline, because to repeatedly punch someone in the ribs till he is black and blue suggests to me a slight overreaction.

I could write pages and pages about this kind of thing, but instead I will tell you about my own story, because I found myself the victim of a violent attack that far surpassed either of these – the difference being that I fought back with an even greater force.

Rifleman Haxiton, one of my closest friends in the regiment, was stagging on at the back gate. Haxiton was a muscular young lad of great humour with a sharp intellect. We got on very well because we had a shared love of weight training and the same sardonic attitude towards 'army bullshit'. When I had been struggling to gain admittance into the Green Jackets, I had bumped into Haxiton at the careers office and had hit it off straight away. He had made it into the regiment a few months before me, and when I turned up, he was pleased that I had made it too.

If there was one person whom I felt I could trust 100 per cent in the Green Jackets, Haxiton was that man, and I hoped he felt the same way about me. Without doubt, he was the last person I would ever expect to fall out with, because nothing seemed to faze him and his good humour always got him through – or so I thought.

One evening, I was the next man in line to relieve Haxiton from his stag duty, so I pulled on my gear and hurried towards the back gate. I was in a hurry because I was anxious not to be late, and I knew that he would be looking forward to finishing his shift. However, I only got halfway there when an NCO called me back and asked me to deliver some urgent paperwork to a senior officer. I told him that it would make me late for stag, but he replied not to worry because he would explain my absence to Haxiton. I reluctantly did as he asked me and ran around like an idiot to make sure I was as quick as possible. Ten minutes later the job was done, and I rushed off to relieve Haxiton. I knew Haxiton was a reasonable and mature guy, so when I got there, I planned to apologise for being late and tell him the reason – I didn't foresee us having any problems.

I ran down the steep stairway leading to the back gate and caught sight of Haxiton chatting to one of the so-called senior bods, Rifleman Yeans. Although I had never had a problem with Yeans, we weren't particularly close, as he was involved with the small gang of senior men who seemed to look down on the rest of us. The pair of them must have heard me coming because they wheeled around sharply and met me with accusatory glares. I could see that Haxiton was pissed off at my being late, and I knew he had every right to be, so I began to apologise and explain my absence. But it seemed that he didn't want to listen, and every time I tried to talk to him, I would be cut down with a series of threats and accusations.

I tried to reason with him and calm him down, but it seemed that my efforts to soothe his temper only inflamed it more. To my utter astonishment, I sensed that Haxiton was psyching himself up to launch an attack on me, and by his sullen expression and cold indifference, I felt that Yeans was encouraging him. But what really worried me, far more than any threats hurled my way, was that a small crowd of Choggies had gathered to watch and were clearly enjoying the spectacle. To see two squaddies engaged in such a vicious slanging match was a rare treat indeed.

The row rumbled on for a while longer and nothing I could say or do would calm it down. When I looked at Haxiton, I could almost see steam coming out of his ears – he was white hot with anger and beyond my reach. Seeing what was inevitably coming, I turned to Yeans and appealed to him to make an effort to calm things down. If he truly was a senior bod, now was the time for him to step in and sort it out, but he proved his colours by clamming up and suddenly losing the power of speech.

As I was 32 years old, I felt like I had a responsibility to prevent any bloodshed, and so I told Haxiton to go off and calm himself down, and we would discuss it later. I told him that if he wanted to fight me that badly over such a non-issue, I would gladly entertain him – but not on the back gate carrying loaded weapons and in front of a crowd of Iraqis.

Somehow my words penetrated the thick fog of his anger, and he reluctantly trudged off upstairs. I breathed a sigh of relief and congratulated myself on my diplomatic skills. Inwardly, I felt sure that Haxiton would see reason once he had cooled down a bit. That had to be better than two friends fighting it out, didn't it? Feeling perhaps a bit smug with myself for averting the crisis, I reflected on how ten years previously I would have just knocked his head off and stamped him into the ground. Yes, I had certainly come a long way now that I could turn away from a fight and talk my way out of trouble.

All of a sudden, I heard an angry cry and a rushing of boot soles on concrete. I spun around on my heels and was confronted by the grimacing face of Haxiton with his rifle in his hands like a baseball bat. Before I had time to blink, he swung it at my face with all his might. I managed to get my forearm up, and the heavy weapon crashed into it with a sickening thud. A second later, the weapon was swinging towards my head again, but this time I ducked, and it slammed into the wall.

In the few seconds it took me to recover my composure, I could see that Haxiton had completely lost it and intended to batter me senseless. Feeling a powerful sense of fear well up inside me, I looked to Yeans and appealed for him to offer me assistance against this weapon-wielding madman. Once again, he showed his true colours by nimbly stepping back and adopting the pose of an interested spectator.

I didn't wait for Haxiton's third swing but instead went for him. With one arm, I managed to lock his rifle down and with the other, I held him off at arm's length. We then engaged in an awkward wrestling match. It was terrifying for me but must have been amusing for the Iraqis to watch. Whenever he tried to swing his rifle, I would slam into him and barge it down with my hips, and whenever he tried to land a punch, I would catch it on the top of my head – which believe it or not is a great way to break your opponent's hand. We waltzed around in our curiously intense 'fighting dance' until we both ran out of breath, and Haxiton lowered his weapon for good. I never took my eyes off him as he backed slowly towards the stairs, turned and sprinted away.

His attack had been so aggressive and unexpected that it had taken everything I had just to keep him off me. He was a strong bastard, and from the way he had writhed around and swung at me, I knew he had meant me great harm. I was pale with shock and shaking with anger at what he had done. To assault someone with a loaded weapon is the most stupid thing a soldier can do. The message you are sending out to your opponent is, 'I have a loaded weapon, and I am not afraid to use it on you.' The fact that it is being used as a bat and the finger isn't even on the trigger is irrelevant, because what happens if someone begins to lose badly, and in a blind panic decides to pull the trigger?

The question now was what was I going to do about it. I had two hours of stag duty left to calm myself down and make a decision. The logical and sensible part of me said to ignore the assault and forget about it – to consider the matter over and done with. Reporting the assault to an NCO was out of the question, and even if I did, they would probably only advise me to batter him anyway. I was sorely tempted to let it go and put it behind me, and if it had happened in any other walk of life, that is what I would have done. At the age of 32, I had worked hard to grow up and put such incidents behind me, but I couldn't deny that I now lived in a hostile environment with a casual acceptance of shocking violence that a civilian couldn't even begin to comprehend. Deep down, I didn't want to strike back at Haxiton, as that would be sinking to his level, but I knew I was going to have to launch a counterattack.

Within one hour of Haxiton's 'successful' attack on me, the news would have spread round camp like wildfire. Indeed, the story would probably get exaggerated to the point that I was curled up on the floor in a ball and begging for mercy, while Haxiton behaved like the Incredible Hulk. Pretty soon I would be regarded as a sniffling coward by everyone in the regiment (and treated as such), while Haxiton would acquire heroic status as a 'brilliant street fighter who takes no shit'. I know it is sad and pathetic, but, unfortunately, it is a true reflection of how things operate in the army.

If I didn't retaliate with swift and overwhelming force, my life in the regiment would become hell. Every mistake or fuck-up somebody else made would be laid at my door, and I would find myself becoming the 'platoon bitch', scrubbing toilets for a living and regarded as fair game for every disgruntled soldier to take a shot at.

Ever wondered why you hear about unhappy soldiers committing suicide? There is often a story like mine behind such events, with the soldier who doesn't retaliate becoming the platoon bitch. Eventually, the shame of his existence overwhelms him, and he kills himself. There is nobody he can turn to in the system, because it is the system that is the problem. Remember, too, that the army only ever rewards strength – it never rewards weakness.

But what really sealed it for me was the fact that Yeans had seen the whole incident. If it had just been Haxiton and me, I might have been able to let it go, but now that Yeans was involved, I would have to sort it out with maximum force. If I didn't, they would paint me as the biggest coward to ever walk the earth.

As I contemplated beating Haxiton up, I felt a mixture of sadness, bitterness and regret. I had always regarded him as a true friend and had given him lifts to go shopping and run errands – his attack on me felt like a betrayal of the worst kind. I could never trust him again, such was the depth of the emotional wound he had inflicted on me.

Haxiton had attacked the mature and reasonable man that was the 32-year-old Rifleman McLaughlin. He had made a mistake in underestimating me and overestimating himself. Now I was going to introduce him to a different me: the 22-year-old doorman who used to knock shit out of blokes like him every Saturday. My old self would only be making a brief one-off appearance, but I would make sure he hung around long enough to get the job done. Haxiton had attacked me in a hot blaze of anger, and he had caught me off guard. I intended to return the favour with a cold-blooded and calculated assault that would pay him back with added interest. Fair play wouldn't come into it, as the rules of gentlemanly conduct had gone out of the window when he smashed a rifle into my arm. I would get him any way I could, and to hell with the consequences.

I made a decision to attack him the very second I next saw him and to only pause to make sure neither one of us had any weapons to hand. I genuinely didn't care if the Queen and Prince Philip were chatting to him – I was going to charge into him like a steamroller and smash his face in.

When my relief arrived, I calmly thanked him for turning up on time and gave him a security briefing on the latest intelligence we had. We then shared a few jokes, as we always did, and I slowly made my way upstairs. In my mind, I had already crossed a bridge to another place and saw no reason to rush. Indeed, my keeping a cool head would be critical if I was going to be successful.

The guard section at Basra airport was situated opposite the fortified entrance to the main building and directly next door to a very busy media control room. Every single visitor to the airport had to come by the guard desk and sign the logbook, and all the world's media would converge on the media ops room next door. Consequently, it was a very busy place and always swarming with bigwigs of some kind. The day before, we had signed in some famous journalists from broadsheet newspapers, and a few days before that, we had welcomed an American film crew. I wondered who would be there to witness my attack on Haxiton and had a chuckle at the possible ramifications of my actions.

I could only imagine the trouble I would be in if my assault was caught on camera and landed on the front pages of the tabloids – which it could well do given the unpopularity of the war and the reputation of the Green Jackets. Before we had even arrived in Iraq, the colonel had warned us to behave ourselves and not do anything that would bring disgrace upon the regiment. Oh well, never mind, sorry old chap and all that bollocks – he wasn't the one that had just been 'buttstroked' with a rifle.

Buttstroking is one of those practices that isn't supposed to go on in the modern army any more – which means that of course it still goes on, but people are more careful not to get caught. The punishment is normally meted out to failing soldiers by young NCOs. Basically, it involves taking a rifle and repeatedly smashing the butt into a soldier's body. The favourite target is the shoulder, chest or back as no visible mark is left, but a particularly brave or offended buttstroker might go for your jaw or face. Of course, the danger with that is that large bruises can be seen, or pesky teeth can scatter on the floor, and that can take some explaining away if a victim complains.

Technically speaking, Haxiton's attack on me had been worse than a traditional buttstroke; he had swung the rifle like a baseball bat, as opposed to the controlled thrust normally used. But that was just semantics; I was going to buttstroke his face with my fists.

I approached the signing-in desk and informed the platoon

sergeant that I was now back off stag. I placed my rifle in the gun rack and removed the rest of my kit, but this time I took off my watch and signet ring as well, placing them snugly in my ammunition pouch. As usual, the signing-in desk was a hive of activity, and I cast my eyes around to see how many spectators would be witnessing my attack. I nodded my head in approval as I counted six riflemen and three NCOs; this would make a good audience and should be enough to make sure that the true picture eventually emerged, once the dust had settled. My heart gave a little flutter when I saw a senior RAF officer and a sergeant-major from the RMP chatting nearby, as these weren't the kind of witnesses I wanted, but, then again, on occasions like these, you can't be too choosy.

My next task was to locate Haxiton himself, and I soon spied him sitting casually in a chair chatting to a friend. I had worked hard to keep my cool up to that point, but when I saw him leaning back in his chair and laughing aloud, my blood began to boil. He looked a picture of innocence and acted as though he hadn't a care in the world. I made my way over to where he sat.

Time seemed to stand still as I found myself standing over Haxiton, looking down on him. He was chattering away to his mate, before pausing when he became aware of my looming presence. If he had been as streetwise as he thought he was, he would have realised how vulnerable his position was and sprung to his feet. But he wasn't, and he merely glanced in my direction before dismissing me with a curt and subtle grin. The very second that he looked away from me, I slammed a heavy left hook into his jaw and swiftly followed it up with a straight right to his chin. His eyes briefly glazed over, and his head lolled onto his chest, but he wasn't knocked out yet. Not wanting to risk breaking my hands on the wall behind his head, I grabbed his hair and began to drag him to his feet. As I was doing this I could feel his strength returning, and he tried to wrap my body in a bear hug, to which I responded with several sharp uppercuts to his face.

One thing I will say for Haxiton is that he was certainly a strong bastard, and he had one hell of a chin. It seemed that the harder I hit him the more determinedly he fought back. But I didn't allow myself to become worried or get flustered, as I knew that with the momentum and speed of my blows, he would soon begin to fold. I had been slamming punches into his face for a long time, but Haxiton impressed me by digging his chin into his chest like a good boxer and only showing me the top of his head, while he continued to apply his bear hug.

This could have been a fight-winning move for Haxiton, but I had been around the block enough times to know not to thump a man mindlessly on his thick cranium and waste my punches. Instead, I employed a trick of my own and decided to use his weight and strength against him, as well as using an ultra-painful technique to finish him off. With my right hand, I gripped his hair and began pushing his head down, while with my left hand, I gripped his ear and began to twist and pull it violently upwards.

The new move worked a treat, and I could feel his body weakening as he let out a loud yelp. Although it felt like an age, our fight had only been rumbling on for a minute at best; the savage intensity of it had meant that it had seemed a lot longer. By that point, I had developed tunnel vision and was focusing all of my energy on Haxiton and his reddening ear. However, in my peripheral vision, I was dimly aware of frantic bodies pulling and tugging at my sleeves. I didn't know what was being shouted or how many sets of arms were clawing at me, but I suddenly felt my feet leave the floor, and I was propelled towards an empty office. I tried to struggle against the tidal force that was pushing me, but, in the end, I sort of blacked out and gave into it.

The loud crashing of doors being kicked open brought me out of my trance, and I found myself returning to the present, utterly amazed at the chaos I had caused. I was roughly flung onto a camp bed in the corner of the room, and a semi-circle of pale-faced squaddies boxed me in. As I sucked in a lungful of air and tried to catch my breath, I noted that my guards were breathing heavily and shaking almost as much as I was. Outside of the room I could hear another commotion going on, amid much shouting and swearing, and I presumed that it was Haxiton being dragged off to cool down somewhere.

The sergeant-major from the military police appeared in the doorway and attempted to enter the room, but an NCO swiftly blocked his way. The MP was red in the face and shouting that I ought to be arrested and charged, but he was told in no uncertain terms that it was an internal matter for the Green Jackets and was none of his business. Over his shoulder peered the beakish profile of the RAF commander, and he too was giving his opinion on what thugs we were and how he would be having words with our CO.

I could hear arguments breaking out all over the place and various threats being issued, but by that point, I was too fucked to care. As far as I was concerned, I had accomplished my mission by fucking up Haxiton in front of all of his friends. I could feel the adrenalin leaving my body, and for the first time, I became dimly aware of the pain I was in. I gave my body a quick once over and made note of my injuries: my fists were covered in small cuts and caked in blood (although most of it was Haxiton's), and my right arm had begun to swell up like a balloon. Where Haxiton had smashed his rifle into my arm there was a hard golf-ball-like lump, and from the pain it was giving me, I knew that it was broken.

For a brief moment, I was worried that the gang of squaddies guarding me might decide to jump me and mete out some justice of their own, but, for once, I had misjudged them, and they stayed glued to the spot. We eyed one another suspiciously, and I noted that a few of them looked a bit wary that I might turn my anger on them. Finally, the tension of the moment became too much, and we all laughed hysterically. It was as if the fear in the room had got up and flown out of the window, and we allowed our shoulders to sag and sighed in relief. The most senior rifleman there was

Doyle, a 28-year-old Brummie with a laconic manner and a nice line in dry wit. He summed up the mood perfectly: 'Fucking hell, Mac. You're one crazy bastard. Remind me never to pick a fight with you.'

I respected Doyle, and I told him the full story of why I had gone for Haxiton like I had. The riflemen surrounding me nodded their heads in sympathy and said that while they agreed with Doyle's character assessment of me, they fully understood and supported the reasons why I had struck out. I was actually quite touched to see a few of them grow visibly angry when they examined my shattered arm, and some of the rougher lads volunteered to smash Haxiton into pieces if he had the cheek to make a complaint against me.

By buttsroking me when I had done nothing wrong, Haxiton had unwittingly violated a code of conduct within the Green Jackets. Although it was considered acceptable for senior riflemen to dish out occasional beatings to new recruits who couldn't cut the mustard (a process known as 'gripping' someone), buttstroking was a far more serious proposition, and it was considered the sole preserve of junior NCOs. By attacking me, Haxiton had put himself on a level with an experienced corporal, which he most certainly wasn't. In doing so, he had alienated two sets of people and made some new enemies.

A senior NCO arrived and placed both Haxiton and me under temporary arrest. This was all a bit of a charade really, as it was more designed to placate the RMP sergeant-major than it was to punish us. We were marched off to face the OC, who made it clear that he was considering sending us home in disgrace. We were charged with fighting on duty and told to reappear before him for sentencing in a week's time, by which point we were expected to have cooked up a story explaining and minimising our actions.

Whenever a serious incident occurs in the army, there is an instant mania about 'getting your stories straight and squaring it away'. The impression given by senior officers' actions was one of

This is what you call being in shape! Here I am posing at the age of 25.

With my black belt diploma at the age of 33. I still have the muscles – but the hair has gone.

A Lynx helicopter with GPMG 7.62 mm fitted. This is the workhorse of the skies in Northern Ireland.

A Lynx takes off for a patrol from Bessbrook Mill base in Northern Ireland. We had some great times in these choppers.

All kitted up at XMG security base. Note the huge aerials on our ECM kit.

The memorial board inside XMG base at Crossmaglen – 63 names in all: RIP.

Inside XMG base, prior to a patrol. Note the writing on the wall: 'Don't worry be happy. Welcome to XMG'.

With my fellow Green Jackets, ready to go again.

The view from the towers in XMG base: 'Stagging on like a bitch'.

United States Marine Hum-Vees in Basra. I loved chatting to the Americans. They were good soldiers and game for a laugh.

This is the Land-Rover Wolf that I drove across Iraq for thousands of miles. We had some crazy times together.

A Sea King helicopter at Basra, of the sort used for 'Eagle VCPs'. Very cramped and claustrophobic inside – not a patch on a 'Chinne'.

This is more like it! A Chinnook based at Basra International Airport.

Damian wins Marine Cadet of the Year, 1989. He made me proud.

Damian looking cold, wet and miserable. It must be the Brecon Beacons – where else could it be?

My brother on a field-ex. He was a top soldier. And for any eagle-eyed squaddies – his pouch was broken.

Damian in Cyprus showing off his physique and LSW 'Crow Cannon'.

Damian had a beautiful heart. Can you
imagine how much I miss his smile?

'I don't care what trouble you get into or what goes on – just don't shit on my doorstep'. I wasn't particularly bothered about how much embarrassment or shame my actions had brought on the regiment, and so I had no intention of apologising or agreeing to be the fall guy when I regarded myself as completely innocent. The truth was, I still felt a deep sense of moral indignation at the way Haxiton had treated me, and that emotion had been the fuel for my attack on him.

I trooped off to the medical centre to get cleaned up and was pleased to see Haxiton there too. I had given him a nice black eye, and his nose was pissing blood all over his face; all in all I felt quite pleased with myself. He offered me his hand, but I waved it away contemptuously; I wanted him to stew in his own juice and reflect on what he had done to me. As far as I was concerned, I was the injured party, and I was taking the moral high ground. I did intend to make friends with him and put it behind us, but it would be at a time of my choosing, not his.

After his examination, the doctor informed me that I had probably broken my arm. When he asked me how I had done it, I told him that it had happened when I was playing volleyball, and he had to reluctantly accept my explanation. I was given a cold compress to take down the swelling, then the next day my arm was bandaged up and put in a detachable cast.

Everybody on camp knew how I had acquired my broken arm, and within two days, the entire company treated Haxiton as a pariah. One happy by-product of the incident was that I was transferred out of 15 Platoon and taken off stag rotation. My new home was in 16 Platoon, and I was received like a conquering hero. As I have said before, it is a sad indictment of the modern army that violence is almost always rewarded, and so it was with me. The trick is to make sure that your violence is morally justifiable – I had, but unfortunately for Haxiton he hadn't.

Previously, I had gone by the nicknames of Grandad or 'Old

Man Winter', but now that I had beaten up Haxiton, I was given the title of 'Mad Mac'. It was like I had suddenly become a different person: I was treated with a lot more respect and people wanted to be my friend or asked me for my opinions on aspects of soldiering. It is really quite sad and pathetic, but in the eyes of many, my assault on Haxiton had proven me to be a 'real man'. Whilst I didn't agree with this new assessment, I wasn't about to disagree with it either, and so I set about enjoying my new status. It was actually quite nice to be treated as a human being with an opinion about things, rather than just another dogsbody to be pushed around.

Sympathy came my way from some surprising quarters, and I found I had no bigger advocate than Cpl. Tradusca, who spoke up for me on several occasions. I cast my mind back to when I had almost come to blows with him during riot training, and I said a silent prayer that I had had the maturity to let that one go.

In my experience, it is likely that all infantrymen will get decked or receive 'a jab' because of some minor indiscretion at some point in their army careers. The key to success and harmony is that the assault must always be justifiable – because if it isn't, situations like Haxiton's and mine can arise. By not making a fuss and 'taking my dig like a man' when Tradusca had struck me, I was now reaping the benefits of his support.

A few days later, when things had calmed down a bit, I was approached and advised to plead guilty in return for a lighter sentence. I got the impression that the powers that be were a bit worried that I was going to go on some kind of moral crusade and request a court martial, which would have brought damaging publicity. I agreed to accept a minor punishment so long as I would have the opportunity to make a statement in my defence and not be penalised for it. I told the officer that my statement would contain some damning home truths about the way I saw the regiment and some of the characters in it, so he had better prepare himself to hear a message he wouldn't like. He said I would have my day, and the OC would listen to my criticisms. He also said that I would only be judged on my actions against Haxiton and not my opinions about the army.

The day of the sentencing came round. I pleaded guilty as agreed and received the fine of a week's wages. The OC was a fair man and agreed to scrub my record clean if I behaved myself for the rest of the tour, and it was an offer I gratefully accepted. I told my story as openly and honestly as I could, and I didn't try to justify my actions to him. The OC said he was offended that I had struck Haxiton while he was sitting down and unprepared for an attack, and argued that it violated the rules of gentlemanly conduct. I agreed completely and told him I was glad that Haxiton had been sitting down as it made my task that bit easier. I added that we were neither officers nor gentlemen and inhabited a world which he could not understand – besides which, when Haxiton attacked me with his rifle, the rules of fair play went out of the window. I also said that I had used military tactics of surprise and superior force to defeat Haxiton because that is what the Green Jackets had taught me to do. Surely he couldn't criticise me for that, could he?

To my mind the OC looked surprised and disturbed by my comments, and he looked distinctly uncomfortable as I gave him my assessment of the regiment in which I served. I told him that while I had been a bit of a jack the lad in my youth, I had worked hard since then to move on, and I had never been an out-and-out thug. I also added that I wasn't particularly enjoying my time in the battalion, and I was beginning to fear that the job was turning me into somebody I didn't like. I felt that if I continued being a soldier much longer, I would become one of those mindless morons that lets his fists do the talking.

He asked me what I intended to do about it, and I replied that I just wanted to do my three years and get out in one piece, as I no longer felt I had to impress either him or anybody else. My little speech went down like a lead balloon, and I could see the OC was very upset about what I had said. The picture I had just painted bore no relation to the army he fondly imagined, and as he dismissed me, I sensed my words had struck an unhappy chord with him.

Despite my displeasure at finding myself in such an intolerable position, I felt glad to have answered the charge and pleased to have been able to get a few grievances off my chest. As regards Haxiton, I never really spoke to him again, and I found it very hard to truly forgive him. Even when I think of it now, years after the event occurred, I still feel a shiver of indignation at how my trusted comrade turned on me. Before the incident we had been friends, but after it we became nothing more than business associates.

I resolved to put my troubles behind me and make a fresh start in 16 Platoon. As much as I disliked the harsh punishments that were routinely dished out to us, one thing that I couldn't fault the army on was how quickly sins were forgiven. My fight on stag might have been an almighty fuck-up, but as it occurred in a different platoon, my new bosses couldn't give a shit, and I knew that it wouldn't be held against me – just so long as I didn't fuck up again. I wanted to make a good first impression, so I upped my fitness training to the point that I was eventually ordered to slow down. It seemed that a few of the lads had already gone down with heat illnesses, and the PTIs were worried that I would pass out while performing my daily jogs.

Although I was in peak physical condition, I was worried about the collection of assorted pills we had to take everyday. Whenever I took a step, I practically rattled. They were supposed to stop us catching malaria and other exotic diseases, which was all well and good, but on some days, they crippled you with diarrhoea and left you feeling like death warmed up.

My increased obsession with supreme fitness wasn't just borne out of a desire to impress my new platoon but also out of a gnawing sense of fear. Up to that point, my tour had consisted of endless stag duty and little else, and as boring and soul destroying as it was, it did provide a degree of comfort to know that you were relatively safe from enemy attacks within the airport grounds. I had been operating in my own little comfort zone and knew that sooner or later I would be forced to abandon it and start doing my share of riskier work.

It was around that time that we began to get our first reports of near misses and skirmishes with enemy fighters throughout the region. Most of the incidents were unfortunate accidents or confused misunderstandings, but the message was getting through clearly enough that the tour had started for real. As a regiment we were spread far and wide across the southern deserts, and I realised that the safe haven of Basra airport was a thing of the past.

By far the worst incident occurred when one of our platoons took on the task of escorting a New Zealand diplomat into the centre of Basra. The lead vehicle was a Land-Rover Discovery, and it contained a couple of diplomats and an Iraqi driver. In the rear, a Land-Rover Wolf (a standard issue army 4x4) with four Green Jackets inside acted as protection. The diplomats had concluded their business and were heading back to camp when the lead vehicle suddenly exploded and leapt 6 ft into the air. When the Discovery came to a rest, it had been torn open like a tin of beans, and there were loud screams coming from the shattered cabin. It had taken a direct hit from a roadside improvised explosive device (IED) and had been completely destroyed.

The Land-Rover behind it screeched to a halt, and the soldiers leapt out to provide a defensive cordon around the stricken vehicle. The NCO in charge was Cpl. Leicester, and he wasted no time in ordering the riflemen to get the injured bodies out of the Discovery and perform emergency first aid. The biggest concern he had was that the terrorists might mount a secondary ambush and attack the Green Jackets as well. It was left to him and him alone to sweep the area and scan the rooftops and alleyways for any potential enemy, but, thankfully, there weren't any, and the lads carried on giving first aid.

The driver of the Discovery was horrendously injured and mercifully died quickly, while one of the passengers in the back was wounded very badly and losing a lot of blood. The dead and injured were loaded onto the back of the crowded Wolf, and as they were out in the open and in an extremely vulnerable position, Cpl. Leicester wisely told Rifleman Bacon to drive back to camp at full speed.

When they finally reached the airport, the medical team took over and slid the bodies out of the back of the vehicle. Rifleman Robinson told me that when he helped unload the vehicle it was so slick with blood that he fell on his arse several times – it was in the soles of his boots, under his fingernails and even found its way into his eyes. He said it looked and smelt like an abattoir.

The lads had been incredibly lucky because if they had been just ten metres in front of where they were, their vehicle would have taken the full blast. Another blessing had been the absence of a follow-up attack as there often was one in such incidents. Sometimes the lead vehicle is taken out first, and when the rear vehicle stops to help, that is taken out as well. The lads had done tremendously well to keep their cool and get the job done. In the same circumstances, I didn't know if I would have performed so well (and I wasn't keen to find out).

I felt particularly bad for Rifleman Pearman, one of our youngest soldiers not long out of depot, who had cradled a dying man in his arms, trying valiantly to hold his shattered body together. As Pearman was giving him first aid, the back of the man's head had fallen off, and bits of brain had dripped through his fingers. It was a heck of an ordeal to go through, but as I told him later, he had certainly proved himself to be a good soldier that day, and we were all very proud of him. Cpl. Leicester had also acted extremely professionally, and his quick thinking and decisive actions had been a comfort to the lads treating the injured; his had been a textbook military response.

I thought that the soldiers on that patrol deserved a medal or perhaps some form of commendation for their actions, but they got nothing. Of course, the lads concerned didn't expect or ask for rewards, and as they pointed out, they were just doing their jobs as best they could. However, the fact remains that they performed exceptionally well and probably saved the life of the wounded Kiwi. Perhaps the greatest testament to their courage and professionalism is that within days they were back out on patrol, passing by the very same spot where they had almost met a grisly end.

The terrorist attack that had almost claimed the lives of my friends was certainly a sharp reminder of the dangers we faced, and as I contemplated venturing into Basra city for the first time, I hoped that I wouldn't be tested in the same way.

7

GIANT CANDLES IN THE SKY

Now that I was part of a patrols platoon, I had to undergo some extra training to get ready for possible operations on the ground. My first task was to learn how to use the Browning 9-mm pistol. Compared to a SA80 it was a breeze to use, although with the short muzzle, you'd struggle to lay down accurate fire from a distance, and the first few times I handled it I ended up with cut fingers and grazed thumbs, as it was very easy to get your digits caught in the fiddly mechanism. Nevertheless, I managed to pass my weapons' handling test after a single lesson. Passing this test means that you can handle the pistol safely but bears little relation to your true level of skill.

As a designated driver I might be expected to carry a 9-mm, so I was pissed off when I found out that I wouldn't get a chance to practise with it on a rifle range. This meant that if I ever found myself in a fire fight with the enemy, it would be the first time I had fired it live!

One of the problems that soon became apparent on our tour was that in terms of manpower and taskings we were being seriously overstretched. As a regiment, we had taken on so much extra work that there was no option but to cut corners. That's why small but important details, like drivers having no live firing experience with a 9-mm, were being overlooked, and VIP escort jobs that required two vehicles were being cut down to one. Part of the problem lay in the prestige of the deployment and the desire of the hierarchy to prove that the Green Jackets were better than anybody else and willing to take on anything. To be sent into Iraq at a chaotic time whilst on Spearhead stand-by was the kind of operation that makes senior officers think of OBEs and other assorted gongs.

As a regiment, we were being stretched to the limit providing security for the whole of Basra, doing all of the donkey-work of escorts and training Iraqi soldiers as well. All of our rest days were cancelled, and we found ourselves taking on an ever-increasing workload. Even some of the junior officers were getting fed up of sitting in on meetings and seeing our commanders sticking their hands up and volunteering for every job known to man. It became a running joke that if ever a toilet needed unblocking or some furniture moving, all you had to do was 'find the nearest Green Jacket'. We weren't complaining about the level of work we had to do – we expected to be stretched on an operational tour; our grumbles were aimed squarely at the other regiments we served alongside.

We shared Basra International with a large contingent of RAF airmen, Royal Engineers, Army Air Corps and a smattering of other units. The harder we worked, the harder they partied. Whereas us Green Jackets worked a 24-hour system and never stopped, the other regiments mostly knocked off at 5 p.m. and spent all night getting pissed in the beer tent.

We would be stagging on at the airport or returning from a night-time patrol at 2 a.m. when we would see the drunken soldiers, sailors and airmen staggering back to their beds. They would often be dressed in Bermuda shorts and Hawaiian shirts and would stop for a chat and ask us why we worked so hard. The reason was because we were on permanent stand-by, took the job seriously and didn't view it as a holiday – but the fact that we were forbidden to drink alcohol probably played a part too! Like I said before, there is the infantry, and then there is everything else.

One of the new tasks we had taken on was implementing Eagle Vehicle Check Points, or Eagle VCPs as they were more commonly known. Basically, these involved a platoon of soldiers jumping onto a couple of Chinook or Sea King helicopters and flying out into the desert. We would fly to a pre-arranged checkpoint and land one of the choppers, whilst the other one would circle in the air and provide overhead protection. The men on the ground would make an effort to hide away in sand dunes or down the banks of the roadside, while the grounded chopper would take off and disappear. As soon as a vehicle approached we would show our faces and one section would carry out a search, while the other provided protection.

We had trained to do this in England as part of our pre-tour build-up, but doing it for real in the desert was a different proposition altogether. To start with, I always hoped before going up that it would be in a Chinook, as I got plenty of space to myself and could gather my thoughts. The Sea Kings, on the other hand, were bloody awful things to travel in: they were cramped and claustrophobic, making an already tense time even more unpleasant. We had to sit two to a seat with bits of kit jammed into our legs or stabbing us in the hips. If we had been flying round for a while, we would begin to get cramp, and then when we jumped out, we'd twist an ankle or fall flat on our faces.

However, the worst part was the tension and the not knowing what surprises might be waiting for us on the ground. I tried not to think about it too much, because my imagination could play tricks on me, but the fears were always there at the back of my mind.

An added problem I had was motion sickness. It was something I had always suffered from, but it had never really bothered me – that is until I went up in a helicopter. The back door of the

Chinook lowers down like a ramp, and as you run into it you are hit by this incredibly hot and powerful rotor blast – it is almost enough to knock you off your feet. Then you sit down and buckle up, and the pilot takes you up very high, very fast, in order to avoid a potential rocket strike. When you fly around, the pilot will occasionally drop sharply or jerk violently into a sharp turn. Again, this is all to avoid an enemy rocket locking on to him. Sometimes when he did this, I would be violently sick and leave my breakfast on the floor, which the lads found highly amusing. Then, just as I would be recovering from my sickness, the chopper would swoop down and land, and we'd bomb-burst out of the back and form a defensive circle.

When you hit the sand running, the heat and draught from the blades caused you to stumble and falter, and it was a relief when you finally found your designated spot. The chopper would then lift off, and the blast of hot sand would mean you had to close your mouth, otherwise you'd get a singeing gobful of grit in your belly. Once the chopper had disappeared and you recovered your composure, you would dash off again and find a nice hiding place by the side of the road, where you would dive down and wait for a vehicle to appear.

The greatest fear I had on these operations wasn't that a suicide bomber or a terrorist would open up on us, but that I would trigger a landmine while I was crawling along the ground. The areas where we did Eagle VCPs had supposedly been cleared of landmines, but I wondered how anyone could be so sure as lots of enemy hardware littered the sands. It wasn't unusual to see the hulk of a rusting tank looming over your shoulder, clearly demonstrating that fighting had gone on in that area, and all it would take to cripple you would be one missed mine.

Other possible dangers came from nearby villages and small townships that overlooked the areas where we landed. You had to have one eye on the road ahead but also one on the ground behind you, as there were often sinister-looking cloaked men wandering about – but I suppose from their perspective we were sinister too!

Another worry that played on my mind was how easily a trained sniper could take off the backs of our heads and how hard it would be for us to spot him. The problem with the Chinooks was that they were so large and noisy; their arrival was announced a long time before they landed. Even employing good infantry skills couldn't do much to minimise the vulnerable nature of our arrival.

I never enjoyed searching the Iraqi vehicles because I always felt like a pest and a nuisance to the local population, and I preferred to use my skills providing a defensive watch. Occasionally, we would find a concealed weapon or some suspect cargo, but as we weren't police and it was considered normal for locals to carry rifles, we were often confused about what to do. A lone driver carrying an AK47 for his personal protection on the dusty back roads of Iraq is not the same as a driver carrying an M16 in Northern Ireland. One is a recipe for instant arrest, but the other is a more complex case. The truth was that we found very little on these Eagle VCPs, and the impression you got from the local Iraqis was that they had nothing to hide. Nine times out of ten their innocent cargo and friendly cooperation confirmed this.

I learned from Eagle VCPs that to be a confident soldier you had to be physically fit and hyper-aware of your surroundings. When the chopper went up, you could cut the tension with a knife, and nervous apprehension was etched into the faces of the men around you. Some tried to hide it with jokes and banter, but underneath it all was a silent understanding that this was about as serious as it could get and that we all had to be completely switched on. And when you hit the ground running, you had better be fit and ready, because the combination of heat and sand with heavy kit on your back meant that you had no reserves of energy to cope with being tired. It was certainly an education, and you had to be ready for anything. The constant tension of doing just a few hours of Eagle VCPs was as draining as spending a whole day digging trenches. At the end of a VCP, you would feel like a worn-out drunk as you staggered back to camp, and just concentrating on eating a chip whacked you out.

It's a strange paradox that while I was up in the air in a Chinook or dashing about in the sand waiting for a car to appear, it was the last place on earth that I wanted to be, but when the VCPs were over and I found myself stumbling out of the chopper covered in a film of sweat and dust, there was no place I would have rather been. When I knew that I had performed well, there was an intense buzz and an afterglow that I couldn't find anywhere else; I felt like there was no better job in the world. It was at those times that my envy of the slacker regiments turned to pity, and I was glad to be a Green Jacket. It was true that we had a far tougher life, but at least we could say we were getting out on the ground and doing the proper work of soldiers, as opposed to sitting in an air-conditioned office or working in a glorified garage. When our tour came to an end, we would have far more meaningful memories to draw on than just a party in the desert.

When we weren't stagging on or doing Eagle VCPs, the remainder of our time was spent doing escort duty. This involved driving for hundreds of miles all over Iraq, and at all hours of the day and night, usually taking important diplomats and generals to various meetings. We'd load up the Land-Rovers with extra pickaxe handles in case we ever had to get physical and just drove on until we were told to stop. A typical cargo would be one driver, one NCO in command, two riflemen in the back and the VIP passenger. Sometimes we'd have up to three Land-Rovers, but more often than not it was just one or two. We always tried to squeeze an extra Minimi (a superbly reliable and effective light machine gun) or light support weapon (LSW) gunner in the back, but most of the time it was just our SA80s and us.

We were supposed to be on a strict system of 'drivers hours' that limited how much time we spent on the road, but as is always the case with these things, the rulebook went out of the window. It wasn't unusual to find yourself dozing off at the wheel, and only a sharp dig in the ribs from your mate would wake you up. Some days we would drive for hundreds of miles, and we'd often be woken up in the middle of the night and told to prepare a vehicle. The biggest single killer of soldiers on operational tours or military exercises is road traffic accidents (RTA), and this should come as no surprise. Typically, the army tries to squirm its way out of this and attributes most accidents to poor driving skills, but a closer examination would reveal that many RTAs are down to simple tiredness behind the wheel.

Before I began doing escort duty I had only ever been on Eagle VCPs to the outskirts of Basra and the surrounding villages and had never actually been into the city itself. I had been given a briefing on what to expect when I got out there, but no amount of warnings could have ever prepared me for what I saw. The scene of utter chaos and total mayhem on the roads could have come straight out of a Mad Max movie, and the abject poverty and clutter that was supposed to be a city looked more like a backdrop from *Black Hawk Down*. Never before or since have I driven a car with such aggression and complete disregard for the normal rules of safety – the streets were like a dodgem track, and I was forced to drive like I was in *Starsky and Hutch*. Before I deployed to Iraq, I had completed a short advanced-driving course in my spare time, and if it wasn't for that, I don't think I could have kept my vehicle on the road, such was the kamikaze style of motoring in Basra.

In Iraq, if you want to drive on the roads, all you have to do is buy a car and go. There are no driving tests, no MOTs, no road tax and no insurance – there are no regulations whatsoever. Anybody can drive a car, and the average vehicle is a '70s Datsun held together by rust and bits of old string. The car would have failed a British MOT 15 years ago, and it will most likely have a few doors missing, no bumpers or bonnet, and tyres that have melted down to the rims. If it has any colour, other than rust, left on it, it will be a mixture of garish purple, lime green or canary yellow.

Basically, it will be several different cars welded together. The lights on the car will have long since gone, and if the driver bothers indicating, it will be with an arm out of the window – or he might just steer into you and try to nudge you aside.

There are no laws of traffic as we know it, and it is not uncommon for junctions to appear out of nowhere or for cars coming in the opposite lane to suddenly cross into your path and approach you head on. And it isn't just battered cars that use the roads: you get tired old donkeys pulling huge carts and even herds of sheep being pushed along by scruffy shepherds. It is a picture of surreal chaos that defies all description, common sense and logic.

On escort duty, we were instructed to drive very fast and aggressively, and as close to bumper to bumper as we could. When we got out onto the open road, we could open the gaps up a bit, but for downtown Basra, it was up each other's arses all the way. None of us enjoyed driving this way, but, unfortunately, it was an absolute necessity. One of the terrorists' favourite tactics was to try and split a convoy up and isolate one vehicle, into which they would then lob a grenade or spray some gunfire. It was a very effective tactic that had been used against us successfully in the past, but we had no intentions of it working on us in the future.

Whenever a vehicle got too close or tried to dart in between us (which, to be frank, was everyday!), we would honk our horns like mad and veer aggressively towards it. At the same time, the riflemen in the back would point their weapons at the offending driver and shout and gesture at him to fuck off. I am aware that this sounds like very unpleasant and unnecessarily aggressive behaviour from us, but trust me when I say that it was justified.

In Britain, all it takes to bring a vehicle to a halt is the flash of a police siren or a blinking of headlights. Unfortunately, in Iraq, compliance takes a lot more than that. The local population has no fear of guns, soldiers or aggressive driving. In fact, all of the above are just simple facts of their daily lives, be it under Saddam's rule or ours. I have seen an old man with only one arm steering a rusty old motorbike, trying to barge into a Land-Rover to force it to give way. Stick a rifle in his face and snarl at him, and he will simply steer at you with greater determination. Iraqi drivers are a combination of the brave, the fearless and the utterly stupid.

Places where we were particularly vulnerable were at police checkpoints and in traffic jams. Whenever we encountered either, we would try and squeeze and nudge our way through, but sometimes it wasn't possible, and you just had to sit there feeling vulnerable. The vehicles we were in were known as 'soft-skin' Land-Rovers, because they had no protective armour. I think the only reason we didn't suffer more attacks was because the locals overestimated us and presumed we were stronger than we really were. While the two guys in the back providing top cover might have looked impressive with their Minimi light machine guns and shades, the reality was that they were incredibly vulnerable and would have made easy pickings for a shooter. To take out a soft-skin vehicle with barely any planning would be incredibly easy.

Basra itself was a sprawling and overpopulated lump of crumbling concrete and abandoned blocks of slum housing. You had to have eyes in the back of your head to keep track of the threats that were always around. While the driver kept his eyes strictly peeled on the road ahead, the other guys had to cover alleyways, pedestrians, surrounding traffic, huge blocks of flats and shop doorways. Whenever you moved, there was an instant hive of activity around you, and 20 sets of eyes couldn't have kept track of all that was going on. Sometimes you would roll to a halt opposite a foreboding-looking multi-storey car park, a narrow back alley with shady characters lurking around it, or derelict buildings with eyes that peered out at you from darkened rooms. At such times, I would look around anxiously and pray that the hold-up would clear quickly, because the longer you were motionless, the better target you became.

The two times of day that you really didn't want to get caught out in traffic was at night-time or rush hour. On the rare occasions that you did, the rulebook was completely disregarded, and you wouldn't hesitate to bash someone out of the way. These were particularly fraught times because darkness and traffic jams were the ideal conditions for terrorist attacks. The name of the game was to never lose momentum or stop the vehicle moving – so we would do abrupt U-turns on one-way roads to confuse the enemy or bounce over central reservations and speed off in the opposite direction.

After a few weeks of driving in Basra's chaotic streets, I soon adapted and began to take suicidal risks that would see me locked up if performed on British roads. I did feel jittery and paranoid, but that was a good thing because it kept me alert and ready for action. I would often hear a quick burst of fire or a long rattle from a rifle as I sped past, but the problem was that I never knew if it was celebratory gunfire from a wedding or if it was aimed at me. In response, I just drove faster and took ever-greater risks.

I alternated between providing top cover in the back and driving the vehicle itself. It made no difference what I did as I felt equally vulnerable in both positions. If an attack ever came, I knew that it would be aimed at the driver first to halt the vehicle and then be switched to the guys in the back to finish us off. It would take no real skill – just a quick burst of rifle fire from a nearby building could rake us to pieces and stop the vehicle. They didn't even need to kill us all in one go: a few rounds sprayed into the legs of the guys in the back would take them out of the game and make us all easy pickings. Behind the derelict and wrecked houses was a maze of back alleys that resembled a rabbit warren. All it would take would be a couple of waiting motorbikes and our attackers could disappear in seconds.

However, the more likely mode of attack would be from a roadside IED. Every clump of rubbish or patch of shrubbery by the side of the road was a potential bomb, and whenever we passed a cluster of any sort, my heart would be in my mouth. Some roadside bombs were quite obvious, and you could see them from a mile away, but they weren't the ones that you had to worry about.

The prevalence of IEDs was clear to see. Although Basra was a large city, there were only so many different routes through it, and after a while it got to the point that whichever road you went down there had been a bomb on it at some point. But the most upsetting thing about IEDs was that their random and unpredictable nature took no account of any military skills I might have. I could be the most switched-on soldier in the world and it would make no difference; I might as well have been a complete mong. If I drove over one, it was tough luck and that was me finished.

One of our most frequent escort trips was a daily run to Basra Palace, which meant a long and risky drive through several terrorist hot spots. Despite the draining tension of the journey, I was always pleased to visit the palace and enjoyed the change of scenery. Like almost everything I had seen in Iraq, the palace seemed bizarre and out of place in a way that my British logic struggled to comprehend. To get there you had to drive through some of the poorest and roughest slums in the city, and you saw poverty on a scale that wouldn't be accepted in the western world. But all of a sudden, and seemingly out of nowhere, appeared this beautiful building at the bottom of a filthy and rubbish-strewn road. In front of it was a fortified entrance and huge gates, but once you drove through them, you were transported into a decadent world of bountiful luxury and stunning surroundings: welcome to planet 'I'm a greedy dictator and this is my wonderful home'.

What struck me as odd about the palace was not its beautiful construction or vulgar excess (as this was what I had expected) but the state of the poverty-ridden slums that surrounded it. Behind its gates lay a world of abundance and fantastic comfort, but only yards away was a hellhole of grinding hardship. It was like taking a brand new Rolls-Royce and parking it in the middle of a scrapyard. I asked myself what kind of values must Saddam and his cronies have had, that they could drive through such deprivation without even a glance over their shoulders. Only someone without a conscience or pity could sleep in the silk sheets of such a palace, while outside his subjects were starving and living in squalor. The slums were so bad that even I felt guilty just driving through them in my Land-Rover – so how Saddam could have breezed through without a care in the world defies human description.

Perhaps the biggest indicator of the poverty that Basra laboured under was the foul and pungent breeze that blew through the air. This was so strong that not even the gold-plated luxury of Saddam's palace could hide from it. The smell was a curious mixture of petrol fumes and rotting garbage, and wherever you travelled, it always hung over you as a sour reminder of the underlying decay and suffering. It was a smell that I don't think you could ever get used to, and it symbolised all that was wrong with modern Iraq.

But it wasn't all doom and gloom, and occasionally we would make a stop in a relatively safe area and try to unwind a little. One section would stand guard while the other relaxed and chatted to the locals. Sometimes we were received as conquering heroes and treated with deference, but on other occasions we would be spoken to with open contempt and hostility. Regardless, I would enjoy these moments because I had a chance to study the culture, and I heard some interesting stories.

I got chatting to one guy, and we sat down on the pavement and shared stories of our lives. He told me that he had been arrested by Saddam's secret police for supposedly spying, when he assured me he hadn't. The police had beaten him up and shot him in the kneecap, and he showed me the scars to back up his story. I looked into his warm brown eyes and saw a lot of sincerity there, and my instincts told me that he was telling the truth. We had an interesting discussion on the rights and wrongs of the allied invasion, and although for his part he was glad we had come and driven out Saddam, he wasn't so sure if the future of Iraq would be much better. The man's open heart and sharp intelligence impressed me, and as we shook hands and parted, I felt a tinge of sadness to be leaving him behind in such a dump. Like the deposed teacher I had met on the back gate of the airport, I felt I had just met a man that would have made a great friend, but the barriers between us prevented it.

I always enjoyed it when we stopped and chatted to the local children. In contrast to the adolescents who spat on the floor or hurled insults at you, the younger kids radiated goodwill and innocent curiosity at our presence. We would have a laugh with them about going to school or what they wanted to be when they grew up, and they in turn questioned us incessantly about life on the other side of the world. Seeing how poor and obviously hungry some of them were broke my heart, and I had to fight my instinct to give them food and water from our own supplies.

In Iraq, clean bottled water was a valuable commodity, because of its unfortunate scarcity. Although we had an abundance of it and always carried boxfuls in the back of the Land-Rovers, we were strictly forbidden to give the people any. This was for very good reasons of safety and security: if we started dishing out bottles whenever we stopped, we would be swamped with pleading adults and children, and it wouldn't be long before terrorists used it as an opportunity to strike at us. It deeply hurt us to have to turn them away, but it was something we had to do.

What really upset me was that many of the kids interpreted our refusal to hand over water as a confirmation of our selfishness and greed, and I worried about what sort of young adults they would become. Most likely they would join the criminal elements of the nomadic street gangs and be ground down into bitterness and anger by years of struggle. I could always spot these kids – they would roam the streets like a pack of wolves and challenge me with their suspicious eyes and aggressive posturing. Unfortunately for them, their true situation was all too apparent from their emaciated arms and pinched faces. Despite their supposed 'strength in numbers', their lives had been reduced to a daily battle for survival that no amount of noisy bravado could hide. Worse still, it looked to me like they had already lost, so who could blame them for rebelling?

I could understand why we were perceived as not giving a shit, but sometimes the nature of the job meant we couldn't help coming across that way. Whenever we went on a long drive, we would often get groups of children or even adults that would run to the side of the road and wave at the vehicle, smiling and hollering at us. When people displayed such spontaneous goodwill and warmth towards us, it was difficult not to respond. In our hearts, we wanted to wave back or reach out and touch them – but because of security reasons, we rarely could. It is a well-known terrorist tactic to distract soldiers with a group of kids or to place a gunman in the middle of a smiling crowd, and then spring an ambush the second you drop your guard. Although 99 per cent of the friendly gestures to us were genuine, because of the 1 per cent that weren't, we had to ignore and rebuff all advances.

I used to dwell on how incredibly cold and arrogant we must have appeared when they ran towards us dressed in tatty rags, without shoes and displaying grossly swollen bellies devoid of food, and we sped past them and brushed aside their good wishes like unfeeling robots. How superior must we have looked with our well-fed faces staring stonily ahead through shiny sunglasses and our ears seemingly deaf to their greetings? They probably got the impression that we didn't give a fuck about them and had come to rape and rob their land of its most precious resources. Even more worryingly, maybe they were right . . .

The only time I really enjoyed driving in Iraq was when I was given a big escort job to do that meant driving to another camp hundreds of miles away. The danger level on the highways was considered nowhere near that of downtown Basra, and so we were given souped-up civilian-type 4x4s to drive. We still took all our weaponry and body armour, but it just meant that we could get where we needed to be with a lot more comfort and speed. More often than not, we'd be driving for some high-powered diplomat or VIP, and some of them were so obese and pampered I don't think they could have endured a long drive in the back of a cluttered Land-Rover. Drivers were issued with a personal vehicle, and for my new toy I was handed the keys to a gleaming silver Mitsubishi Shogun. It was an absolute beast of a car, and I hammered its V6 engine to the limit.

Whenever we visited Nasiriyah, we'd stop off at the Italian HQ and get something to eat. There was an unspoken agreement between all the different nations serving in Iraq that whenever a foreign patrol stopped by they'd be treated with the maximum respect and given a warm welcome. It was a system we all benefited from, and it did add to the general feelings of warmth and mutual respect that we had for one another. Whenever the Italians dropped into Basra, I know they enjoyed tucking into the British cuisine, and the same went for us whenever we visited their base. We got to know a few of the soldiers by sight, and it was nice to exchange a few words and handshakes when we met up. The Italians had a sizable force in Iraq, and we always seemed to be driving intelligence officers and diplomats to and from their base.

Having become friendly with the Italians, I felt pretty sick when I heard that they had been hit by a devastating suicide-bomb attack. To get into the Italian camp you had to negotiate an awkwardly positioned gate and guard post, which was designed in such a way that you couldn't just drive straight in. An ingenious team of suicide bombers had overcome this by ramming the entrance with a heavy truck, leaving just enough space for an explosive-laden van to nip alongside and drive in. The Italian soldiers had naturally assumed that the big truck was the main threat and moved to counter it, but, actually, the little van had most of the explosives on board, and in the confusion, it managed to sneak in and detonate itself. The larger lorry only added to the carnage.

I was very saddened for the Italians because I realised how vulnerable and tempting a target they must have been. As someone who had done more than his fair share of guarding a gate at Basra, I was well aware of how susceptible to attack you could be. Sixteen men died on the Italian gate, and although I didn't know any of them personally, the law of averages told me I must have shared a chat and a joke with some of them. It was a sharp reminder to us all of how dangerous the tour really was, and the fact that you could be smiling and laughing today, wouldn't protect you from a gruesome death tomorrow. I also felt exceptionally lucky not to have been caught up in the blast myself, because I had visited the camp many times.

The attack on the Italian HQ had a notable effect on security in Basra. Whereas before we had been merely strict in our methods, we now became draconian. Huge slabs of concrete were placed at either end of the airport to prevent any unauthorised vehicles getting through, and Warrior armoured personnel carriers were stationed permanently outside the gates. The numbers of men on guard were doubled, more routine checks were made and the Choggies were searched and questioned whenever they arrived for work. Of course, the downside of all this was that the poor bastards on guard now had to do more stag than ever, and their lives became a world of sleep-deprived torture.

Ever since the brutal fist fight with Haxiton, my fortunes had looked up, and I had enjoyed a series of lucky breaks. The suicide bombings on the Italian HQ had signalled the beginning of a marked upsurge in violence across the whole of Iraq, and this meant there was going to be a change in how we were used. For the unfortunate souls who remained on duty at the airport (which was mainly my old platoon), it meant longer and more intense periods of stag, but for the rest of us on patrols duty and escorts it meant a welcome change of scenery.

The regiment had received requests for assistance from the British HQ in Baghdad and the Danish forces in the Salt Marsh region. In response, the company split down into three sections: 14 Platoon was despatched to Baghdad, 15 Platoon remained in Basra (stagging on!) and 16 Platoon was sent to help out the Danes.

I was over the moon at this as it meant I would escape from the 'head sheds' in Basra and experience a few weeks away from all the usual bullshit. I would also get the chance to work alongside some of Denmark's best soldiers. Any extra tasks like this were always welcome because the different experiences and surroundings recharged your batteries. As much as I enjoyed blasting down the highways to Nasiriyah, or dodging and weaving through the chaos of downtown Basra, I had to admit that I was getting fed up of constantly repeating the same old journeys with the same old faces. I was starting to feel like I knew Basra better than my own home town, and the guys I patrolled with were starting to bicker like old married couples that needed some time apart. The trip couldn't have come at a better time; it would break up the tour nicely. By the time we returned, we would only have six weeks until it was all over.

We loaded up the vehicles and snaked out of Basra in a long convoy for the 100-mile journey to 'Danebat', as the Danish HQ was known. The long drive would probably pose the greatest risk of our time with the Danes, because long and slow-moving convoys are notoriously vulnerable to attack, no matter how well protected they are. We would also have to pass through several towns and former roadblocks where terrorist militias were known to operate and had launched successful strikes. More worryingly, we would have to pass through an infamous stretch of empty wasteland known as 'Sniper Alley', where roadside bombs and wrecked cars littered the landscape like pebbles on a beach.

The Danish area of command stretched for endless miles across abandoned villages, impoverished towns and desolate country known as the Salt Marshes. Unlike the British HQ, their camp was situated in the middle of a barren wilderness, and you had to drive for a good half-hour until you came across even the tiniest of villages. From a security perspective it was a good idea, but from a human one it left you feeling very isolated and removed from the people whom you were supposed to be policing.

In comparison to the British camp, Danebat had a cosy and intimate feel, and was much smaller, being designed to support a single battalion of troops only. They didn't employ any Iraqi workers, and there were no other soldiers there apart from Danes until we arrived. You got the feeling that for them it was a home from home.

It was late afternoon when we arrived and were shown to our accommodation. Most of the Danes lived in box-like container houses, similar to those on a building site but surprisingly comfortable and well equipped. Unfortunately, no such luxury awaited us, and the tents we were placed in were decidedly grotty.

Living in a tent for a few weeks shouldn't present any real hardship for a soldier, but when it came with the 'extras' that the Danish camp provided, it was a different story. In all my time in Basra I hadn't seen a single spider or creepy crawly (and I was always on the lookout), but within minutes of our arrival at Danebat, we were becoming intimately acquainted. The tent was crawling with them. You had to be very careful where you put your kit down, because if you plonked it near the corners, you would often find a set of beady eyes staring back at you when you went to pick it up.

Apparently, the Danebat area was a haven for camel spiders, and they turned up in boots, lockers, kit bags and bergens – anywhere that was dark and warm. For some of the lads who were scared of spiders, the damn things were a bigger worry than the Iraqis!

As a self-confessed greedy bastard, I was particularly pleased with the fresh Danish food on offer, and I immediately set about demolishing a massive meal. At Basra we had to put up with the same old dry vegetables, greasy chips and stodgy puddings everyday, but here we had a feast of chilled seafood, exotic cheeses, spicy sausages and fruit juices. I didn't stop to think what effect all this unusual fare might have on my gastric juices, and I tucked in greedily. Our first task was going to be assisting the Danes on a familiarisation patrol of the local area, and I reckoned if we were covering a lot of ground, I would be wise to get some calories down my neck. I was anxious to make a good impression, and the last thing I wanted to do was embarrass myself by running out of fuel in front of my new colleagues.

The Danish infantry troops weren't just ordinary run-of-the-mill soldiers but belonged to one of the finest reconnaissance regiments they had. Because the Danish presence in Iraq was relatively small – at just 1,000 troops – their government had decided only to send the very best they had. You could tell they weren't regular infantry by the weapons they carried, and it was a little embarrassing to compare our clumsy and heavy SA80s to their matt black M4 Carbines, complete with laser sights and collapsible stocks. Before we hooked up with them, our platoon commander had told us to ignore their Gucci kit and to get out there and impress the hell out of them with our skills and proficiency. We considered ourselves to be every bit as good as them and intended to show it on that first patrol.

I was buoyed up by what the boss had said and agreed with every word of it. To a British squaddie, 'Special Forces' means the SAS and nothing else, and while we rated the Danes highly, with the greatest respect in the world, they weren't the SAS.

For our first patrol, the Danes decided to take us to a safe area; the plan was to allow us to gradually familiarise ourselves with the ground rather than to chuck us in at the deep end. This was a good idea, based on sound common sense, and as I prepared my kit, I felt quietly confident that we wouldn't have any dramas unless someone really fucked up – and I knew that it wouldn't be me.

Before a patrol I always felt a bit sick and nervous, but this didn't bother me as I equated it with my mind readying my body for action. I would have been more worried if I hadn't felt anything. We climbed into the back of a Mercedes 4x4 and were driven to a Danish-controlled police station on the outskirts of the nearest town.

I wasn't surprised to see that Danish squaddies drove every bit as badly as their British counterparts, and as I slid around the back and bounced out of my seat, I had to smile at how some things are the same wherever you go. What did worry me though, were the increasingly nauseous feelings that were growing in my gut, and the way my body was beginning to shiver as if it was a cold winter's day. At first, I put it down to pre-patrol nerves, but as it got rapidly worse and my stomach began loudly rumbling, I knew it was something else.

I jumped down from the vehicle and made my way into the police station on shaky legs. A dreadful weakness had taken hold of my body, and I could barely put one foot in front of the other. The Danish sergeant in command of the patrol was pointing to a map on the wall and giving us a security briefing when, without warning, I began to vomit violently. A fountain of rotten fish and cheese projected out of my mouth, and I made a feeble effort to run from the room. I failed utterly and collapsed in my own pool of stinking sick.

There was a stunned silence before spontaneous applause and laughter broke out. I dragged myself to my feet and began stammering an apology to my Danish hosts, before being stopped mid-sentence by another stream of sick. This time even the Danes found it hilarious, and a few of the guards from outside couldn't resist coming in to see what the commotion was about.

So much for making a good first impression and not fucking up; I was off the patrol before it had even started. I was in a complete shit state and had to be helped to a nearby camp bed, where I was laid down like a sick child. Within minutes, I was reduced to a shivering and murmuring wreck and had to suffer the indignity of a medic being called to watch over me. By the time the patrol got back, I could barely walk and had to be helped to the medical centre. The doctor took one look at me and pronounced that I had food poisoning, probably caused by gorging myself on unfamiliar fish and cheese. He put me in an isolation room, and I slept solidly for two days with a pounding headache and growling tummy, only waking up to eat a tiny bowl of ice cream and a few sips of water, which was all I could keep down.

I felt bloody awful for putting myself in that position, because it meant my section was a man down, and I had succeeded in giving the Danes the worst possible impression of us Brits. But it had been a genuine accident and purely down to my own bad luck (and greed), so I knew it wouldn't be held against me. My being 'on the sick' would just mean that I would have to work harder when I was well again.

One lesson I had learned was to never go near the Danish food again – from then on, cold pasta, uncooked fish and spicy sausage were strictly off the menu. Even if it meant living off bread and butter, I had no intentions of going near that crap again, and I never did.

Once I had recovered, I rejoined the platoon on daily patrols. The first time I went out, we visited the famous Salt Marshes and spent some time assessing the local population. In Iraq history, the Salt Marshes were famous for one very unfortunate reason: Saddam Hussein had coveted the land for political and economic reasons. The indigenous people had made the fatal mistake of opposing him and had managed to scupper his plans. In retaliation, he drained the once-lush marshes and razed the settlers' humble homes. Where once had stood flourishing markets and crystal-clear lakes, all that now remained were polluted brown puddles and crumbling shanty towns. To my westernised eyes, the poverty was truly shocking, and it even managed to surpass Basra on the suffering scale by a distinct margin.

As we cruised past their flimsy homes and watched their children playing, the locals would crouch in the sand and wave at us or run to the side of the road in the hope that we would throw them some food or water. It struck me how fortunate I was to have been born an Englishman and to have had freedom of choice. While a class divide between rich and poor undoubtedly exists in Britain, it is nothing compared to the gulf between rich and poor in Iraq. In Britain, even the poorest and most deprived child will have a chance to educate themselves and develop their talents, but in Iraq, you cannot say the same. I wondered how much talent and potential had gone to waste or met a premature end in the ruined marshes – even a charismatic and gifted leader would never escape the confines of those cruel lands. You could be born there, live there, dream there and die there, and nobody would ever know you had existed. It was like living on another planet. Yet despite all the suffering and hardship the people had endured, they still had the capacity to radiate goodwill and optimism, and on the few occasions I chatted to them, I always came away feeling guilty about my own good fortune and ignorance.

Perhaps now that Saddam has gone, the Salt Marshes will have a chance to recover and recapture some of their former lustre. I certainly hope so, because I believe that given half a chance, nature can repair almost any damage that man cares to inflict on it. That belief was reinforced by the rugged beauty that persisted in the marshes and hinted at their eventual recovery. For example, when leaving the camp for an early morning patrol in the area, I was continually hushed into a respectful silence by the ghostly mist that hovered over the clumps of green bush – it was a truly stunning sight.

The welcome peace of the Salt Marshes would be shattered as soon as we turned onto the motorway or ventured into a nearby town. There, as it seemed to be wherever we went, the usual noise and chaos reigned. We would form a two-car convoy and do 'Snap VCPs', in which we would pull up on a random stretch of road and do searches on suspect cars. As it was the Danes' area and they seemed to know what they were looking for, we usually stood back and let them do the talking, but we would make our presence felt if someone started to get stroppy or aggressive.

Even though the Danes were notionally in command, I couldn't help but notice that the Iraqis seemed to defer to British soldiers more. I don't know if it was because we were viewed as a 'warrior race' or because there were more of us, but there was a definite respect for us that the Danes didn't seem to receive. On a number of occasions, a Danish sergeant would be very obviously in command of a VCP, but the Iraqis would address their complaints to the British lads – even if we were standing in the background. Sometimes it got embarrassing because we were only guests in Danebat, and this was very much their turf.

But aside from the occasional awkward moment, we got along well, and there was mutual respect. They made a big effort to make us feel welcome and included, and it added to the nice multi-national vibe that we had going on. We were all in the shit together, and it felt good to be able to laugh and enjoy the absurd moments that frequently sprang up.

One such moment came on a stretch of busy motorway when a minor traffic accident and some ultra-aggressive Iraqi drivers split our convoy up. It was no big deal and happened all the time, but it was important that we hooked up again quickly, because you never knew what might happen. The only problem was that whenever I pulled out to overtake, a stream of oncoming traffic would meet me or the vehicles surrounding me would pen me in and refuse to let me out. This farce went on for a few miles, and the Danish sergeant started to get very agitated. He was shouting and swearing at the swarm of drivers around us and was all for bashing them off the road. I didn't fancy doing that as I had three of my mates doing top cover in the back, and I felt responsible for their safety.

The Dane was getting more and more pissed off, and the Land-

Rover in front was disappearing into the distance. I asked him if he had any better suggestions, rather than pulling out into a stream of oncoming traffic or barging someone off the road. He thought for a moment before advising me to 'undertake' the traffic by using the hard shoulder. The hard shoulder bore no resemblance to one you would find in Britain: it was more of a rubbish-strewn dirt track that was covered in potholes, small boulders, blown tyres and rusty bits of engine. I asked him again if he was serious, and he screamed at me, 'Fuck it, just do it, just do it.'

I pulled onto the hard shoulder, and the thick gravel immediately slowed us; I had to drop a gear and really floor it to start overtaking. We clattered through all kinds of debris, and the vehicle bounced along like a giant Tonka toy. We were shaking about so much that I thought it would fall apart, and I had to swerve to try to avoid holes and rocks but more often than not ploughed straight through them. The guys in the back were loving it and whooping with laughter – to them it was a boy racer's wet dream come true, but to me it was a bit more worrying. The manoeuvre was taking so long that I was worried we were going to crash into an approaching bridge support before we caught up with the guys in front. As the bridge loomed ever closer, I decided to indicate and pull back into the traffic lane – but it seemed that the nutty Iraqi drivers didn't want to make a gap for me.

The bridge was getting closer and closer, and the Dane was hanging out of the window screaming at the Iraqis to give us room, but instead of making space for us, they just stared back with cold and impassive eyes. Finally, when we were only metres from the bridge, I sharply steered my vehicle back into the traffic. I took the bumper off the car in front of me, and the guy behind ran into the back of us and lost his bumper too. I couldn't give a fuck about the damage we did to their vehicles, as they were quite happy to see us run straight into a wall and had given me no choice but to barge them out of the way. Anyway, the good news was that we had caught up with the vehicle in front.

Once we had got to know the area, we started to go out on patrols by ourselves, and the Danes seemed eager to unload some of their work on us. It was on these patrols that some of the most magical and unforgettable moments of the tour occurred, and I found myself wishing that it would never end. We were free from the hierarchy that ran our lives so strictly in Basra, and as guests of the Danes, we could pick and choose what we wanted to do.

One of the problems the Danes faced was providing daily patrols to deter the 'pipeline bandits' who siphoned oil or routinely sabotaged the dozens of oil plants. As a result, the surrounding area, dominated by acres of arid desert, was full of blazing oil wells and abandoned refineries. The boss told the Danish commanders not to worry as we would be more than happy to take the bandits on in return for having daytimes off. The Danes hastily agreed, and we were given a series of pipeline patrols to perform on a nightly basis.

We would wait for it to get dark and then leave the camp at about 10 p.m. We didn't need a map to see where we were going because mile upon mile of blazing oil wells lit up the sky like giant candles. Flames soaring hundreds of feet into the air and illuminating the landscape created a striking image. The closer we got, the more awesome the sight became, and we could actually feel the powerful flames heating up the cool night air. There was fire everywhere as far as the eye could see, and a column of burning oil would meet you whichever way you turned.

Creeping through the Salt Marshes in the eerily quiet mornings, I was struck by the power of nature, but as I plodded along the desert highways at night, I was struck by the power of man. The flea-ridden dump that was Iraq by day was transformed into a mighty machine-like furnace by night. It positively glowed with purpose and intent, the huge flames angrily licking the sky.

Most of the refineries had been badly damaged by the war, overrun by bandits or abandoned and left to crumble – but the burning never stopped. Occasionally, we would pull up outside and patrol through the shattered grounds, before returning to the vehicles and hitting the road again.

You could drive for countless miles at night and not see another living soul; nothing seemed to exist except those hungry flames that dominated the moonlit landscape. Even the stars seemed to disappear in the presence of such power. We would cruise the deserted highways for mile after mile, the cool breeze blowing through our hair and the light from the infernal fires illuminating the scrubland. Normally, the vehicle would be a hive of loud chatter and crude jokes, but at times like those, none of us dared utter a word in case we spoiled the magic and broke its spell. It was serene, it was peaceful and it was a time that none of us will ever forget.

8

BASRA BY NIGHT

Our time in the Salt Marshes drew to a close all too quickly, and as we bid goodbye to our Danish hosts, we all agreed that we had been profoundly moved by what we had seen. At the same time that we returned from Danebat, 14 Platoon came back from Baghdad. They brought with them the usual collection of war stories and tall tales that soldiers always do, and we spent the next few days catching up on one another's experiences.

When I had at first heard about the deployment to Baghdad, I had been green with envy, and I reckoned that we had lost out by being despatched to the Salt Marshes. However, when I heard about how Baghdad had been, I realised that we had been better off. It turned out that 14 Platoon had been criminally underused, and they had spent most of their time doing escorts or getting pissed. Although they had seen the capital city and worked up close and personal with the huge American war machine, I felt that we had seen the real heart of Iraq, with its giant oil funnels spewing flames and its acres of flat desert.

Because the roads to Baghdad were considered too dangerous to travel, 14 Platoon had flown there from Basra airport with only their weapons and minimal kit. When they had arrived at

Baghdad and were getting off the plane, they noticed that they were getting a lot of admiring glances from the Yanks and wondered why. As they strolled towards the terminal, groups of American soldiers gave them salutes and exchanged high-fives with each other before whooping and hollering. The Green Jackets went to collect their baggage and a group of waiting soldiers respectfully stepped back. Then, a few lads went to queue up to buy some goods and were ushered to the front. When our boys asked why they were being treated like royalty, they were told that the United States military had the greatest respect for Britain's famous Special Forces and that they were just glad to have them on board.

It turned out the Yanks had mistakenly thought that the Green Jackets were elite Special Forces, purely because they wore green berets. When 14 Platoon saw how well they were being treated and how all the Yanks bowed down to them, they decided to play along with it and milked the fantasy for all it was worth. Several of the lads ended up shagging American girls who were desperate to hear of their heroic deeds 'all over the world'. US Marines would come up to them, shake their hands and ask for advice and tips on how to become 'the best of the best'.

Because they had no vehicles, the platoon was met by a fleet of brand new armour-plated Range Rovers at the airport, and these vehicles only added to the impression that they were 'something special'. It was in these cars that they would drive British generals around and pick up diplomats from the airport. They would blast down the main roads and whiz through US Army checkpoints with a wave and toot of the horn – as befits the status of elite 'green berets' on special duties. Americans would often ask if they could try on Green Jackets' berets or have a photo with them, and the US troops would rave about what an honour it was to be serving alongside such great soldiers. I must admit, I would have loved to have been up in Baghdad fooling the Yanks and having a laugh at their expense, but I don't think I would have been able to keep a straight face at some of the bullshit that the Green Jackets were coming up with.

Back in Basra, we slipped into the old routine of being used as a taxi service for anyone who needed to be someplace else. We didn't mind driving VIPs to important meetings and acting as their bodyguards, because, after all, that was what we were there for, but we did resent being used as a convenient chauffeur service for lazy-arse intelligence staff who should have known better. A lot of tension was bubbling below the surface whenever we dealt with the support staff, because it had become clear to us that they had no concept or understanding of the dangers we faced out on the ground. They sat in air-conditioned offices all day, waffling on the phone or analysing reports, and then, at a click of their fingers, they expected us to be at their beck and call.

What especially galled us was that our own opinions and judgements were being ignored, and we were being fobbed off with bullshit whenever we questioned the need to travel. Some fat, snotty-nosed officer would tell us he needed to be at Basra Palace urgently that night for an 'important briefing about terrorist activity', but when we got there, we would find a reunion party going on at one of the compound mansions. The problem was that these office dwellers rarely ventured out of their comfortable abodes, and when they did, it was always under our protection. They spent hours each day cocooned in a nice office studying intelligence reports, but they never actually got their boots on the ground and 'pounded the beat' for real. Consequently, they had very little idea or respect for the dangers we faced when we were driving them off to a jolly somewhere; it was all theory to them.

There was a growing feeling in the regiment that the support staff were pushing their luck and that sooner or later we would come under attack on one of these pointless journeys. We knew it because of the vibe on the streets, the hostile looks we received and because it was common fucking sense. None of us wanted to die in Iraq, but if you died while protecting an important general on a critical task, at least there was some glory in that. But who the hell wants to lose his life driving a snobby diplomat to Basra Palace so he can have a natter with an old pal?

Thanks to the bomb attack at Nasiriyah, we were spending less time there, and most of our daily business took us to destinations that were nearer, such as the Shaibah logistics base. The journey to Shaibah was only a short one, but it was a tense experience nonetheless, as the roads were in a very bad state. You would often come across suspected landmines or bombs and be forced off road into the thick sand. It was a difficult choice to make because going off road carried its own risks, and there could be buried ordnance waiting for you. The thick swirl of dust that billowed up from the vehicle in front obscured your vision and meant you would often be driving blind. Sometimes, my heart would be in my mouth and my eyes straining to their limits as I tried to avoid suspect debris or odd bits of junk that appeared in my path. Inevitably, there would be times when I was too slow to spot things and had to drive over them, hoping for the best. I was always lucky and never triggered anything, but I knew that other patrols hadn't been so fortunate.

One task that we did take pride in and regarded as worthwhile was when we were awoken from our beds at 1 a.m. and told to drive a Portuguese counter-terrorist team to Shaibah. They had flown into Basra that same day and were going to be involved in releasing a Portuguese journalist, who was being held hostage in Nasiriyah, for a ransom of $5 million. We had to take them to Shaibah under the cover of darkness and in absolute secrecy. Once there, they were picked up by another section and driven to the Italian camp at Nasiriyah, where the operation would be planned. We had a good old chinwag and bit off a piss take on the way down, and they gave as good as they got. But mostly we were just grateful to be involved in something worthwhile again, even if it was only in a small way, because we were getting heartily sick of driving support staff to Basra Palace for tea and scones.

But however much we railed against the pointless and unnecessary tasks, they still rumbled on, and we doubted things would change unless a serious and possibly tragic incident occurred. It wasn't a question of if, but when, and we only hoped that we wouldn't be the ones to bite the bullet.

Perhaps it was a bad portent of things to come when we found ourselves manning a VCP on the outskirts of Basra. A patrol from the RAF Regiment had found a cache of AK47s and concealed explosives, so a cordon had been thrown around the city, and we were checking all vehicles going in and out. Most cars stopped without incident and didn't give us any hassles, but we got a few that grumbled loudly or did an abrupt U-turn and scampered out of sight. Occasionally, we'd jump in the vehicles and give chase, but most of the time we just let them go, because we couldn't spare the time or manpower to indulge in cross-country races.

The frustrating thing about some people was that they would act guiltily and make you think they had something to hide, even when they had done nothing wrong. We learned this when we caught up with the cars trying to evade us: nine times out of ten it would just be an innocent family, who for some unknown reason liked to behave as if they were bank robbers on the run.

The most ludicrous incident that occurred that day was when a truck laden with gas canisters in the back came careering towards the patrol. The sergeant stepped into the road and firmly put his hand up for the driver to slow down – but in response, the Iraqi accelerated towards him, and the sergeant had to dive out of the way. The driver swerved across the road and looked at us with a panic-stricken, ash-white face, before barging into a fence and sliding to a halt. Instantly, our weapons were in our shoulders, and we adopted a firing position, screaming at him to get out of the cab. He climbed down wearing a wild-eyed expression and advanced towards us as if he hadn't a care in the world. Clearly, he wasn't intimidated by the guns or our loud screams. We all looked to the sergeant for guidance about what to do next, as we were all thinking the same thing – suicide bomber.

Fortunately, we had an Iraqi translator with us, and he managed to calm the man down and establish why he had steered into our patrol so aggressively. The answer was typically absurd and underlined how you could never assume anything in your dealings with the local population: the man's speeding lorry, which had been loaded with highly explosive gas canisters, didn't have any brakes! Only in Iraq!

We had been out all day on the VCP and were dead on our feet, so when the call came through that the operation was over, we were extremely relieved. We wearily drove back to camp, still in a state of shock at the stupidity of the lorry driver who had almost hit the sergeant. It seemed that just when you thought it couldn't get any crazier and you had seen it all, Iraq would throw up more surprises. Life was so cheap that a lorry without brakes and carrying gas was considered normal, and nobody batted an eyelid at the dead dogs and fly-ridden carcasses of livestock lying on the city's streets. Everything seemed rotten, old and decayed, and I desperately wanted to go home.

Unfortunately, our day wasn't over yet. We were dozing on our beds at 10 p.m. when the ops officer came in and shook us awake. He looked embarrassed and was apologetic as he told us that he needed us to run two important figures to Basra Palace for a meeting. The platoon commander sighed heavily and asked him for more details, because it was getting late, and we weren't supposed to go out at night unless it was absolutely necessary. The ops officer shrugged his shoulders and said he was only doing as he was told, and he had to assume that the meeting was urgent otherwise we wouldn't have been roused. Feeling more than a little irritated, we pulled our kit on, started up the Land-Rovers and headed for the airport.

A colonel from the support staff and a diplomat from the foreign office met us. The colonel wore thick glasses and carried a briefcase, and the diplomat had a blue blazer and beige slacks on. They looked like a pair of pale-faced bureaucrats. I hoped they realised that our trip wasn't just a casual jaunt and that there was an element of real danger involved.

The colonel clambered into my vehicle, and the diplomat was seated in the one behind. We tried very hard not to show our resentment at this tasking, but, in our own way, we made it clear that we weren't happy about it.

As we sped down the highway and past the huge concrete blocks that protected the camp, we picked up a lot of speed. Whenever you left the safe zone, you were vulnerable to attack, and the best way to prevent it was to use speed. We ploughed down the empty highway with our pedals planted firmly to the metal, and the wind blasting through the cars shook us violently. As we climbed the steep hill that led us into Basra city, the riflemen in the back stood up and readied their weapons. A few seconds later, we were once again playing dodgems with the heavy night-time traffic and having to weave crazily to avoid smashes. I glanced in my rear-view mirror and saw that the colonel was being flung about like a rag doll, so I deliberately accelerated some more. Judging by his startled expression, he had no idea how chaotic Basra became at nights, so I made sure he was given a rude awakening.

Basra by night was one of the last places on earth that you would want to get lost or have a crash, and I just hoped that our unwanted passengers realised it. If you were vulnerable by day, it was nothing compared to the threat you faced at night, and you didn't want to be out there unless you had a bloody good reason.

The insurgents were clever bastards and knew that whenever a Land-Rover streaked past them on its way to the palace, they usually wouldn't have to wait long for it to come back on the return leg – and with the limited number of routes open to us, they had a good chance of scoring a lucky strike. If you became separated from your vehicle at night-time, a rescue force would have a hell of a job finding you, and you could easily get lost. But the most worrying moments would come if you were stopped in heavy traffic and had to wait around like sitting ducks as Iraqi youths jeered and menacingly encircled the vehicles. The pavements would be as crowded as a Saturday night in Blackpool, and the same potential for violence hung in the air. There is something about the night that gives courage to cowards and makes fools do things they wouldn't normally contemplate. If a gang of idiots decided to rush the Land-Rovers or to take a few pot shots at us, it would more than likely be at night.

Mercifully, we made it through the city without incident and drove into the relative safety and welcome peace of Basra Palace. However, we didn't go to one of the busy offices at its centre, as we should have done if there had been a real meeting going on, but instead circled around until we found a cul-de-sac of luxurious mansions just inside the compound wall. We pulled up outside the biggest house, and a cherry-faced officer came bounding out to greet us. None of us said a word but just looked at one another and raised our eyebrows – it looked very much like another fucking party. The colonel jumped down and headed off into the house (almost forgetting to pick up his briefcase) with a cheery smile and wave of his hand. He told us to relax and chat amongst ourselves while we waited for him to conclude his business inside.

The front door of the house was wide open, and loud music was coming from the living room. There was a constant stream of soldiers going in and out, and many of them were carrying wine bottles. We didn't know what they were discussing, but from the constant laughter and loud chatter we guessed it wasn't business. We didn't mind that they were letting off steam and enjoying themselves – truth be told, we were a bit pissed off at not being invited in – but what we did resent was the manner in which we were being used. In the army, there is a time and a place for everything – and if they were having a party, which it seemed they were, this wasn't the time or place for it. Also, if that was the case, then the colonel and his friend, who were presumably mature and intelligent men, had taken the decision to drive miles across a hostile city when it wasn't necessary. If they wanted to have a get-together, they should have had one with their colleagues at Basra airport (where they lived and worked) and have contented themselves with that. Furthermore, there were numerous escorts and trips to the palace in the daytime, and if they were so desperate to see their friends, they could have jumped on one of those. As it was, we believed that they had placed both themselves and us in danger. To say we were spitting mad was an understatement.

A few hours later, they emerged from the house in a fit of giggles and said a flamboyant farewell to their hosts and fellow officers. It was past midnight by then, and we weren't best pleased at having had to wait for hours while a gang of toffs seemingly had a chatter about the good old days and 'oh, what a lovely war' it was. We faced a hot day of stressful driving to Nasiriyah, while they would be recovering in the comfort of an air-conditioned office. Thanks to what appeared to be their little jolly, we had lost out on a good night's rest. For infantry soldiers, sleep is the most precious commodity of all, because a lack of rest equals a lack of awareness, and a lack of awareness equals potential death.

We pulled out of the palace compound and drove towards the city centre. The lads in the back resumed their normal fire positions, standing up to face any threats. It was a beautifully cool night, and the cold air made the hairs on my arms stand to attention. Despite the late hour, the streets were as busy as ever, and the traffic didn't thin out until we reached the outskirts of the city. I was glad when it became a little less hectic, because it was a sign that we were almost home and an accident became less likely. Everyday in Basra, squaddies were crashing Land-Rovers, and although they were usually able to coax the damaged vehicles back to camp, it wasn't a chance I wanted to take.

I glanced across at Cpl. Norris and was relieved to see that he was scanning the streets and flicking his eyes towards the rooftops and dark alleyways that I as the driver had to ignore. My job was to keep the vehicle moving no matter what, and I had to strain my eyes into the distance to check for roadblocks, crashes or anything suspicious that might slow us down. I had a good team in the Land-Rover, and I felt about as confident with those blokes as I did with any others in the regiment.

Norris was a gruff Yorkshireman, who had a blunt manner and a quirky sense of humour. I knew that he rubbed some people up the wrong way, and they weren't sure what to make of him; they could never work out if he was taking the piss or being serious. But his skills as a soldier were second to none, and I had grown to appreciate his off-beat style and dry wit. Some people just seem to be good at their jobs and you feel you can trust them, and Norris was one of those types.

In the back of the Land-Rover were riflemen Quardis and Dennis. They were a couple of gruff cockneys and as close as two peas in a pod. The two of them had joined the army at the same time and had been childhood friends. They were utterly army barmy and forever getting into scrapes and causing mischief. On their own they were just about manageable and could be quite pleasant, but once they got together, they were like a pair of unruly twins, always egging each other on and trying to get one up on you. Wherever Quardis and Dennis went, drama invariably followed, and it was a full-time job trying to avoid becoming a victim of their constant practical jokes. But as was the case with Cpl. Norris, you felt you could rely on them to do the business when it mattered, so I tried to ignore their worst excesses and developed a thick skin.

As we drove along, I was grateful for the cold air snapping against my cheeks, keeping me fresh and alert. Normally, we'd have to contend with a cloud of irritating flies that had a habit of darting in your mouth when you spoke – and the hotter it became, the braver they got.

I stared at the red lights of the Land-Rover in front and tried to keep a reasonable distance between us. The roads were quieter than usual, so there was no need for us to be up each other's arses. The rows of shops and businesses that had bustled so noisily in the day were now boarded up, and in the unnerving silence, Basra took on a more threatening tone. I squinted into the grey shadows and blackened doorways as we roared past them, feeling like an unwelcome visitor in an alien land.

Aside from a few battered jeeps weaving about in front of us, we seemed to be the only living souls in Basra. There were no lights on in the houses, and the feral dogs that roamed the streets by day had seemingly disappeared. The sound of the tyres rolling on the tarmac gave us comfort, because it meant we were making progress and getting closer to home. We then turned onto the road that would lead us back to camp.

I glanced across at Norris, and he regarded me with a quizzical expression. It was quiet – perhaps a little too quiet, even for the outskirts of town at that ungodly hour. Neither of us said anything, but I knew we were both thinking the same thing, as an eerily silent hush enveloped the streets around us. Norris returned his gaze to the darkened side streets and alleyways, and I peered ever harder into the distance ahead. I felt my knuckles involuntarily tighten on the wheel and saw them whitening. It took an effort to loosen them. Something about the deathly silent street wasn't quite right, and I had to stifle a growing sense of unease bubbling in my gut. Even the noisy pair in the back had quietened down for a change, whereas normally they'd be firing insults and jokes at each other.

I calmed my inner turmoil by telling myself that perhaps the silence was a good thing: at least it meant we were all switched on, when we could all have been forgiven for feeling sleepy at that time of night. I glanced across at Norris again and saw the same look of concern on his face that had rattled me only moments before. This time he caught me looking at him and read my mind, and he told me to keep my eyes peeled on the road ahead. It was good advice, and I returned my gaze to the direction we were travelling, inwardly chastising myself for letting the deserted streets spook me. I told myself that the only reason we were feeling a bit jumpy was because we weren't used to travelling through Basra so late at night. It was actually a peaceful evening, and the silence and stillness, which we found so threatening, were probably normal for that area. When we got back in, we'd all have a laugh about it – and we'd no doubt deny that we'd ever been bothered!

Then, out of the corner of my eye, I saw Norris kick open his door and wondered what the hell he was doing. A split second later, he slammed his rifle into his shoulder and began firing into the darkness. His body was arched awkwardly in its seat, and his back was pressing against the dashboard. As he was putting the rounds down, he was screaming, 'Contact left, contact left!' Almost instantly, I heard the same cry from Quardis, and he started firing too. I was aware of a loud clump in the back of the vehicle, and Dennis was snarling at the colonel, 'Get fucking down, get down!' before his rifle joined the fray and started spewing out rounds at a ferocious rate.

Someone then shouted, 'Fucking drive, Mac, drive!' I didn't need to be told twice; I ground the pedal into the floor as hard as I could, and the vehicle lurched forward. The acceleration was painfully slow, so I dropped it into third and lifted off the gas for a second – before slamming my foot down and feeling the vehicle at last respond. We bolted forward like a rocket, and I tried to blank out the sound of the blazing rifles from my head. I felt utterly powerless, and I was frustrated that I couldn't pick up my rifle and return some fire myself. I was angry at the position I found myself in and cursed God, the heavens, the Green Jackets, the Iraqis, my colleagues and anything else I could think of. However, I realised that the only thing I could do to help was make sure that we didn't crash and that we got out of there as quickly as possible.

My eyes zeroed in on the road ahead, and I tried to blot out the chaos and noise erupting all around me. I shrunk my head into my shoulders, tucked my elbows tightly into my body and hunched down in my seat, trying to make myself into a smaller target. I stared intently at the road ahead and felt all my senses sharpening up and sparking into life. All of this happened involuntarily and within seconds, and I felt pleased that I was responding as I always hoped I would.

All of a sudden, I felt hot stings biting into my arms and legs, and I wondered for a second if I had been hit. It wasn't too painful, and it certainly wasn't about to distract me from driving, but it crossed my mind that this was how it might feel when you were about to die. Maybe it wasn't so bad after all — just a few stabs of pain and then a flash and almighty bang and you were dead and gone. I was jolted back to reality by the sight of two battered vehicles chugging along in front of me. They might have been part of the attack or nothing to do with it, but, either way, I could take no chances and had to get past them. I saw a narrow gap open up between them and dived through, skimming by with only inches to spare.

I gunned the accelerator and flew by the Land-Rover in front of me, only briefly pausing alongside to make eye contact and ensure they understood what was happening. With our colleagues behind us, we had to stop firing in case we hit them, but the good news was that we had miles of clear road in front of us, and I intended to hammer it all the way. We shot across junctions and roundabouts, and I drove the vehicle so hard I began to worry that it would fall apart. In the back of my mind, I was worried about a secondary ambush team waiting for us, and I wanted to make us an impossible target.

At that point, the only sounds were our own heavy breathing and Dennis periodically yelling at the colonel to stay down. I was driving so fast that I almost lost it a few times, and my tyres clipped the kerbs. At other times, I applied the brakes a touch too enthusiastically, and we'd slide into a screeching skid. When we were certain that nobody was following us and we were out of the danger zone, we pulled into a lay-by and did a quick 're-org' to check our bodies and equipment.

I still hadn't a clue what had gone on and was desperate to know what we had been running from. I asked Norris what the fuck it was all about, but he only punched the windscreen in a fit of rage and frustration. The glass splintered, and I could see that his face was bright red and livid with anger. The lads in the back were very pale and agitated – I could see their limbs trembling due to the adrenalin coursing through their veins – while the colonel just sat there mutely.

I ran my hands down my arms and legs, checking for wounds where I had felt the hot stings. All I found was a pile of empty shell cases that had been expelled from Norris's weapon, and I realised that it was these that had caused me to flinch. None of us were injured, and apart from the fact that there was steam coming out of Norris's ears, we all seemed to be OK. We composed ourselves and drove back to camp in relative silence, apart from Norris, who loudly berated the colonel and hurled insults at him for putting us in such a dangerous situation.

When we returned to camp, we parked the vehicles and trudged off to the canteen to get a coffee and start writing our contact reports. Nobody felt like talking much, as the experience had left us physically shattered, but procedure dictated that a contact report had to be produced immediately. As we sat down, the colonel and his friend approached us to thank us for looking after them and getting them back safely. He shook our hands and looked more than a little contrite and embarrassed about the whole incident, and, to his credit, he didn't make a fuss about the abuse that Norris and Dennis had heaped on him.

From a military viewpoint, the way that the colonel had been spoken to was outrageous and insulting, and, technically, we had shown him great disrespect. But from a common sense point of view, we had behaved appropriately. Thanks to him we had faced enemy contact in a place where we had no business being. He was very wise to let it go and not kick up a fuss, because he would have ended up the loser.

When the colonel left us, I asked Dennis how he had handled him during the contact, because from where I was sitting, it had sounded pretty rough. With a gleeful smile, he told me that he had flung the officer to the floor, planting his boot firmly on the colonel's chest. He had then used the inert body of his superior as a 'fire support stool' and had started to put some rounds down. Dennis said that it had felt wonderful chucking a colonel about and speaking to him like shit, and all the while knowing that he was just doing his job and couldn't be punished. His comments broke the tension, and we dissolved into fits of laughter.

Norris then told me why he had initiated the contact and exactly what had happened. As we had driven past a side street, he saw a cloaked figure emerge from the shadows and crouch down on the corner. The assailant had a rocket propelled grenade (RPG) launcher in his arms and brought it up to his shoulder as if he was about to fire it. Norris immediately sensed the danger and started firing at the man. As the rounds began flying towards him, the cloaked figure staggered over and promptly fell on his arse. He then scrambled wildly to get the RPG into a fire position but, in the end, thought better of it and dived for cover down the alley. Norris kept him pinned down with a barrage of shots, and by that time, the lads in the back had spotted him too. They didn't know if they had hit him, but their feeling was they hadn't, because hitting a moving target in the dark whilst travelling quickly is almost impossible.

Fortunately for us, the colonel had seen everything, so if we had any comebacks or complaints about our aggressive tactics, we were well covered. Similar incidents had happened in the past, and local clerics were shameless enough to portray dead or wounded terrorists as innocent passers-by. If we had hit the guy and he washed up dead somewhere, the last thing we wanted was the local religious militia pitching up on our doorstep and inciting riots.

We reported the confrontation to our commanders and handed in the contact report. The incident caused a stir amongst the intelligence and support staff based at HQ, and I noted that they got their official explanations in pretty quickly. It seemed that we weren't the only ones writing reports and covering our arses. Just in case we had forgotten, an officer from HQ gave us a reminder that the trip to Basra Palace had been for an important meeting to discuss 'security issues', and any scurrilous rumours about a party were to be ignored. We told the officer that we were 'on message', and he didn't have to worry about us making a fuss, but we would appreciate it if we were used 'more sparingly' in the future.

Nothing further was said, and we all knew where we stood. After our close shave, all unnecessary trips were cut, and if there were any last-minute jobs that meant travelling across the city late at night, a chopper was usually used. At the end of the day, it was all too easy to become a casualty in Iraq, and our incident had been a sharp reminder of that – we only hoped that certain elements of the operation would now start taking it more seriously.

For the last few weeks of the tour, we tried to keep our heads down and dodged as many tasks as we could. History has shown that towards the end of an operational tour soldiers have a natural tendency to start switching off and to become slack, leading to increased casualties. None of the lads in my section had any plans to follow that trend, and if it was a toss-up between a boring shift on stag or a long drive to Nasiriyah, the stag would win out for once. I didn't dare allow myself to start thinking about going home, and instead forced myself to become hyper-vigilant and ultra-defensive.

But try as we might, we couldn't get out of doing work

altogether, and the final week saw us being hit with an avalanche of escorts to every corner of Iraq. It was on these trips through small towns and hidden villages that I got my first real look at the Americans and how they operated. I am not in a position to criticise or judge their overall effectiveness, because I never worked alongside them as colleagues, but I did see enough to form my own opinion. It seemed to me that one of the problems the Yanks faced was that they were perceived as 'aggressive invaders', rather than 'helpful peacekeepers', in the eyes of the Iraqi population.

Whether this was by accident or design, I don't know, but they did come across as being a very dominant force. When an armoured Hum-Vee rolled through a small village, it was a menacing sight, and they were so wide they covered over half the road. On top would be a burly soldier manning a 50 calibre machine gun, or an M60 with rolls of 7.62 mm link ammunition pouring out of its side. The overall image they projected was one of brute force and supremacy, and I could see how the local population would be intimidated.

When the British Army had first deployed into Northern Ireland in the late 1960s, it had adopted a similarly aggressive style and tried to dominate the ground by sheer force and weight of numbers. It took 20 years for the powers that be to realise that those tactics don't work and that the only way you can force a reluctant people to bend to your will is to employ diplomacy, tact, consideration and coercion. I had an awful feeling that the Yanks were making the same mistakes that we had in NI and would be forced to endure a long and bloody guerrilla war against an invisible enemy. Quite simply put, it is impossible for a regular conventional army to defeat a determined and faceless terrorist force. History has shown this time and time again – how can you kill what you cannot see?

The difference in the overtly aggressive American approach and the subtler British one was perhaps best demonstrated by the names we used for our operations. We would use a simple tagline like 'Op-bumble bee' or 'Op-telic', but the Americans chose grandiose titles that sounded like they belonged to a Hollywood blockbuster. I began to lose count of the operations given names such as 'Iron Hammer', 'Steel Fist', 'Eagle Strike', 'Flames of Justice', etc. These titles sounded suitably spectacular and heroic, but they failed to live up to their billing, and the body counts kept on rising.

The vast majority of American servicemen I spoke to were very unhappy about the way in which they had gone to war, and they were desperate for it to end. I spoke to Rangers, Marines, guys from the 82nd Airborne and countless other units. The message I got back never changed: this is a fake and phoney war and none of us know why we are here – apart from to secure the oil, of course. Special anger and resentment was reserved for President Bush, and on more than one occasion I heard him described as a 'draft-dodging, lying son of a bitch!' I felt the same way about him, so we got along great and would put the world to rights over a burger and fries.

I don't want to give the wrong impression about the Americans here: it is not the soldiers I criticise but the war effort itself. My opinions on the US military are that they are first-class, talented soldiers, and I have a huge amount of respect for their capabilities and courage. Nonetheless, I do feel that they received bad advice and poor intelligence and, as a result, were employing the wrong tactics. The commanders seemed to lack the ability to distinguish between conventional and guerrilla warfare. They made the error of trying to fight terrorist insurgents, who wore smiles, jeans and trainers, in the same way that you would fight a column of enemy tanks and uniformed infantry. The two are completely different, and simply razing a city isn't always the best approach.

Killing one terrorist is a fine victory that deserves to be celebrated – but is it worth it if you have to kill a whole town of innocents just to get to him? Is it worth calling in an air strike to flatten a whole street and destroying countless lives just because you think a terrorist might be there? Is that a good way to win hearts and minds? Indeed, is it possible to win hearts and minds in a fundamentally flawed war where the local population sees you as aggressive invaders, who care more for oil than basic human rights? Time will tell, although I think the answers are already clear.

Before we left Iraq, I was sent to Kuwait to pick up a translator from the airport, and I had a glimpse of what Iraq could become if it is allowed to flourish and succeed. The luxury and wealth that is displayed in Kuwait is the most decadent I have ever seen. The place is awash with money. Once you cross the border from Iraq into Kuwait, the difference in living standards is both stark and disturbing. You cruise down a well-lit motorway before the capital city itself looms into view. Once you enter the city, you are struck by the rows of fabulous mansions that fill the landscape. And I am not talking about regular-sized English country piles here – I mean huge white palaces with Rolls-Royces and Ferraris in the driveway.

It is hard to comprehend that Iraq is just a few miles down the road. Its people labour under the most extreme poverty imaginable, yet it is a country with even more oil wealth than Kuwait and much of the Middle East put together.

There was more money in just one of those Kuwaiti mansions than in entire towns and villages in Iraq. No wonder Saddam wanted to get his grubby hands on Kuwait, and no wonder Bush and the oil companies want a piece of Iraq. Kuwait is a highly polished jewel that is run like an efficient business, but Iraq is like an even larger uncut diamond that with a bit of care and attention could out-dazzle its tiny neighbour.

I crossed the border back into Iraq feeling profoundly depressed at what I had seen. Despite its huge potential for wealth and success, I cannot see Iraq improving much any time soon. The country is a hundred years behind Kuwait and the western world in socio-economic terms. Kuwait can only be described as a bountiful paradise, and Iraq is a vast cauldron of despair in comparison. Thirty years of iron-fisted rule by Saddam has sapped the confidence of the country and bled its natural wealth dry. American bombs, which have reduced cities to rubble and destroyed the country's infrastructure, have only compounded the problems.

The hurdle that I think will scupper Iraq is religious extremism and inter-tribal warfare. Now that the terrorist insurgency, purportedly led by al-Qaeda, has taken hold, I cannot see it loosening its grip. From the point of view of the Islamic fundamentalists, there is now too much for them to lose. Iraq has become a recruiting sergeant and cause célèbre for Islamic extremists across the world. Whereas before they wouldn't dare show their faces in Iraq, they have now taken up permanent residence, and they can point to the map and say to eager recruits, 'Look at what America has done to Iraq. It invaded it for no reason and stole its oil. Join us and fight.'

America had enormous worldwide sympathy and support in the wake of the 11 September attacks. If it had chosen to act strategically and diplomatically, I think a new era of goodwill and mutual understanding could have been born. But when the Bush administration rushed into attacking Iraq for selfish reasons, the well of goodwill and sympathy evaporated, and it was replaced by a simmering resentment and distrust. By choosing to attack Iraq when it did, America may have opened up a 50-year conflict with Islam, not dissimilar to the struggle with Communism but potentially deadlier, because I believe religion to be a more powerful force than political ideology. I am convinced that in years to come historians will look back on the debacle of Iraq and regard it as grand folly on an epic scale.

While serving in Iraq, despite being an atheist, I took the time to read and study the bible. I came across a short passage that I feel holds particular relevance for President Bush and Prime Minister Blair, who both claim to be committed Christians:

> For what shall it profit a man,
> if he shall gain the whole world,
> and lose his own soul?
>
> Mark 8:36

9

BANDIT COUNTRY

None of us could quite comprehend that our Iraq tour was ending. It was a moment that we had fantasised about for months, and now that it had finally arrived, we could scarcely believe it. I cast my mind back to the endless nights on stag duty, when I would turn my head to the sky and longingly gaze at the aircraft heading for home. I worried that my turn would never come or that when it did, it would be in a flag-draped box. But here I was – here we all were – heading home at last.

The steel-grey RAF VC10 took off under the cover of darkness, and we weren't allowed to turn on the lights or pull back the curtains until it had reached a certain height. On previous flights, terrorists had attempted to rip out the guts of the aircraft with RPG strikes. They hadn't got lucky yet, and the flight crew told us that they had no intentions of becoming the first victims. None of us wanted to tempt fate or start celebrating too soon, so until the pilot told us we were safe, we sat in mute silence.

At last came the words that we had been waiting to hear for three unbearably tense months: 'Gentlemen, we have now left Iraqi airspace.' A loud cheer went up inside the plane, and broad grins broke out everywhere. Some soldiers shook hands and exchanged high-fives with their friends, while others simply closed their eyes and sighed. It was over. We were going home – but more importantly, we were going home with no casualties. Every single man who had started the tour would make it back in one piece, and that was the biggest relief of all. It also meant that we could celebrate with a clear conscience and look back on our time in the Middle East with nothing but pride and satisfaction. Several blokes were carrying minor injuries, and several patrols had come under enemy attacks, but thanks to a combination of hard work, skilful soldiering and sheer good luck, the most we would be taking home were scratches.

I don't know why it is, but whenever I take a flight anywhere, the male stewards seem to be incredibly camp. It seemed that the RAF was no different, and whenever the steward walked past us, he would be subjected to a chorus of catcalls and whistles. To his credit, he took it well and didn't complain, but I could see that he was a bit pissed off, so I decided to turn it to my advantage. I had enjoyed my time in Iraq, and I wanted to end it on a memorably high note.

The next time the steward passed me, I stopped him and asked him in my most polite voice if he could do me a favour. I could see that he was relieved that somebody was addressing him as an equal and showing him a modicum of respect. He asked me how he could help me, and I explained to him that I had always had an interest in aviation and would love to visit the cockpit. The steward smiled and nodded enthusiastically, before disappearing into the captain's cabin.

A few minutes later, he returned and told me he could do better than that: the captain would be happy for me to spend the remainder of the flight in the cockpit! I couldn't believe my luck, and as I made my way to the front of the plane, several envious colleagues asked me how I had swung that one. The steward seated me in the spare seat and gave me some headphones to listen in on. The captain was an American on secondment from the US Air Force, and he seemed flattered that I had made my request. He gave me a quick lesson on how everything worked, and we chatted about our careers.

When the plane flew into English airspace, the pilot pointed out various cities to me, and they glittered in the blackness like lights on a Christmas tree. He then showed me the runway that we would be landing on at Liverpool John Lennon Airport, and I was amazed that you could see it from miles away. As we began to descend, the plane was met with rows of red and green lights, and the sharp details and sparkling brightness of the ground rushing towards us was both comforting and reassuring. The dusty landing strip at Basra had been dry and lifeless, but the multi-coloured display at John Lennon Airport suggested warmth, comfort and security. I was home.

I shook hands with the captain and thanked him for an unforgettable experience. I could not have thought of a better way to end the tour, and it made it all the more special. As I stepped off the plane I felt like kissing the ground, and I sucked on the air like a dying man. The air tasted crisp and clean and pure. There were no flies, there was no heat and there were no nauseating smells – just pure fresh air. It was 3 a.m., there wasn't a cloud in the sky and I felt like I had died and gone to heaven.

The coach journey back to camp was a blissful experience, and it was a joy to be able to just sit back and watch the world go by, although it did feel strange. Whenever we had ventured out onto the roads in Iraq, we had lived in constant fear of sniper attacks, ambushes and roadside bombs. It felt good not to give a shit anymore; from now on, all we'd have to worry about were old ladies crossing the road or stroppy traffic wardens giving us a ticket.

As the coach crept back to camp at what seemed an absurdly slow pace, I had to fight the urge to tell the driver to step on the gas, and whenever we hit a traffic light, I felt like ordering him to blast through. I wasn't the only one having such feelings, and I realised that readjusting to the slower pace of normal life would take some time.

We were given five weeks of post-operational leave, and the only time I had to come back to camp was to do a Christmas Day guard. I didn't mind having to work on Christmas Day, because no matter how shit it was, at least it wasn't Iraq. I did a lot of thinking on leave about my experiences in Iraq and the unfairness of life in general. It felt like a luxurious indulgence just to be able to walk the streets and not have to worry about being shot or blown up, and then to be able to drive home at 30 mph and not have to worry about being forced off the road.

Whenever I visited the city centre to do some shopping, I would look at the fat, pasty faces of the people around me and wonder if they realised how incredibly lucky they were. I registered the bulge in my own wallet and realised that the wad of notes inside it made me a wealthy man by Iraqi standards. In fact, in relative terms, both the soft-bodied shoppers and I were multi-millionaires – we just didn't realise it.

Gazing in the well-stocked windows of a shopping mall, I allowed my mind to drift back to the chaos and poverty of post-war Iraq. The shattered country was three hours ahead of Britain, and I looked at my watch and tried to picture the scene at Basra airport. A couple of squaddies would be standing at the back gate, bitching and moaning about how shit it all was, and trying and failing to keep track of all the mad Choggies who were running around like hyperactive children. If they were switched on, they might notice a middle-aged man staring at them with intense eyes and how the young tearaways were careful not to disturb him as he went about his menial work. He would be slowly and methodically sweeping the back gate or stacking some heavy boxes, but most of all he would be dreaming of a better life than the one he currently had. Perhaps he would be dreaming of a life like mine. I hoped my friend the teacher would find his place in the new Iraq.

* * *

Whenever an operational tour is completed or another one is about to begin, there is always a big shuffle in the platoons and companies. I said goodbye to my friends in F Company and moved over to G Company, where I would remain for my last year of service. I arrived at G Company with a somewhat tainted reputation, thanks to my fighting with Haxiton and my barely concealed criticisms of my old commanders. My new sergeant-major made it crystal clear that if I had any such grumbles about his decisions, I would wind up with my teeth on the floor and my bollocks somewhere in my chest cavity. I received his message loud and clear – work hard, don't complain, keep your gob shut and we will get along fine. It sounded fair enough to me.

My spirits picked up when I met my new company commander, and I was given a much warmer welcome. Maj. Weatherall had been my brother's OC in Kosovo, and when Damian had died, we had shared several long telephone conversations. By sheer chance, he had just arrived at 1RGJ as we were coming back off Christmas leave, and he had no idea that I had joined the army. The last time we had spoken was when we were arranging Damian's funeral, and when I stood before him as a fellow Green Jacket, I could see that he was a little taken aback. He enquired about my family, whom he had also grown close to, and he wished me well for my time in G Company. Bumping into Maj. Weatherall at such an opportune time seemed like a stroke of good fortune, but I knew that I wouldn't receive any favours, and I would still have to perform well if I wanted to be accepted by my new colleagues.

We began preparing in earnest for our upcoming Northern Ireland tour. Our training package was basically the same one that we had used to prepare for Iraq, but it was a condensed version. I am aware that this might sound like we were cutting corners, but believe me when I say we weren't. For the whole of the previous year we had been training for Spearhead, and when we were crashed out to Iraq, we had been doing the job for real. Our levels of military preparedness and physical fitness were still sky high, but, at the same time, we were feeling tired and jaded. The Christmas leave had allowed us to recharge our batteries, and we were ready to deploy again. Our minds and bodies just needed a quick tune-up, as opposed to being put through the mill. If we had beasted ourselves again and gone berserk with the riot training, it would probably have done us more harm than good. As the saying goes, 'Sometimes, less is more.'

We had known that we would be going to Northern Ireland for well over a year and had had plenty of time to get used to the idea. We were still nervous and apprehensive about it (as you are wherever you go), but there wasn't the same 'wow' factor that had come with the Iraq deployment, which had been a true bolt out of the blue. When I had been sent to Iraq, a shiver of raw, naked fear had run through me, and that was something that the threat of Northern Ireland couldn't match.

From a professional soldier's perspective I felt confident, because in Northern Ireland we had managed to devise a set of very effective tactics that had been proven to work – whereas in Iraq we were learning from our mistakes as we went along. There was also an added factor of experience, as most of our NCOs already had at least two or three successful NI tours under their belts.

However, one thing I couldn't ignore were my own ambiguous feelings about the presence of British troops on Irish soil. In my younger days, my sympathies had lain with the loyalist cause, and like most Englishmen, I had never felt the need to revise my opinions. All of that changed when my brother entered the army in 1994, and I began my love affair with books and education. As a Royal Green Jacket, I knew that there was every chance my brother would have to serve in Northern Ireland, and at an especially dangerous time because the fledgling peace process was yet to take hold. For his sake as much as mine, I decided to read up on the history of the conflict and to try and get an understanding of it.

In the past, I had always considered myself a stern patriot when it came to matters of state and security, but I was disturbed when my new-found education began to threaten those beliefs. I felt torn inside, as if acknowledging that I might have been wrong about Northern Ireland was an admission of treason. As the brother of a serving soldier, I had felt honour bound to support him wherever he went, but I was now morally compelled to question that blind support. The conclusion that I reached, after studying the conflict from both points of view and struggling to remain impartial, was that Britain had no right to claim Northern Ireland as its own.

As for the IRA and its offshoots, I regard them as murdering fanatics. I respect and support their cause, but I detest and deplore their methods. No matter what political beliefs you have, there is no possible justification for blowing up shopping malls and killing children. It requires no courage or military skill to murder soft targets with bombs and ambushes, and I am neither impressed nor moved by such shows of force. That was my opinion in 1994 when I first took a serious look at the problem, and it remained my opinion in 2004 when I was about to deploy there myself.

Something I will always be grateful for is that my brother never had to face the republican threat and that he escaped duty in Northern Ireland. Damian's service took him to the Balkans three times, and I feel proud that he served a far more worthy and noble cause.

Although it turned out that my worries about Damian serving in Northern Ireland were groundless, the knowledge I had picked up wouldn't be wasted, because now a full decade later, it was finally my turn to serve in Northern Ireland. In a way, it felt curiously apt that I was serving in that conflict, because if I hadn't, I would have felt cheated out of an essential experience as a soldier. As a child of the '70s, I had grown up in a time when the troubles dominated the nightly news, and I had watched my soldier friends being called there one by one.

It was a curiously intense, very British sort of a conflict, and for soldiers of my age, serving there had been a rite of passage. I was in a strange position, because although I marched alongside teenage riflemen and was commanded by 20-something NCOs, I was, in fact, the same age as many of the sergeant-majors who had seen NI at its very worst.

So, despite my republican ideals, and despite my beliefs that Northern Ireland was a fundamentally flawed and impossible-to-win conflict, I felt relieved to be going out there and vowed to do the best job that I could. That said, I had no romantic illusions about the place: the IRA wouldn't give a fuck that I was a republican at heart and would still view me as a legitimate target, and as a British soldier patrolling Irish streets, I wasn't exactly in a position to complain! At the end of the day, I had volunteered to join the army, and I knew that NI was a place I would most likely serve in, so I would just have to put my personal feelings aside and get on with it.

The soldier's unattainable dream is to be able to pick and choose the wars he fights in, but, unfortunately, real life isn't like that. When you join the army, you are taking a chance and making a wild gamble as to where you might end up serving. If you are lucky, you might end up doing something in which you truly believe, and I know my brother felt that way about his time in Bosnia and Kosovo. He felt that he was protecting minorities from the horrors of ethnic cleansing – it was simple, it had clarity in its purpose and it was noble. If he died doing it, he would have at least died for a good cause, and to a soldier in the firing line that means everything.

But, unfortunately, you are sometimes asked to participate in a conflict that you bitterly oppose, and that's where the gamble comes into it. For many British soldiers, Northern Ireland has long represented a stumbling block and a cause of resentment. At the height of the Troubles it symbolised a soldier's worst nightmare – potential death without purpose or meaning. From my time in Iraq I knew that the Americans were having to wrestle with a similar crisis of conscience. But it is at these times that your professionalism and common sense have to kick in, otherwise you wouldn't be able to function.

The fact that I believed in the cause of Irish republicanism was irrelevant: I was a Royal Green Jacket, and I knew where my loyalties lay. For the duration of the tour, I would do all I could to detect and disrupt any mischief that the republicans cared to get up to – and I would do it with a clear conscience.

Up until the mid '90s, Northern Ireland had been one of the most dangerous places in the world for a soldier to serve, and, over the years, the British Army had lost hundreds of good men there. Although the tour still carried with it an inherent danger, I wasn't kidding myself that it was anything like the threat level of the old days. Since the 1994 ceasefire and peace process of the late '90s, it had become a much less dangerous place, and direct attacks upon British soldiers had virtually died out. But the threat from the IRA and its various offshoots had never really disappeared, and I would have to patrol under the assumption that an attack could come at any time.

The IRA still had its active service units, and it still kept a close eye on British patrols and movements on the ground – the only difference was that for the time being they were choosing not to strike. I hoped that this was the way it would stay, but I wasn't foolish enough to presume it.

The main threats that we as a company would face on our tour were spontaneous riots and pre-planned demonstrations that were designed to catch us out. While it was true that the threat of enemy snipers and IRA booby traps had temporarily receded, it was equally true that you could still be very easily maimed or killed by a baying crowd of rioters or a carefully planned violent ambush of boots, bats and fists. These grim possibilities would be a particular threat to us because of the area in which we were being deployed: South Armagh – otherwise known as 'Bandit Country'.

South Armagh is a semi-rural area situated right on the border of the Republic of Ireland and the disputed North. More soldiers have been killed in South Armagh than in any other area of Northern Ireland, and it is considered to be the IRA's heartland. The small towns and villages that make up the area are almost 100 per cent republican, and the British Army are about as popular and welcome as a colony of lepers.

Even in today's supposedly enlightened times, South Armagh represents a dangerous and worrying deployment for a British soldier, but I felt lucky to be going there under the banner of a shaky IRA ceasefire, because back in the bad old days it must have been a nightmare scenario. Even though I knew our chances of running into trouble were greatly reduced, I still felt my stomach performing somersaults, just as it had done before I left for Iraq. Whichever way you dressed it up, ceasefire or no ceasefire, Northern Ireland was a fucking serious place.

We flew into Aldergrove Airport and were met by a large coach. Because we were very obviously squaddies about to begin a tour, we couldn't go through the normal departure lounge. Instead, we were dropped off on the edge of a field and told to wait for our transport to arrive. In the distant sky, I saw the familiar silhouette of a giant Chinook helicopter, and as it got closer, the distinctive 'thwack, thwack' sound of its rotors became deafening. A platoon of soldiers spilled out of the back and passed us by with jeers and catcalls. We gave them a bit of abuse back, but, to be honest, our hearts weren't really in it; their tour was ending and ours was just beginning, and the joke was very much on us.

We scrambled up the ramp into the chopper, and it felt just like old times as the hot downdraught seared our throats. Despite the Chinook's size, it was a hell of a squeeze inside, and bagged up GPMGs and L96 sniper rifles littered the floor. It was a comfort to know that the IRA could never match the quality of the kit we carried, but I reflected that it would be even more comforting if we didn't have to bring it.

As the chopper whizzed across the sky, I felt the same sensations of doom and gloom clouding my horizons as I had done in Iraq. For some reason, whenever I found myself inside a helicopter, a deep sense of unease and foreboding settled into my bones. Perhaps it was paranoia or just an overactive imagination, but the sound of spinning blades and heavy machinery clattering away hit me like a punch in the guts. All of a sudden, my job felt very real and painfully raw – reality bites!

We made a brief stop-off at Bessbrook Mill military base (the busiest heliport in Europe), where we had to transfer to a Puma helicopter and pick up even more hardware. The peace process was supposed to be in full swing, but judging by the amount of kit we carried, you would never have known it. The army wisely chose to ignore the fragile ceasefire, and we soldiered on under the belief that a devastating attack could be launched on us at any time. It was a clever move, because if the current stalemate ever broke down, the first we would know about it would be when we came under attack. And if that ever happened, which we hoped and prayed that it wouldn't, then we would be as well prepared as ever. To put it bluntly, nothing had changed for the soldiers on the ground.

Our final destination was the small town of Crossmaglen (XMG in army speak), where we would spend the remainder of our tour. As the cramped Puma circled the camp, the sight of a fortified barracks in the middle of a market town struck me as an incongruous and bizarre image. After a short pause, the chopper swooped down at breakneck speed, and we were on the ground within seconds. We practically spilled out of its sides, falling over ourselves as we struggled with the extra weapons and bulging bergens. As the last man left the chopper, the pilot was already beginning his ascent; within seconds, he had disappeared from view.

Where the chopper had landed there was now a large empty square, with tall watchtowers at each corner overlooking the town from all angles. In between the towers there were huge walls of corrugated iron that made an unsurpassable fence line and stretched 40 ft into the sky. Beneath the steel walls was about 10 ft of reinforced concrete, and on one strip of wall some bright spark had written in huge letters, 'Don't worry be happy, welcome to XMG'.

The remaining walls were painted with huge murals and badges dedicated to the various units that had passed through over the years. Apparently, it was a sacred tradition, and before we left, we would also be expected to produce a 6-ft high dedication to the Royal Green Jackets.

We were ushered inside the base itself and shown to our rooms. The accommodation was very basic and claustrophobic – everything had been designed to withstand a powerful mortar strike. The walls were made of thick reinforced concrete, and the doors were similar to those you would find on a submarine, made of thick, heavy steel. The complex itself was about the size of an average sports hall and was encased in a heavy coating of mortar-proof concrete. Inside it was a maze of narrow corridors that led off into either dorms or offices, with no sense of order or logic. It had a '70s feel to it, and the only considerations were for function and safety – the idea of being comfortable didn't even register on the scale.

Because of its heavy construction, dampness and oppressive heat were a real problem at different times of the year. To combat this, air conditioning had been installed, which would have been great if it ever worked. We were crammed into our rooms like sardines in a can, and bunk beds were stacked three high. Walking into a room full of a dozen sleeping squaddies is not a pleasant experience as the bad air can't escape and just sort of sits there. If you got up in the middle of the night to go to the toilet, you would sometimes struggle to get back to sleep, because breathing in the stale air was like sucking on CS gas. It was as cramped and basic as it was possible to be, and it was to be our home for the next few months.

The two areas of consolation in XMG were the gym and the NAAFI (in this instance, a small tuck shop and lounge). The gym was like a medieval dungeon that looked like it belonged in a Rocky film. Like everything else in XMG, the equipment was old, rusty and very basic – but it did have a magical atmosphere that inspired you to push yourself. It was a spit-and-sawdust type of place, and the second I laid eyes on it, I knew it would become like a second home to me. The place radiated energy, and after a long night on stag or a particularly stressful patrol, it represented a sanctuary where I could sweat out my demons and rage against the world. By the end of the tour, previously skinny squaddies would be parading around with muscles bulging from their T-shirts, and it was always a give-away that they had been based at XMG.

The NAAFI was a sanctuary of a different kind. It was a haven for those times when you were too fucked to move, or too tired to even care. You would just plonk yourself down in front of the TV and watch MTV or some cheap satellite shows – anything to take your mind off the reality you inhabited.

I was introduced to my new teammates and placed in what is referred to as a 'multiple'. It was explained to us that our radio call sign for when we went out on the ground would be 'Three Zero Bravo'. Also, we would be sharing our tasks and duties with the other multiples on a rotational basis, and it was very much a case of mucking in and making the most of it. We had been given plenty of warning to expect a tough time of things, and that is exactly what we got. Our tour was going to be split into three distinct phases, and we would be working like dogs until the very last day.

The first phase was a two-month period of guard (stagging on again!) and general duties at XMG security base. Before we even started, we knew that this phase would be a killer because 'general duties' covered a multitude of sins. As well as stagging on like bitches for 24 hours a day, we would be expected to assist with patrols, unload choppers, wash pots and pans (dixies), and any other shit they cared to find for us. It wouldn't be unusual to find yourself with a spanner in hand trying to fix a leaking sink or banging nails into shelves that had collapsed.

In XMG, being just a soldier wasn't enough; you had to be a handyman and toilet scrubber as well, because you couldn't just call out a plumber when something went wrong. If something broke and we couldn't fix it, we'd have to wait weeks for a security-cleared tradesman to arrive.

Phase two would be a two-month residency in one of the observation outposts that scattered the hilltops of South Armagh. We were anticipating an easy time of it there as you were very much left alone to do your own thing. Our only task was to log and record all the daily movements of known republican activists and to report any suspicious activity. In a twelve-man team we would have six on duty for the day shift, and the other six would cover nights. It would be a pain in the arse and there would be lots of stagging on (no surprises there then!), but, at the same time, it would be a welcome break from the sergeant-major and his ever-watchful eyes.

The final phase of the operation, and potentially the most dangerous, would be when we became the primary patrols multiple for two months. We would be spending a lot of time out on the ground, doing VCPs, assisting the police on arrest jobs and generally putting ourselves about a bit. This would be the most exciting part of the tour – we'd be flying about in Lynx helicopters confronting demonstrators – but it was a long way off yet. By the time we got there, we would be suffering from cabin fever from having spent too much time living in one another's pockets, and our minds would be numbed from the endless hours of twilight stag. The best way to overcome this would be to take the tour one day at a time and reduce it in your mind to bite-sized chunks.

My new teammates were a motley bunch of characters, but I felt that we would gel well. Before I had arrived in Northern Ireland, I had lain awake at night worrying about getting stuck in a shit section. I had struck it lucky in Iraq when I ended up in 16 Platoon, and I wanted to keep the good vibes going. Having to live and work alongside characters that you don't necessarily like or respect can be a dispiriting ordeal for a soldier.

On an operational tour you have an enormous amount of stress and tension, and precious little privacy or free time. If you're not getting along with somebody or feel that your feelings are being trampled on, it can result in a hostile and emotional atmosphere. Petty squabbles can blow up into heated arguments, and if the boil isn't lanced, a full-blown fistfight often erupts. It isn't nice, it isn't pretty and, unfortunately, it happens a lot more than you might think.

But as I scrutinised my new colleagues, I had no such worries: there wasn't a single bad egg or weak link amongst them. I breathed a sigh of relief as I realised my luck had held out again. Although most of G Company were a decent bunch, there was the usual smattering of nasty bastards and moaners that you find in any group of random soldiers. The self-styled 'bad boys' were never a problem for me, and I tried to get along with them, but I knew all that could change if they were put in my section – so I was extremely thankful when they weren't.

Three Zero Bravo had a nice blend of youth, experience, professionalism, fitness and, most importantly of all, humour. I was particularly pleased with the commanders in charge of us, because we had managed to get blokes with high professional standards but an aversion to pointless army bullshit. Amongst the notables in the team were:

- Capt. Stringer – a laid back 'Rupert' with a squaddie's sense of humour and a relaxed but serious approach. He had passed the Commando Course and had spent time in Afghanistan with the Royal Marines on attachment.

- Cpl. Eprry – a highly qualified reconnaissance soldier who was completely 'army barmy', but in a good way. An utter fitness fanatic and a very professional soldier, he was a man whom you felt was definitely going places and was without doubt a future RSM.

- Lance Corporal (L/Cpl.) Preston – a proud Liverpudlian who made a big effort to be scrupulously fair and reasonable to everyone. Solid and reliable, he was just the sort you want on an operational tour.

- Rifleman Payne – a 20-year-old Brummie who had a twin brother serving in 2RGJ. He was a likeable lad who took a real pride in his work and was very keen to progress. Tall and slim, he was popular with the lads because he took his job seriously but liked a piss up as well. He enjoyed getting stuck in and having a go, and because of that he was respected amongst his peers. I saw him as a young guy with a lot of potential, and I knew that if the shit hit the fan, he could do the business.

- Rifleman Kinivuwai – an old Fijian friend from back in basic training. He was very dependable, as strong as a bull, a real team player and a good man to have alongside you in a ruck. His tall and intimidating appearance was a very handy attribute for patrolling in Crossmaglen, as were his exceptional military skills.

- Rifleman Steele – a 22-year-old Jamaican with American parents and an obsession with the rapper Tupac, whom Steele was convinced was still alive. We were always making jokes about 'spliffing it' and 'smoking the weed' and constantly took the piss out of each other. Steele's humour and goodwill provided us with morale for the tour – a priceless asset.

- Rifleman Roberts – a 21-year-old Grenadian with an infectious laugh and a bright outlook on life. 'Robbo' had joined the army to escape from a tough upbringing and a 'guns and gangs' culture that had threatened to draw him in. He was relieved to be away from it all and had no intentions of going back, but he was still a little nostalgic for the crazy days of his youth, and he would often regale us with hilarious stories.

- Rifleman Stevenson – a soldier on his last tour and looking forward to getting out. Highly professional and very reliable – but like me a bit jaded and tired of it all. He had an interesting life story: his father had served with the army in Borneo and had adopted two little girls he found abandoned in the jungle. Stevenson was a good man to have around if things got serious.

- Rifleman Edwards – a very quiet and serious soldier who had a reputation for being honest and reliable. Edwards was one of those characters that you instinctively felt you could trust and someone who garnered a lot of respect. Physically fit and mature of mind, he was what I considered to be the ideal rifleman. He had worked as a security guard before joining up, and he felt he had found his calling in the army. Like Eprry, he was someone you felt was going places. Edwards' main ambition was to be a sniper, and his locker was stacked full of books on the subject.

Making up the rest of the team were L/Cpl. Broom, a former army boxing champion, Rifleman Mills, a likeable five-year veteran who was always game for a laugh but also very good at his job, and Rifleman Shaw, who had joined us straight from training depot and came from a family of soldiers.

Once we had settled in and been split down into our new multiples, we were given an extensive intelligence briefing on Crossmaglen town and the possible threats that we might face. We would only receive this big chat once, and anything new that developed would be passed on to us in short daily operational briefings (DOB). It was a chance for us to get an understanding of the causes of the conflict and to ask any questions we felt were relevant. For many of the younger lads, and especially the Commonwealth recruits, this would be their first introduction to the potential terror of the IRA.

As things stood at that time, the IRA had split down into three constantly squabbling factions, and their opinions were sharply divided on how to advance the cause of Irish republicanism. The most powerful and respected faction was the original mainstream IRA to which Gerry Adams and Martin McGuinness were linked, referred to as the Provisional IRA (Provos). It was the Provos that had terrorised the British Army in the '70s and '80s, and it was the Provos that controlled the area of South Armagh with an iron fist. For the time being, they were on an official ceasefire, but we knew from our intelligence sources that they were still hoarding weapons and training for future operations. The current political climate boxed them in very tightly, but as with all things, circumstances could quickly change.

The next faction that we had to worry about was the breakaway dissident republican movement that called itself the Real IRA. They had managed to attract quite a few major players from the Provisional IRA cause, but their effectiveness had been greatly damaged by the Omagh bomb atrocity in 1998. The blast had been intended to only damage property and disrupt the security forces, but thanks to a bodged coded warning, 29 innocent people were killed. After that monumental failure, they became about as popular as the Royal Ulster Constabulary (RUC), even amongst their own hard-core supporters. Apparently, their money-raising efforts had been terminally crippled, and they had been reduced to using their own vehicles for attempted operations and 'dicking' jobs (spying on security bases).

The final group that we would have to keep a wary eye out for was the Continuity IRA. This group was formed from defectors of both the Provisional and Real IRA. They were hard-core republicans who were implacably opposed to the peace process on ideological grounds, and they were itching to 'off a few squaddies'. Lack of money and fear of reprisals from the Provos kept them in line, and mainstream republicans heavily marginalised them.

Our approach to the smaller organisations was to keep a watchful eye on them and maintain as safe a distance as possible. None of their players would dare launch an attack on us whilst we were in Crossmaglen, because if they fucked up the peace process without prior approval, they themselves would become Provisional targets. Crossmaglen was a 100 per cent Provo-controlled heartland, and it would be a brave and foolish man who decided to do his own thing on someone else's turf.

It was ironic that we were relatively safe in South Armagh precisely because it was the Provisional IRA's home base. Of course, if peace talks broke down, we would be in the worst place of all, but as it stood, the Provos would be our greatest protector.

We were given a massive catalogue to study that contained hundreds of pictures of known Provisional IRA associates and players. It was astoundingly well detailed, and it had names and addresses, occupations (both real and false ones), and dates of birth for almost all of the faces. We were even told what make and model of cars they drove, and what their daily movements were. Basically, if you were anyone of importance in Crossmaglen, you couldn't take a shit without us knowing about it.

The catalogue was the product of years of intensive intelligence work, and we were told that the army had one for practically every street in Northern Ireland. I had always assumed that it was the IRA that had forced the British government to the negotiating table, but thumbing through the catalogue made me wonder if it wasn't the other way around.

I asked the Intel officer how they had managed to assemble such a document and what the current state of the IRA was. His refreshingly honest answers surprised me: the IRA was absolutely riddled with paid informers and double agents, many of whom had no more interest in Irish unity than a Japanese tourist did. The new generations of young IRA volunteers were far more interested in making money from illicit and criminal enterprises than they were in achieving a united Ireland. If you asked many of the up-and-coming young 'stars' of the IRA to choose between prospering from crime or achieving a republic, they would take the money any day of the week.

It was true that there were still some 'true believers' within their ranks who were passionately committed to the cause, but, unfortunately for them, the lure of hard currency was eroding their influence. In the new and modern IRA cash was king, and republicanism came a poor second.

However, we were cautioned against relaxing and taking it for granted that we were safe from attack. While it was true that most of the Provisional IRA membership had chosen to embrace the business possibilities of a 'peaceful' era, it was equally true that there were plenty of young guns looking to make a name for themselves and grab their own piece of republican history.

A lot of the older generation who were now preoccupied with making money and smuggling diesel had been cold-blooded killers in their youth, and they had made their mark and earned their stripes as committed murderers. But most of the younger members had missed out on that phase of violence, and while they were happy to make money from old-fashioned crime and drug dealing, they also wanted the distinction of taking out a British soldier. Some of them had lost family members to skirmishes with soldiers or violent feuds with fellow republicans, or they had been victims of loyalist attacks themselves. For these IRA members, a British squaddie would always remain a tempting target and killing one would be a feather in their cap.

Before I joined the army I viewed the IRA as a terrifyingly distant and invisible force. The fact that you could walk past a member in the street and not realise it had both comforted and frightened me. They weren't a group of people that I wanted to spend time with or come into daily contact with – I was very happy with them being miles across the sea in a foreign land. Now that I was being forced to acquire an intimate knowledge of them and put names to their faces, I felt uncomfortable and disturbed. It felt like I was getting to know them and becoming a part of their lives and problems; it was a truly awful feeling. As a British soldier, I was now officially 'enemy number one'.

My personal feelings about the conflict made me feel like a traitor to the British point of view and a hypocrite and fraud to the Irish one. But I wasn't the only soldier who felt that way: from the constant sarcasm and black humour of my colleagues, I got the feeling that I wasn't alone in my opinions. I think that there are a lot of closet republicans in the British Army, especially amongst the senior ranks and old hands. Anyone with half a brain can see that we are trapped in an unsustainable conflict that can't be won – it is painfully and embarrassingly obvious to us all.

In XMG security base, there is a mural on the wall that lists all of the soldiers killed in Crossmaglen town. There are sixty-three names, and the first one belongs to Cpl. Ian Armstrong of the King's Royal Hussars, who was killed on 29 August 1971, just two days before I was born. I have no doubt that he was a fine young man and a superb soldier in the prime of his life and that his death was a shattering loss. There were lots of Green Jackets up on that board, too, and I tried to imagine the pain if I saw one of my colleague's names up there. What a pointless and tragic waste it would be.

The only way that the base could be replenished and restocked was via army helicopters. Every couple of hours, a Puma helicopter would swoop down and drop off boxfuls of food or pick up huge crates of waste and rubbish. It wasn't safe for us to transport supplies on the roads, so we were forced to take to the air. The cost of it all must have run into the millions, and it was another reminder of the unsustainability of the British presence.

My first impression of Crossmaglen town was that it was a peaceful and quaint sort of place to live. The only reminder that it wasn't, other than the hostile glares of the locals, was the huge security base that sprouted up awkwardly in its centre. I could well understand the local's hatred of the place because it was an ugly monstrosity that dominated the skyline and looked down into their backyards. The constant noise of choppers and military clatter must have driven them mad as well. Officially, the place was supposed to be a police station, but this was a bit of a joke when you considered that it resembled Fort Knox and only housed a couple of coppers at any one time.

Our official role was to patrol the border, prevent smuggling and assist the police in going about their daily business. As ludicrous as it may seem in the twenty-first century, a lone policeman still cannot venture out onto republican streets by himself because he will be torn to pieces. Whenever a policeman wants to so much as take a stroll through Crossmaglen Square, he needs a full multiple of soldiers to protect him. It is actually a very sad state of affairs, because while this ridiculous stand-off exists, the soldiers cannot be pulled out.

By far the worst part of being based at XMG was the relentless stag duty. Unlike when we had been in Iraq, we were in relatively secure positions, but we had to remain just as alert and switched on, and the tedium of the routine was mind blowing. It is difficult to describe to a civilian just how dispiriting stag duty is, but the sad fact is that it represents a big part of your life as an infantryman. If the army recruiters came clean about just how much stag a soldier has to do, then they wouldn't be able to fill their quotas. If you want to get an idea of just how boring and soul destroying it can be, I recommend you get out of bed at 2 a.m. and go and stand in a car park for six hours. Don't talk, don't listen to music, just stand there and squint into the darkness for six hours. Welcome to the glamorous world of the infantry stag bitch!

At XMG we did a straight eight-hour shift, spread equally across four watchtowers. To reach the guard post you had to climb up a steep flight of stairs and metal ladders, at the top of which sat a small box-like structure. In the lookout point, you had just about enough room to stretch your legs and take a couple of paces, and it was here that you watched the surrounding area from four bullet-proof windows protected by wire mesh.

The towers were a frequent target for bricks thrown by demonstrators. Despite their strong construction – they were designed to be blast proof – you still felt vulnerable, because they were a static target.

It was frowned upon if you had to come down for a piss, so we were encouraged to take plastic 'piss bottles' with us, which we stowed in our webbing (a thick belt with a number of pouches on it for storing essential personal equipment, such as water bottles, rifle-cleaning kit, emergency rations and magazines of ammunition). Empty Lucozade bottles seemed to be the favourite choice.

Once inside the tower, you had a powerful telescope and binoculars and had to make sweeps of the area every 15 minutes and log any suspicious activity. We also did regular mortar base plate checks (MBPC) on areas from where previous strikes had been launched. As trouble rarely kicked off, you spent a lot of time peering into people's backyards and bedroom windows, hoping to catch a glimpse of bare flesh. Most residents had become wise to our antics and had installed frosted glass throughout their whole houses, so there was no way we could spy on them.

Fortunately for us, there was one particular house where a gorgeous young girl lived, and she took great delight in parading around her bedroom in just her underwear. She knew we were watching and would occasionally give us a smile and a wave. We were just grateful that she hadn't inherited her father's prejudices against squaddies, and it was considered good etiquette to set up the telescope in prime position for the next man on duty after you.

But aside from our female friend, the duty was something we loathed and constantly 'ticked' (complained) about. It wasn't too bad in the daytime, because there was plenty of activity for you to watch, but nights could send you into a deep depression. Early evening was OK, because you got to see all the drunken revellers and half-naked girls staggering across the streets, but once the pubs closed and the town went to sleep it became a battle to stay awake. If your shift coincided with the early hours, we called it the 'drag stag', and the only way to stay awake was by talking to yourself or singing at the top of your voice. Another tactic was to drink gallons of coffee or hot sweet tea, but no matter what you did, you still felt like an anaesthetised zombie.

From our vantage points, we witnessed some curious phenomena in Crossmaglen. In particular, it became clear that the pubs closed whenever they wanted, and drink driving was rife. We realised this after a couple of weeks in the Sangers (the name for the watchtowers) watching drunks stagger out of the pubs at 2 a.m. and brazenly driving off. It was quite unbelievable to see and came as a bit of a culture shock, but it was understandable that it was allowed to happen. Because of the huge potential for violent disorder and riots that existed on the streets, and because of the need to preserve the fragile peace, the police had adopted an unofficial policy of ignoring minor crimes.

From the point of view of the Police Service of Northern Ireland (PSNI), it simply wasn't worth the aggro to go into a pub and force it to close at a reasonable hour. Hard-core republicans frequented some of those pubs, and if the police went wading in and kicked people out, they would have a riot on their hands. The truce that existed between the hated PSNI and the local republicans was both fragile and tenuous, and it could fracture at any time. Unless someone was doing 'donut' skids around the square and knocking people over, we turned a blind eye to any illegal behaviour. The local population had the potential to make our lives very hard and miserable, and for the sake of peace and quiet, many incidents that would get you arrested in Britain had to be ignored.

Another factor that prevented us from providing effective policing was the time it took us to get out on the ground; unless it was a catastrophic incident, we couldn't just burst out of the doors. For a policeman to deliver so much as a parking ticket required hours of planning: he had to organise a full multiple of soldiers for back-up, he had to liaise with high command so that he could move onto a piece of turf and he had to work out escape routes and likely ambush spots before he even stepped out of the station. Police work in Crossmaglen was a laborious, complex and ultra-sensitive issue, and much of it was left to the local Provisional IRA.

The area was almost entirely self-policing, and there was very little petty crime. No yobbos dared get too out of hand, because a local Provisional IRA bruiser would pay them a visit and relieve them of their kneecaps. Also, Crossmaglen was entirely Catholic and had no loyalist contingent, so trouble was highly unlikely, and punishment beatings rarely had to be dished out. When they were, they were unfailingly savage: victims would lose eyes, teeth and, in some cases, limbs. If a Provisional IRA gang wanted to break your legs, they didn't just snap them – they tried to grind your bones into powder and turn your muscles into mush. So, as you can imagine, they carried rather more influence in the town than we did, and they were a lot more feared.

Being in the towers was a voyeuristic paradise, and although I felt uncomfortable passing the time spying on other people's lives, I still went ahead and did it because there was nothing else to do. The towers were incredibly intrusive, and I wasn't surprised at the hostility they generated. If an old lady was sweeping her backyard, she would pause and wave her fist up at you, or if mums were watching the kids play Gaelic football, they would make time to give you the finger and a baleful glare. Sometimes they'd push the kids forward and encourage them to throw stones at you or a brick even, if one was to hand.

It upset me that things had been allowed to continue for so long that young mothers who share our language and customs regarded us as barbarian invaders. How fucked up and distorted have things become that an old lady who has a Virgin Mary statuette on her mantelpiece thinks it's OK to blow up a squaddie? The whole situation is absurd, and I wanted nothing to do with it, but as a soldier, I was an intimate participant.

The atmosphere of the tour took on the same sense of timelessness and inevitability that Iraq had. Nights melted into days, weeks drifted into months, and all without us noticing. Because our routine was so grinding and repetitive, we even had to be reminded what day it was sometimes. For us there was no difference in a Saturday night and a Monday morning – it was all just the 'same old shit'. What did worry me was that some squaddies started to get complacent. It would usually be the young guys, or some of the Commonwealth recruits, who had little respect for the terrorism of years gone by.

I nearly got into an argument when I found a young lance corporal reading a book on stag. He was sat on his arse with his feet on the shelf, and he had his head buried in the pages. He didn't even look up when I climbed the ladder and asked him what he was doing. When I began to remind him that the IRA still existed and we were living in their backyard, he waved me off with a dismissive laugh and confidently advised me that they were now standing down. I felt my blood begin to boil but had to let it go as he was senior to me, and it wasn't worth fighting over. The problem was he wasn't old enough to remember how bad it had been back in the '80s and judged the place as it was then, post ceasefire. Well that attitude was fine if the ceasefire held – but if it broke, he would be in a world of shit. There was simply too much history and bad blood in Crossmaglen for us to be able to relax, so why take the chance?

Some of the lads had actually fallen asleep on stag, and there was an official and unofficial way of dealing with it. The first time it happened, a hefty dig in the ribs was considered sufficient punishment. The second time it happened, you still got the punch, but you also got charged with dereliction of duty and sent to Colchester Military Prison. It happened to two guys in Crossmaglen, but, thankfully, they weren't in my section. A lot depended on how you had fallen asleep: if you had genuinely nodded off with the binoculars and pen still in your hand, you might even be offered sympathy, but if you had taken off your kit and lain on the floor, you would get a beating, and rightly so.

When the end of our stag rotation came round, we were in a state of ecstatic relief. It had lasted for a full two months and eaten up a third of our tour. Initially, we had been grateful for the relative safety of the steel walls that surrounded us, but by the end of our watchtower assignment, we were itching for a change of scenery. Physically we had noticeably deteriorated, and the lack of a regular sleep-and-rest pattern had reduced us to shambling wrecks. We had lost weight, our eyes were ringed with dark circles and our skin took on a pale and pasty pallor. It was a good thing there was a ceasefire in place, because if the IRA had chosen to launch an attack on us, we would probably have been too tired and sleepy to even notice. Our listless voices and shuffling, lethargic steps matched the glazed expressions on our faces. We were fucked, we were broken and we were ready for a change.

10

TOWER LIFE AND PATROLS

For the second rotation of my Northern Ireland tour I was assigned to a watchtower out in the countryside. A plethora of these towers are scattered all along the border of South Armagh. These lookout stations are usually situated on the top of a hill or other piece of high ground, and they provide us with the ability to observe a certain area of suspicion very closely. A typical tower is about 60-ft tall, at the top of which perches a room-sized 'stag box'. At the base of the tower is a walkway leading to a helicopter landing pad and an underground tunnel to the accommodation area.

The accommodation area is made up of large steel containers that have been sunk into the ground and covered up with grass and bushes. There is a separate kitchen, bathroom, communal space, exercise room and sleeping area. All of these areas are linked by a series of underground corridors. There is also a small garden for you to stretch your legs in and get some fresh air, and there is usually a sandbag-covered outside gym, full of rusty weights and rowing machines. The outside area is dug out of the hillside so that you always remain below ground level and out of the range of snipers. Rolls of thick razor wire and a heavily padlocked gate surround the helipad and tower compound.

There is no way that an IRA hit team can get in, and we know this because they have tried to several times over the years. Their best chance of scoring some success would be in a well-timed mortar strike – and they have tried that too.

The towers contain some pretty sophisticated cameras and tracking devices, though they are nowhere near as space age as the local Sinn Fein councillors claimed. Using this equipment, we kept close tabs on the movements of local Provisional IRA suspects by compiling what are known as 'sighting reports' and radioing them on to the next relevant tower. For example, a known player would drive by, and once out of sight, you would alert your next-door neighbour that he was headed their way. Most of the time we just took the details of lorries we suspected of smuggling fuel, but, occasionally, we'd track a stolen car or note the build up of hostile crowds. Pre-ceasefire I imagine the work had a sense of urgency and importance about it, but in these new, enlightened times, it was merely boring and repetitive.

The highlight of our day was when a Lynx helicopter would swoop down and drop off our mail or bring us our supply of food and newspapers. This was important because in the towers there were really only three things that boosted morale: the generously stocked kitchen, where we could gorge on biscuits, donuts and ice cream to our heart's content; the rickety old gym where we could blast away at the weights and make as much noise as we wanted; and the daily drop-off of newspapers and magazines that kept us in touch with the outside world. Aside from that, it was a very claustrophobic and unnaturally enclosed existence. Miles of countryside and winding country lanes surrounded us, and it was only through our powerful telescopes and cameras that we could see what was going on in the distant villages and towns.

I volunteered to do the nightshift, because although it would be more tiring, it was a lot less busy and would give me a chance to relax in the sun during the day. The shift involved six hours of stag duty in the tower and then six hours of 'general duties' in the accommodation. To be honest, the whole thing was a breeze and not at all hard work, apart from the need to stave off boredom and stay awake on stag. The greatest stress we faced, and one that was very real and damaging, was the threat of 'cabin fever'. It might sound like a joke, but it wasn't, because when you are living in each other's pockets for twenty-four hours a day, seven days a week, heated arguments and dislikes can develop. I considered myself to be hugely lucky in that I was a member of a chilled-out multiple, because there was an abundant supply of pricks available in the army to spoil things for you and poison the atmosphere.

In many ways, tower life was similar to what you would find in an arctic research station or on a reality TV show like *Big Brother*, because you couldn't just walk away or shut yourself off from someone if there was a personality clash. Daily life was a delicate balancing act, and you had to be sensitive and respectful of the moods and boundaries of your colleagues. It wasn't a huge effort for me, because I did have an exceptionally good team around me, but even so, I tried to tread carefully.

With experience I got to know everyone's idiosyncrasies and likes and dislikes. Everybody developed their own little routines and habits, and some of them were quite amusing. Capt. Stringer was a fanatical fan of *The Simpsons* and the whole tower had to descend into a respectful hush whenever it came on. Cpl. Broom was a former amateur boxing champion, and we always let him have first refusal on the punch bag, on which he would happily tap away for hours. Cpl. Eprry loved to watch cheap, straight-to-video films that featured actors nobody had ever heard of and were universally crap; he had a suitcase full of them. Kinni always liked huge portions of food, and seconds and thirds as well. Rifleman Mills loved to spend hours on the Internet, chatting up gullible girls and telling them about his exploits (with a view to meeting up, of course). Riflemen Payne and Edwards enjoyed reading army books and would spend hours poring over titles about the Vietnam

War and various other campaigns. Riflemen Steele and Roberts had a fascination with street gangs and rap culture, and would spend hours discussing the benefits of being a 'Crip' or a 'Blood'.

But perhaps the greatest idiosyncrasy belonged to me and my adoption of a kitten. Because of the countryside settings of the watchtowers they were plagued with field mice and assorted vermin. To combat this the army had provided each tower with a couple of resident cats. None of us could resist spoiling the cats rotten, and happier and more contented cats you could not find anywhere. They would spend the days roaming in the surrounding fields and farmyards, and then come in at night and curl up on our laps.

We had just taken delivery of a beautiful silver-and-grey kitten, and it was so cute I couldn't keep my hands off it. I soon became the kitten's new best friend, and whenever it wanted titbits, it would come straight to me. I used to love cuddling her, because she always smelt of fresh summer grass and reminded me of more innocent times. It seemed the feeling was mutual, because whenever I crawled into my sleeping bag to get some kip, I would awake to find my little friend asleep on my chest. As pathetic as it must sound, the comfort and affection that kitten showed me was a major factor in getting me through the tour.

You had a lot of time to think in the towers and a lot of time to really get to know someone. During the daytime, there was always lots of traffic and helicopters passing through to keep you busy, but at night-time, it all died off to nothing. We would sit in our stag box and stare at the infrared cameras, but we rarely saw any activity. It was at these times, during the silent night hours, that we would chat about our hopes, dreams and aspirations. Most of the lads were desperately fighting homesickness, marking time till they could leave the army for good, but others were hoping to stay in and make a career of it.

I liked hearing other soldiers' stories, and the more I heard, the more I realised how impossible it was to pin down and characterise any one definitive squaddie type. The fact was that all kinds of people joined up for a variety of different reasons, and the regiment was like a microcosm of any society – but with a few more 'rough-and-ready' types thrown in.

A good example of the often contradictory images of professional soldiering was Cpl. Eprry. On first impressions, he came across as an extremely dedicated professional soldier. That would be an accurate description, and it would be one that pleased him. But he also had another side that only showed itself when he was off duty, and it hinted at hidden depths. In his spare time, he was a student of psychology, and every spare second he had, he would bury his nose in his books and shut himself off from the world.

Eprry had a fascination with the subject of parapsychology, and this area formed part of his academic studies. He would regularly read palms, deal cards and tell people's fortunes. And I am not talking about a passing fancy here but a deep level of knowledge and understanding of all things paranormal. The subject had never really grabbed my attention before, but I developed a tremendous respect for Eprry's sincere curiosity and impresseive knowledge on the subject.

As I got to know Cpl. Eprry better and saw at first hand his considerable understanding of a variety of subjects, I reflected on how he smashed the squaddie stereotype. In many ways, he was like a chameleon, and I felt that he could have blended in and succeeded within any organisation. At that particular moment in time, he was a NCO in the Green Jackets, which demanded a dedicated physicality and a robust frame of mind – so that is what he gave it. But I had no doubt that if a job required a sensitivity and sophisticated knowledge of culture, he could have provided that just as well.

At the other end of the spectrum was Rifleman Leamer. He had joined the regiment as a brash teenager and was primarily out for a good time. His attitude was to live for today and not worry about tomorrow; he didn't waste time analysing things too deeply. However, for a lad who claimed not to give a shit about where the army sent him he surprised me, because he had an instinctive and natural grasp of world affairs that few could match. He had an irreverent attitude to the army, and I detected he was becoming jaded with it all. I asked what had drawn him to the Green Jackets, and he told me he had seen a television documentary about the Balkans and the Green Jackets' role in the conflicts there. There was a scene that showed a platoon of Green Jackets arresting a war criminal and kicking down the door to his flat. They gave the bloke the rough treatment, and Leamer said his initial reaction was, 'Fuck me, that looks good. I fancy some of that – kicking fucking doors down!' I had to laugh at Leamer's refreshingly honest answer and candour, because that was the kind of scene that would have impressed me as a youngster – and to a lesser extent it still did.

Over the years, I have learned that a soldier really lives his life and experiences his emotions on a far deeper level than most people could comprehend. It is almost a primal thing, and you feel love, hate, fear, cold, tiredness, hunger, anger, joy and resentment on a scale that few civilians ever experience. The nature of the job means that it takes a lot out of you, because it feels like you are living on your nerves and having to utilise all your inner resources just to keep on an even keel. The job is a drain on your emotions and sensibilities, and you have to project your mind to the future just to make the present bearable. The discussions with my fellow soldiers in the watchtowers, in which we frequently bared our souls to one another, only emphasised this to me.

Another frequent topic of conversation in the towers, and one that sparked off much heated debate, was the emerging prisoner abuse scandals involving British and American troops in Iraq. The scandal had been unfolding before our eyes on the nightly news, and it had sent a shockwave of anger throughout the battalion. Although we felt sympathy for the unfortunate positions that the prisoners found themselves in, most of our ire was caused by the likelihood of reprisal attacks against allied soldiers. The general consensus seemed to be that the abusers were a bunch of ill-disciplined, unprofessional and inadequate pricks, who had brought shame on our uniforms and placed our colleagues in great danger.

My own personal feeling was that the bastards who abused prisoners should be hung out to dry and immediately booted out of the army. And I don't believe the waffle that they were only following orders and didn't realise the seriousness of their actions – that is complete and utter bullshit. The abusers knew full well what they were doing, and they were clearly enjoying themselves. If they were only following orders, as they claimed, that shows how weak and unsuited to army service they really were. If any senior officer within the British Army had ordered me to start playing silly buggers with a cowering prisoner, I would have told him to piss off and challenged him to charge me – and so would any other decent soldier I knew.

By the time our stint in the towers came to an end, I was as mentally lethargic and burnt out as I had been on stag at XMG. The problem in the towers wasn't one of overwork but one of boredom and isolation. I had grown so dispirited and fed up with tower life that towards the end of our stint I actually tried to sleep away the tour – whenever I was off duty, I would retreat to my bed and try and dream away the days. When that didn't work, I would go to the gym and pump iron till my arms felt like falling off. It must have been an incongruous sight and sound in the middle of the beautiful countryside – a huge tower sprouting out of a hillside and rave music blasting out of an invisible gym. We didn't care because nobody was around to complain about it or tell us to turn it down, and as far as we were concerned, we were bringing a little piece of English culture to the Irish hills.

I was desperate to get out on the ground and start doing some patrols, because being cooped up like a bird in a cage was beginning to drive me mad. If we remained locked up for much longer, I felt sure we would get cabin fever – no matter how well we all got along. 'This is fucking shit,' had become our tour anthem, and it was about time we got a new song. So far, all we had done in Northern Ireland was stag on and watch CCTV screens, and I didn't want that to be my abiding memory of the tour. I wanted to take something a bit more substantial home with me and to be able to say that I had done a worthwhile job.

One of the things that had made the Iraqi tour rewarding was that every now and then it would throw up a special moment and you would experience some magic. In the watchtower, the only distinguishing feature was a complete lack of memorable moments and in its place a dreadful sense of boredom and isolation; I felt like we were completely on our own. There was no racing along desert roads at midnight or cruising through the back streets of Basra with kids running along after you and shouting and waving, it was just the same old faces and the same old shit. For all the interaction we had with the local community, our 'Golf One Zero' watchtower might as well have been on the moon. All I wanted now from our final phase of the operation was a sense of purpose and a dash of excitement – not too much, but just enough to get us to the end with a feeling of accomplishment.

Before we took over as the XMG patrols multiple, we were brought up to date on all that had happened whilst we had been stuck in the towers. It was certainly an eye-opener, and it reminded us that despite an ongoing peace process, there was still plenty of danger on the streets. South Armagh covered a big area, and it seemed that every day there was an incident of some kind that was linked with violent republicanism. A lot of the attacks were directed against their own kind and little more than inter-party feuds, but a good deal more involved the ongoing surveillance and disruption of the security forces' ability to operate in Northern Ireland. We had only been in the towers for two months, but in that space of time a number of incidents had occurred. For example, a large bomb had been found in a trailer parked in a local farmyard. A 'cordon op' had been called, and the Royal Engineers were forced to seal off the area and defuse the bomb. A routine VCP had also uncovered a sniper rifle and full magazine of ammo inside the boot of a vehicle, a young Jamaican soldier had let the distance between himself and his patrol get too big, and he had been surrounded by yobbos and given a brief beating in Crossmaglen, and in another demonstration of poor patrolling skills, the rear man on one patrol had allowed himself to become separated from his multiple. Even worse, his colleagues hadn't noticed that he was missing until they were back inside the base, by which time they had no idea where he was. Unbelievably, the lad decided to bluff it and completed the patrol by himself, walking past crowds of people as if he had a whole team behind him. Eventually, he found his way back to camp, where a mega bollocking from the sergeant-major greeted him. It was actually pretty funny, but it could have had fatal consequences.

Meanwhile, the Provisional IRA continued in its efforts to present itself to republican sympathisers as a legitimate 'alternative police force', and it continued to administer its own special brand of justice to anyone who crossed its path. Because of the iron grip of fear in which it held its subjects, minor crimes went unpunished and gangsterism and thuggery were allowed to flourish within its ranks.

What disturbed me most about the above list of incidents, which are only a taster of what had been going on, was that they only related to events in our own area and things that we knew about. The intelligence officer told us that there were similar things going on in many areas of the North and that some events were a lot more serious than the ones he was permitted to tell us about. The underlying message was that yes, the peace process was very much still on, but there was still a dangerous hotbed of republican resentment on the streets. I didn't need reminding of this, but I was glad he had jogged my memory.

Once the security briefing was over and we were fully up to date, we began to prepare ourselves for the patrols phase of the tour. However, before we were allowed onto the streets we were issued with some extremely heavy and cumbersome bits of kit known as electromagnetic countermeasures (ECM). These were basically large radios that weighed about 40 lb apiece, and they were carried in special backpacks that had 3-ft long aerials poking through the zips. The heaviest and most important piece of ECM was the Chubb, and it was such a pain in the arse to carry that it was universally loathed and avoided like the plague. Because of its size and weight it tended to fall onto the shoulders of stronger soldiers, and so it was that I came to be burdened with the blasted thing for the remainder of the tour. But not only that, because I was also the official platoon medic I had to carry a cumbersome and well-stocked med pack, which conspired with the Chubb to crush me into the ground. I estimated that by the time I packed in all my other bits and bobs and got my boots out onto the floor, I was carrying well over 70 lb on my back.

You had to guard the ECM kit as you would guard your own life, because if the IRA ever captured it, we would be in a world of shit. The kit contained a series of top-secret electromagnetic codes that could detect explosive devices from a considerable distance. If ever you got near a bomb, an incessant bleeping would warn you to back off or guide you to its location. It was a priceless piece of kit that had gone a long way to nullifying the IRA's threat, and they were desperate for their own engineers to get a look. Whenever a piece of ECM was captured by the IRA, an incredibly expensive set of new codes would have to be developed, as the old ones became useless. If a soldier ever managed to lose a piece of ECM kit when out on patrol, he would be in very serious trouble with his bosses: unless you were fighting for your life and it was torn from you, your career would be over.

The first time I ever entered Crossmaglen town was on a foot patrol from the security base. Although it was 2004 and the peace process was well established, I forced myself to think back to the bad old days, when nightly riots featured on the news and Northern Ireland was going up in flames. All of the skills and drills we had been taught prior to deployment I used exhaustively: every 20 m or so I did a full turn and checked what was going on behind me (doing your 360s); whenever we encountered a thick bush, I peered into it closely (looking for bombs); whenever the patrol came to a halt, I searched out a piece of cover and went down on one knee (going firm); and so on. I basically tried to be as totally switched on and professional as I possibly could. My motivation was a fear of the unknown and powerful childhood memories that refused to go away.

My attention to detail and excessive caution didn't go unnoticed. Even the PSNI officer was a little taken aback by my patrolling style and couldn't resist a gentle dig at my expense: 'Fuck me, young fella, I haven't seen anyone take that much care since Bloody Sunday – what are you expecting, World War Three?' I laughed along at his joke, but I had no intention of loosening up my patrol style, and I had no intention of slacking off. The way I saw it I was the last man at the rear of the patrol, and I was also carrying the heaviest piece of kit, so I was therefore the slowest moving and most vulnerable target for an IRA sniper – and I had no desire to make his job easy.

We moved through the town in what is known as a 'four man brick', with a soldier acting as the point man and me bringing up the rear. We patrolled in a constantly moving zigzag fashion, and we tried to keep the spaces between us to about 20 m. The officer from the PSNI walked in the middle of us, and sometimes he would circulate around the multiple and spend time with each man. This system of patrolling had evolved from years of practice, and it was widely regarded as the most effective way to reduce the threat of attack or to defeat an actual assault. It was simple, fluent and flexible, and it allowed for speedy reactions and quick counter movements if anybody tried to take us on. Each man in the patrol knew exactly what his role was and what to do in the event that something out of the ordinary occurred.

On every level, patrolling through Crossmaglen was hard, and it really took it out of us. We moved along at a fast pace, taking long strides and often making sharp and unexpected turns. That, combined with the weight on our backs, meant that we would often be panting and dripping with sweat. But most tiring of all was the emotional stress of constant concentration and vigilance being stretched to breaking point.

You couldn't just walk down a road or cross a field and enjoy the scenery with your 'thumb up your arse'. You had to squint into the distance and scan rooftops and tree lines for suspicious movements; you had to make brief eye contact with every single soul you saw walking on the pavement; you had to watch where your feet fell and walk around empty Coke cans; and you had to veer away from pub doorways and back alleys. Basically, you had to have 100 per cent awareness of your surroundings at all times. It was an extremely draining and intense method of working, but history had shown that it was the best course to take.

Although the local IRA were on an official stand-down and claimed to be inactive, that didn't stop them sending out runners to do dicking operations on us. Dicking is the term given to IRA surveillance methods. Whenever a group of soldiers are out on the ground, the Provos will get a junior member to follow the patrol round and observe their patrolling tactics. If the soldiers appear to be professional, alert and switched on, that message will be relayed back to the IRA commanders, and it might just foil a planned attack. But if the soldiers are sloppy and disinterested, the IRA will be informed that they have an easy target if they want to have a go. That was another reason why we chose to patrol professionally and assertively (with a subtle hint of aggression), because we were sending out a message to anyone with silly ideas: 'Don't fuck with us, we are serious soldiers.'

It is when soldiers start to get lazy and slacken off that they are most vulnerable to an attack. For example, in Crossmaglen there is an abundance of hedges, crumbling stonewalls and barbed-wire fences. A good soldier will inspect the obstacle and choose to go over it at its most difficult point, but a lazy one will take the easiest route — and that is when the terrorists will strike. In South Armagh, the IRA were notorious for booby-trapping farm gates and fences, and such devices have blown up dozens of squaddies. The IRA knows full well that if a tired and pissed-off soldier is given the choice of opening a simple little gate or climbing a steep and crumbling stonewall, he will be inclined to take the easier option — and that is when they will blow him up.

To confuse and intimidate potential snipers or IRA dickers, we had a formation to suit every occasion, and at a subtle signal we could move to either the diamond formation, the staggered file or the arrowhead movement. Out in the open fields, if we ever felt the need to go firm, we wouldn't just drop to one knee and have a brief look round but would get on our belt buckles and intensely scan the hills with our SUSATs (Sight Unit Small Arms Trilux, the optical sight that sat on top of our rifles with an adjustable times four magnification).

Whenever we entered a particularly dodgy area, or one where a previous patrol had run into trouble, we made a conscious effort to put on a 'skills display' and move through at a brisk pace. Anybody watching us would find themselves confused and puzzled as they tried to keep pace with our seemingly disorganised moves. In actual fact, we would be performing a rigorously rehearsed and perfectly choreographed pattern. At any one time, we would each know where the other was, and we would have a good 'all round defence' with our weapons covering every possible angle of attack.

To the untrained eye we were just a blur of bodies, but our movements had a clarity and purpose that had taken years to develop.

Any fat that you had on your body soon melted away after a few patrols, and after an hour on the streets, you felt like you had run a marathon. It was a good way to get fit, but the physical stresses and strains wreaked havoc on your body. Your knees were permanently sore and bruised from crouching down and going firm on every corner, and although we all tried to kneel on a piece of grass or soil, it soon made no difference. The Americans were routinely issued with kneepads to protect them, and why the British government wouldn't go to the same expense was a constant source of irritation in the battalion. But worst of all were the debilitating effects of lugging around the ECM kit on your back, and after a few weeks, your spine and hips felt like they were ready to fall apart. Throw into the mix the ordeal of tabbing along for endless miles over hills and dales, and you can see why so many soldiers ended up being medically discharged after a couple of years.

The first time I ever encountered a dicker I came away feeling very vulnerable and uncomfortable at the position I had found myself in. The army had a policy of 'assertively confronting' them whenever possible – not to intimidate or scare them off but just to let them know we were aware of their presence. We had been conducting a routine patrol when it came over the net (slang for radio) that a large man was paying unusually close attention to the security base, and we were rerouted to intercept him. By the time we caught up with him I was the nearest man, and so the job of 'chatter upper' fell to me.

I could see the guy was big, but I didn't realise just how big until I came face to face with him – or rather face to chest. I kept a wary distance and eyed him up before speaking. He must have been at least 6 ft 5 in., and he was built to match, with shovel-like hands and an angry ginger beard. The guy resembled some kind of crazed Celtic Viking, and as I approached him, I prayed he would behave himself.

It dawned on me that with all the kit I was carrying I wouldn't stand a chance if he chose to fight it out with me: it would be like fighting in an Eskimo suit. Far from giving me confidence, the SA80 that I cradled in my hands felt like a burden, and I had to fight the urge to chuck it on the floor and heave off my backpack at the same time. But, as ever, soldiering in Northern Ireland was an endless game of bluff and counter bluff, and it was critical that I didn't show any fear.

In a polite but firm voice I asked him what he was doing hanging around XMG security base. The man was obviously a seasoned campaigner, because he didn't answer but merely gazed back at me with an even and calm glare. I asked him if I could have his name and address, so that I could be certain there was no way in which I could help him, but, again, he didn't reply, and casually ran his fingers though his hair and grinned at me.

Before I left him to his own devices, I asked him one last time if he wanted to have a chat with me, and, again, I got the same mischievous glare and contemptuous silence. We were getting nowhere, so I bid him farewell and asked him to be more careful where he spent his time in future. For the first time I saw a flicker of anger in his eyes and he shot back at me, 'No, you watch where you go. This is a free country, and I'll go where I please.' I paused mid-step and whirled round to face him again, trying to think of a pithy parting shot of my own, before realising he was right and there was nothing more I could say. The best I could come up with was a nod of my head and a grin of my own, so I departed, and we left it at that.

Whenever we were out on patrol, I always found it interesting to observe the local population and their attitudes towards us. If I ever got the chance, I would try and reach out to them, even though I knew it was more often than not a futile gesture. Generally speaking, the old people were completely against us, the middle-aged studiously ignored us, refusing to acknowledge our existence, and the young had a stilted and wary tolerance of us. I realised that for some of the older generation the bitterness and hatred ran so deeply that there was no way they could ever get past it. It struck me as odd that otherwise friendly and God-fearing people could harbour such intense hatred towards us, but I suppose it was a natural reaction to living with the Troubles for so many years.

On one occasion, I strode by a baker's on a mid-afternoon patrol. It was a gloriously sunny day, and I saw an old man leaning against the wall eating a pie. The man hadn't yet seen me, but I had clocked him from a distance, and as I scanned his face, I could see he was the sort of jolly, warm and humorous old soul that children love to have as a grandfather. As I walked towards him, he looked up and beamed at me with a generous smile. I nodded my head at him and asked him how he was getting on, and he replied, 'Fine, thanks.' I think I must have caught him off guard, because as soon as he realised that he had said hello to me his expression took on a hateful glare. He then spat on the floor and cursed himself, before slinging his pie to the ground. I was shocked at the sudden change in him, and it knocked the wind out of me.

The old man's reaction had been an impulsive and uncontrollable surge of anger – but what really disturbed me was that his anger was directed at himself rather than me. In his mind, his natural and friendly human response towards a soldier's cheery hello was an unforgivable betrayal of his republican ideals.

The town was full of contradictions and ambivalent attitudes that meant I often scratched my head and came away puzzled and confused. The locals professed to hate the Brits with an unrivalled passion, and at no time was this more prevalent than at pub closing time on a Friday night. If ever we were patrolling through the square at that time, we would be showered with a hail of beer bottles and sectarian insults, and people would shout, 'Fuck off back home, you Brit bastards!' or 'Shame on you, Protestant scum!'

Aside from the sticky beer and smashing bottles, I always had a private giggle at these moments, and I enjoyed the confrontations because of their absurdity. For a start, a number of my patrol was from the Commonwealth or Catholic – so how they whittled us down to a bunch of 'Brit bastards' and 'Protestant scum' was beyond me. But what was truly comical, and undeniably ironic, was that these 'Sons of Ireland' were often wearing English football club shirts! It seemed that every other yobbo I set eyes on was sporting a Manchester United or Liverpool shirt, and they displayed their allegiances with a beaming pride.

If the young men of Crossmaglen harboured a lot of hostility towards us, it certainly didn't extend to the women. Whenever I patrolled past a young girl, her reaction depended on who she was with: if a male accompanied her, we received a careful indifference, but if she was with a girlfriend, you would normally get a cocky hello and perhaps even a suggestive comment. I got the impression that the girls enjoyed having a bit of a wind-up and teasing the soldiers, because they looked at us from a different perspective than the men. To the girls we were a bunch of strange and forbidden men from across the sea, and I think they were perhaps intrigued by our 'outsider' and 'bad guy' status in the eyes of the local community. In contrast, the young lads viewed us through a fog of testosterone, in which male rivalry and a sense of territorial rights combined, and it was understandable that they felt threatened.

But perhaps the saddest indictment of the British military presence in Northern Ireland was the attitude of the children. There was definitely a sense of hostility towards us from the kids, but how severe and how twisted it was depended on how much hatred their parents had instilled in them. I can only presume that the indoctrination process begins from when they are toddlers, and it is ingrained more thoroughly the older they get. But there were glimmers of hope and humanity from these hardened kids, and the reactions you provoked usually depended on whether they were alone or in a gang.

I think children the world over have a natural curiosity about and fascination for soldiers, and even more so if the soldiers themselves appear to be friendly. If the kids of Crossmaglen were in a group, they were more likely to throw stones at us than say hello, but if they were walking down the street on their own, their good nature and openness would inevitably win out.

On countless occasions, I would go firm on a street corner or tuck myself in behind a nice thick tree when the patrol came to a halt. Sometimes, I would see a child walking towards me, and they would nervously glance over their shoulders before saying, 'Hi soldier' or giving me a little wave and a smile. Whenever this happened, I always returned their greeting as warmly and discreetly as I could, because I knew if a passing adult clocked them saying hello to a squaddie, they would get a clip round the ear and a lecture on how evil we were.

It must be confusing and upsetting for the children growing up in these circumstances, because they are conditioned to believe that British soldiers are big, bad monsters who will snatch them off the streets and beat up their daddies. When they see for themselves that this isn't necessarily the case, it must provoke some awkward feelings in them. From what I saw, I would say the 'nice and curious' phase lasts till they are about ten years old, and then it is swiftly replaced by stone-cold hatred and peer-driven anger. The pressures of community life and looming adolescence mean they are honour bound to change, because if they maintained their tolerance of us, they would be publicly shamed and ostracised from everything they know.

I had a great deal of sympathy for the people of Crossmaglen, because even if they wanted to ratchet down the tension and normalise relations with us, the burden of the town's history would make it impossible. Nothing less than the immediate tearing down of the security bases and watchtowers would appease the general public – not only that but you would have to disband the PSNI and withdraw the army as well. In all but name, the whole region of South Armagh belongs to the Republic of Ireland, and no amount of peace talks or negotiations will ever change that. Too much blood has been spilt and too many lives have been torn apart for any half measures to be considered.

Most of the IRA members killed by the security forces, or blown up by their own bombs, are hardened and committed terrorists, and they know the risks when they take up arms and get involved. But it has to be said that not all of the people caught in the crossfire are terrorists, and a lot of innocents have been dragged into the Troubles and have lost their lives too. It is because of the sacrifices and deaths of these two different groups of people, who ultimately believe in the same cause, that no false dawns or half-hearted peace accords could ever be accepted.

The majority of republicans in South Armagh don't discriminate between an IRA bomber who is blown up by his own device or an innocent Catholic drinker who loses his life to a pub bomb – they are both victims of the Troubles and the British are to blame for their deaths. The fact that most reasonable people can see that one brought about his own downfall, whereas the other is an innocent bystander, is an irrelevance to the staunch republican. 'If there were no troops, there would be no bombs, and they would both be alive,' is their logic.

In the middle of Crossmaglen Square there is an elaborate and very impressive memorial statue that highlights the impossibility of British rule in a republican heartland. Indeed, many of the smaller towns and rural villages that line the border have equally grand and expensive-looking memorials, complete with flags and IRA battalion banners. At first glance, you could mistake them for the typical war memorials and cenotaphs that can be found in many British towns – but you would be very wrong. The statue in

Crossmaglen depicts a slave-like figure breaking free from his chains of bondage, staring defiantly at the sky, and the inscription reads:

> Glory to all you praised and humble heroes
> Who have willingly suffered
> For your unselfish and passionate love
> Of Irish freedom.

It is a powerful statement of intent and succinctly sums up the mindset of Irish republicanism.

Fuel and contraband smuggling in South Armagh remains a huge, multi-million pound business. Now that the peace process is in full swing, the old hands of the IRA have switched their attentions to building up their own personal fortunes – albeit with a friendly nod and a wink from the British government, who will turn a blind eye to anything if it preserves the ceasefire. I have to say, I agree with the unofficial policy. Over the decades, too many good people have died in this needless conflict, and too many communities have been torn apart for the status quo to remain.

In all my time in South Armagh, I never saw a single fuel tanker from a major multi-national company like Shell or Texaco. Small family firms and private businesses ran all of the tankers and oil companies, and it says a lot for the intimidating power of the Provisionals that they are able to keep massive corporations out of their small and rural heartlands. Many of these tankers actually smuggle illegal red diesel and other goods, and a huge profit is made by all concerned. We knew the registration numbers and details of the owners and operators, but unless we stumbled around a corner and caught someone red-handed, we merely logged details and turned a blind eye. In the old days, we would have come down on them like a ton of bricks, but in trying to preserve the ceasefire, we were working for a higher cause.

However, there were occasions when confrontations inevitably occurred, and every now and then, we would catch someone in a compromising position that we couldn't ignore.

On one unbearably hot day, my multiple was coming to the end of an exhausting three-hour patrol, and it felt as though we had covered half of South Armagh. A PSNI officer called Patrick was leading the patrol, and he was one of the few policemen I encountered that seemed able to get along reasonably well with the republicans on his patch. He was an old-fashioned community copper in his late 50s, and he had the aura of someone that had seen and done it all. Despite the opposition he met on his daily rounds, he retained a friendliness and youthful optimism about the area on his beat. It seemed that he would stop and chat to virtually every person we came across, which meant that we had to go firm and get sore knees, while the patrol moved along at a snail's pace.

As the point man for the patrol rounded a corner he yelled back at us and began running frantically. The rest of us, who up to that point had been crawling along at a leisurely pace, broke into a fast run and followed him down the quiet country lane. As soon as we caught up with him, we were confronted with the hilarious sight of a huge oil tanker trying to reverse in the narrowest of roads. The point man was jumping up at the cab and repeatedly banging his fist on the window. The frantic driver had absolutely no chance of making his manoeuvre work, and as his wheels began sliding into a steep ditch and he demolished the leafy hedges, he wisely decided to call it a day and gave up. In a flash, the point man leapt into his cab and seized the keys and, at the same time, barked at the terrified driver to dismount. I noticed that the point man was shouting furiously and seemed on the verge of exploding. I think the driver sensed it too, because he couldn't get out of his cab quickly enough.

We sealed off the road, and Patrick did a quick search of a nearby farmyard. Surprise, surprise, we found a hefty quantity of red diesel hidden in horseboxes in the yard. The driver was arrested and carted away, but not before he had recovered his courage and threatened to have us all shot. We laughed off his threats because if anybody was going to get shot, it would be him and not us. He was the one who had fucked up and led us to a nice little haul. The irony was that if he had just kept on driving slowly and sensibly when he stumbled across us, we would have stepped aside and let him pass.

Although I didn't enjoy patrolling around Crossmaglen town, mainly because we frequently encountered hostility from the locals and never knew what was waiting for us around the corner, on a typical day we'd also get to do a rural patrol. I particularly enjoyed the countryside patrols, because they were a chance to get out of Crossmaglen and experience a change of scenery. We would be picked up from the security base in either a Lynx or Puma helicopter and would be flown at great speed to a 'grid reference square' on the map from where our patrol would begin.

The flights themselves were always hugely entertaining, and the pilots flew in a daring and unpredictable fashion. One minute we would be flying high and steady with the GPMG poking threateningly out of the open doors and a combination of wind and gravity pinning us to our seats; the next minute we would be pitching into a suicidal, rooftop-skimming dive and grabbing at our mates' arms for support. On the surface it was all fantastic and childish fun, but the pilots assured us that it was absolutely necessary and that they were flying to orders. Just like the infantrymen on the ground, the pilots had to operate as if the threat of an IRA attack was as strong as ever, and the constant turns, dives and swoops were carefully designed in order to avoid rocket strikes.

Once at our destinations, the chopper would set us down in the middle of a field, and we would jump out and sprint for the nearest hedge line, which provided us with cover and protection. When the chopper was safely out of sight, we would rig up our ECM kit and form up in our 'order of march', ready to begin our patrol. At the signal of the platoon commander, we would fan out and move off, and the patrol would officially commence.

South Armagh is primarily a rural area made up of acres of beautiful countryside and farmyards, interspersed with small towns and villages like Crossmaglen. At its best, it is an area of stunning natural beauty, resplendent with green hills, clear lakes and a quaint, old-world charm. But at its worst, it is a virulent hotbed of republicanism and a graveyard for British soldiers. More soldiers have been killed in South Armagh than any other area in Northern Ireland, including Belfast. It is a heartbreakingly beautiful place but, at the same time, frighteningly dangerous.

The countryside patrols were physically very tiring, as we would be trudging up and down steep hills for hours and be climbing over rickety barbed-wire fences that tore at our hands and had a nasty habit of collapsing under our weight. They were psychologically wearing too, because out in the middle of nowhere we were vulnerable and tempting targets. Every tree line or hedgerow hid a potential threat, and we had to patrol in a defensive style that countered this.

In the past, most IRA attacks had been made from the high ground on troops occupying the low ground, and it was a difficult position to fight back from. We tried to minimise this threat by splitting down into three multiples and sending two teams up into the nearby hills to provide 'over-watch' protection, while the remaining team went about its patrols business searching farmyards and engaging with the locals. This tactic was called 'satelliting', and it meant that the middle 'roads-multiple' had a 360-degree defence against any assault. But while this style of patrolling offered us a reasonable level of protection from attack, we had to accept that it still didn't provide complete safety; if a skilled sniper had us in his sights, there was very little we could do about it. That was one thing that pissed me off about patrolling in the hills – the fact that even if I did everything correctly, I could still get dropped at the click of a trigger.

It was all too easy to drop our guard and let the peaceful surroundings lull us to sleep, but past experiences had shown us that the fields could erupt with gunfire at any second. Whenever I felt myself slackening off or enjoying the scenery a bit too much, I made a conscious effort to jolt myself awake. The trouble was that after a leisurely couple of hours strolling through the fields and valleys, it was hard not to feel like I was in the Kent countryside or on a field exercise in Salisbury Plain. I had to constantly remind myself that the dozens of charming farmyards and miles of enchanting green hedges and leafy trees weren't just attractive features for me to enjoy but also positions for deadly sniper attacks.

A good trick I used to keep my alertness levels up was imagining how long it would take to raise a chopper if one of us got shot and was lying in a field with his guts spilling out. The answer was that it would take a fucking long time, a thought that perked me up and kept my eyes flicking from side to side, scanning the bushes for a flash of flesh or a hint of gleaming gunmetal.

Whenever we moved through a town, I always presumed we would come under attack, and I forced myself to make the same presumptions in the field. Deep down in my heart I knew it was unlikely, but I was a big exponent of the philosophy 'train hard and fight easy'.

One of the blessings of our Northern Ireland tour was that it took place in the summer, so we were at least spared the ordeal of getting up to our eyeballs in shit and muck whenever we crossed a patch of land. Patrolling through beautiful countryside on a gloriously hot day is no real hardship, but doing it in the driving rain, freezing snow and biting winds of winter must be an ordeal from hell.

As for the unfortunate soldiers who had to patrol those hills in the darkest and bloodiest days of the Troubles, I have only admiration and respect. I can't imagine how emotionally draining it must have been to be a soldier in South Armagh in the '70s and '80s, and I would never compare my experiences as a soldier to theirs. The tour that I went through was tough and it was hard work, but I only saw flashes of the hardships that my predecessors had to endure for months at a time.

However, while patrolling in the countryside, we did become uncomfortably familiar with all the small towns that interrupted the green hills, and we tried to move through them as discreetly and quickly as we could, because the last thing we wanted was trouble. I would have liked to have seen these villages from the perspective of a civilian and had the time to really explore them, because, in their own way, they had a huge historical significance that belied their tiny size.

For example, Cullaville, perched right on the Irish border, was a notorious spot for Provisional IRA attacks and fuel smuggling. A bit further along and you came across the village of Cullyhanna, which had a large memorial to the IRA on top of a small hill overlooking the village. The memorial was made up of solid black marble with gold lettering, and had a row of battalion flags hanging over it. The cost of it all must have run into the thousands, and it would have done any army proud, let alone the IRA.

No matter how hard we tried to be discreet and go unnoticed on our patrols, the reality was that it was almost impossible. At the first glimpse of a British soldier setting foot into a village or a helicopter landing in a distant field, the children would stop playing games in the street and rush off inside to inform their parents. But the most effective early warning system was the dogs, which the locals had helpfully trained to bark at us and harass us wherever possible. Most of the time it wasn't too much of a problem, just so long as you kept your awareness up and didn't let them see you were scared, but occasionally you would get bitten.

Some of the more hard-core republicans had actually trained

their mutts to attack squaddies, and whenever you entered their streets, the dogs would fly at you like Exocet missiles. I couldn't work out what was more disturbing – the dog gnawing away at your leg or its owner silently watching it with his arms crossed and a grin on his face. Fortunately for us, most of these 'attack terriers' were small Jack Russells or elderly mongrel dogs, and a swift boot or stamp of the foot was sufficient to send them scurrying off. But there were other dogs that caused a great deal of anxiety and sent a shiver of fear through the patrol, and we often wondered how we would fight them off if they ever got a hold of us.

We frequently encountered a huge Rottweiler that would go berserk and crash itself against the gates that penned it in whenever we tiptoed past it. The dog was absolutely fucking massive, and when it stood on its hind legs, its head easily cleared the 6-ft gate. Once it caught sight of us, it would howl and snap ferociously, lunging at you in an effort to take a bite. Equally frightening was a gigantic Alsatian that one of the locals kept chained up in his back yard – the thing resembled a werewolf more than a dog, and whenever we went past, it just growled and slavered menacingly instead of barking.

The only reason the owners of these fearsome beasts didn't turn them on us was because they had been told in no uncertain terms that we would shoot or stab their pets at the first sign of trouble. I accept that this might sound extreme, and it isn't the best way to win hearts and minds, but those two particular dogs could kill you if they got hold of you. What was more worrying was that their owners would be happy to just stand back and watch them savage you – so they were told the score very early on.

It might sound like a bit of a joke worrying about dog attacks when there is a threat of an IRA sniper, but just consider how much damage two crazed pit bull terriers could do. The republicans stopped using serious dog attacks as a disruptive strategy after some of their beloved pets were shot with plastic baton rounds back in the '80s, which had caused a mini riot. An old Jack Russell nipping at your heels can be laughed off, but a 10-st. Doberman going for your throat is not so easily dismissed.

On the long patrols you really got to know the PSNI officers, and that was another eye-opener for me. A lot of them were ex-squaddies, and they would actually try and recruit you if they felt you were interested. They said that being a policeman in Northern Ireland was nothing like being a copper in Britain, and I had to agree with them from what I had seen. The majority of the PSNI were Irish born and bred, and however much they tried to disguise it, the tension of sectarianism was always there. But just because a policeman held strong loyalist beliefs it didn't prevent him from being a fair man, and I have to say that the majority of coppers I saw were scrupulously even handed with the republicans. Of course, there were quite a few who yearned for the 'good old days' of ruling with an iron fist, but to say they were all like that would be a gross misrepresentation.

I did dozens of rolling VCPs with the PSNI, where we would patrol along a stretch of road and the policeman would wave down cars at random and have a quick word with the drivers. Far from being the sort of aggressive interrogation that had gone on back in the '80s, from what I could see, it was more like a friendly chat. The copper would usually have a brief laugh and a joke with the driver, and he might ask to see their licence, but that was as far as it went. There was no searching of boots or tearing up carpets and threatening the passengers, as had happened in the past.

One justifiable complaint that the locals made about VCPs was that they disrupted their local routine and inconvenienced their journeys. That's a fair comment, but the VCPs in South Armagh had a purpose and sound reasoning behind them, and we made them as quick and hassle free as possible. Because of the lack of a strong police presence on the ground, a lot of minor traffic offences and more serious road crimes were ignored, and the PSNI wanted to get a grip of the problem. A lot of younger drivers in

South Armagh had neither licences nor insurance, and they had no intention of purchasing either. The PSNI were always getting complaints about hit and runs, unreported accidents, false number plates, drunk drivers, joy riders and near misses. A lot of the victims were innocent members of the public, and they were as pissed off about it as anybody.

There was no denying, though, that some drivers hated the VCP checkpoints, and rather than go through them, they would reverse away and find an alternative route. I noticed that whenever we were out on the ground, cars would flash their headlights at each other to warn other vehicles that a checkpoint was coming up, in much the same way that we do in the UK when we see a policeman doing speed checks. And even if the majority of residents handled our VCPs with a modicum of uneasy tolerance, I wouldn't pretend for a second that they supported them, because they represented yet another display of unwanted British rule.

Occasionally on a VCP I encountered some of the most extreme idiocy it was possible to imagine. On one of our stops, the PSNI arrested a youth driving a car erratically with false plates and without a licence. He looked like a snivelling scrote-bag, and he would have been well advised to keep his mouth shut, lest he get himself into more trouble. In a rather pathetic attempt to intimidate and impress us, he rolled up his sleeve and showed us his IRA tattoo, informing us that it was his life's ambition to become an IRA sniper and take out a few Brits. The PSNI resisted the impulse to give him a clip round the ear, and we all had a good laugh at him instead. The kid was just a sad wannabe, and he was advised that it wasn't a particularly good idea to tear around Crossmaglen boasting of his connections (of which he had none). If the local Provisional IRA found out that he was name dropping and bragging at vehicle checkpoints, he might have a different sort of encounter with his heroes than the one he wished for.

* * *

Because of the ever-present threat of terrorism and the large number of IRA sympathisers in the area, we often had to get involved in activities that wouldn't arise in the UK. South Armagh was an area that had profited from the peace process, and in the surrounding hills there were new homes and villages sprouting up on what seemed like a daily basis. The building contractors used explosives for digging out holes in the ground, laying foundations or taking out small chunks of hillside. Once they had finished their work, we would come along and supervise the destruction of the surplus charges – otherwise the local Provisional IRA would volunteer to do the job.

The explosives were placed in the back of a wagon and taken to a huge quarry, where certified engineers would bury them and blow them up. The explosives were called Energel charges, and they resembled long pieces of thick sausage. We called this process an 'op justice' day, and we had to observe the whole thing and take up secure positions in the surrounding hills, just in case the Provos decided to grab some free supplies for themselves. It would always be a spectacular experience as the ground rumbled beneath you and huge slabs of the quarry were blown into dust.

When I look back on my time patrolling across the fields of South Armagh I do often find myself smiling. The sights weren't as glorious or stirring as those I had witnessed in Iraq, but they were just as special in their own way. For both me and my colleagues, the 'Iraq experience' was most often seen from behind the wheel of a Land-Rover on some barren desert road. In contrast, the NI tour was all about a small, tight unit of friends and comrades patrolling for endless miles over hills and dales. South Armagh was all about getting 'grass under foot' and employing our skills in a 'green environment', out in the fresh air. I was never what you call an army barmy sort of soldier, but I have to admit that patrolling in NI brought out the purist in me, and it was an intensely satisfying experience.

11

HIT AND RUN

In the '80s, the streets of Northern Ireland had been a bloody battleground where frequent riots and impassioned protesters often seemed to materialise out of thin air. Gangs of youths roamed the streets, and middle-aged men hung around outside community centres, sullenly waiting for the next army patrol to walk by. The threat of violence was all-pervasive, and both the security forces and the general public existed in a permanent state of opposition, agitation and denial.

In the early years of the new century, times had supposedly changed, and we were all meant to have moved on. However, I would often experience things in Crossmaglen that would make me pause and wonder. It was true that much of the violent discord that characterised the previous decades had gone, but there remained a chilling hatred and searing resentment towards the Brits that would occasionally flare up.

The whole purpose of our being there, and the manner in which we were forced to interact with the locals, struck me as like being trapped in a tragic farce; it was like Groundhog Day everyday. We coexisted in a constant game of brinkmanship and one-upmanship. A patrol would enter a heavily republican area and come across a gang of protesters. To avoid a confrontation, the patrol would be ordered back to base, which would be considered a victory for the residents and a defeat for the security forces.

In order to counter this, and to avoid the estates becoming no-go areas, the next day the army would send out a massive patrol and flood the area with soldiers – as well as having platoons on stand-by within the base in case of trouble. The name for this was 'framework patrolling', and we would be sent out as much as a dozen times in a 24-hour period. The residents would view this a victory for the army, as we had 'taken back the streets', and this would put us at honours even – until the next time. Of course, all this did was inflame passions on either side, and it sent us further down into the bottomless pit of stagnation.

Just as I was beginning to think we might be lucky enough to get through the tour without any casualties, I was given a harsh and bloody reminder of the capacity for violence that still existed in Crossmaglen. The first incident involved Patrick, the old-fashioned community copper, and the second incident involved me. On both occasions, the day started out as normal, and on both occasions, it ended amid much spilt blood.

The levels of drink driving had reached such a high level that normally hostile locals had begun demanding that the PSNI do something about it. In response, a series of night-time patrols were set up with the express purpose of catching pissed-up drivers red-handed. Under the guidance of Patrick and one of his colleagues, we would sneak out of the station as quietly as we could and make our way across pitch-black fields under the cover of darkness. Once we had reached a certain point adjacent to the main road, we would then climb over the walls and hide ourselves away in the ditches that ran alongside.

The reason that we had to trek across the fields to reach our destination, as opposed to just strolling through the square, was because if the local boozers saw that a patrol was out on the ground, they would just wait until we had returned to the base or drive home using an alternative route.

We would set up a hidden VCP, and by the time drivers realised they had driven into it, there would be no means for them to escape. Two soldiers would form the entrance to the VCP by ducking down into a shallow ditch at the side of the road and stretching a thin 'Stinger' device across it, which they would pull to activate if anybody tried to escape. Approximately 80 m down the other end of the road, another pair of riflemen would do exactly the same thing, except with a much bigger device known as a 'Skiball', which could reputedly stop a truck. Whereas the Stinger only offered one solitary row of spikes to puncture a set of speeding tyres, the Skiball was designed so that when you went over it dozens of tiny nails ripped the rubber to shreds. In the middle of the VCP itself, would be the PSNI officers and the platoon commander.

The first night that ended in violence started off smoothly enough, and we managed to stop several cars without incident. As soon as I saw a vehicle approaching, I would get on the radio and send a message to the corporal, and once the car passed me, Patrick would step into the road and wave a red torch at them to make them slow down. It was a simple and supposedly foolproof system that had been used for many years without incident, and if anybody tried to aggressively evade it, I presumed we would be safe. I had obviously forgotten the golden rule that you should never presume anything in NI.

A white taxi van approached, and I relayed the message to the corporal. Just as I expected, it slowed down as soon as Patrick stepped into the road and began waving his red torch. All of a sudden, I heard a loud screech of spinning tyres and saw a red Peugeot hatchback flash by me, before braking sharply behind the stationary taxi. I passed another message down to the corporal that there was now a second vehicle in the VCP area, so be ready to check him out. Once Patrick had finished with the taxi, he waved him past and beckoned the car driver to move up and take his place.

It was at that point that we got our first hint of trouble and sensed that something wasn't quite right. Instead of inching forward slowly as he should have done, the driver sat there revving his engine.

Patrick was in the middle of the road beckoning him to move forward and enter the VCP area, but for some reason the driver didn't want to cooperate. I looked at Patrick standing in the middle of the dark road, with one hand on his hip and the other waving his little torch, and I realised how incredibly vulnerable he was. After a few moments, he seemed to grow tired of the stand-off, and he approached the red car. As Patrick casually strolled towards him the driver slammed down his accelerator and the car shot forward like a bolt. I could see all of this happening in slow motion, and I felt sick and powerless at not being able to intervene.

Patrick was trapped in the middle of the road, and the car was hurtling towards him. He rocked on his feet as if he couldn't make his mind up which way to go, and when he finally lunged to one side, it was too late. The driver cynically and deliberately smashed his vehicle into him, and I heard an almighty thud that sounded like a door slamming. Patrick was lifted clean into the air, where his body performed a neat somersault, before landing on the floor like a sack of spuds.

At the top of his voice, I heard the platoon commander scream out, 'Deploy Skiball, deploy Skiball,' and I could just make out the figures of the two riflemen frantically diving out of their hedge and dragging it across the road. Once the driver had gotten rid of Patrick, he turned his attention to the struggling riflemen and pointed his car towards them. Luckily, they realised the danger they were in, and as he swerved crazily towards them and gathered even more speed, they dived headfirst into a ditch. For a dreadful moment it looked like he was going to follow them into the ditch, but, at the last second, he veered away and shot off in the direction of the border. The whole incident was over in seconds, but as I squinted into the darkness at Patrick's lifeless body, I knew that the shit was only just beginning to hit the fan.

In the immediate aftermath of the incident, I sat by the side of the road gawping like a fish in a pond. I seemed momentarily paralysed by the shock of it all, and it was only the sound of the corporal's boots running towards me that woke me up. As he was running he was shouting into the radio that we had a man down and needed urgent assistance. And then came the moment that I hoped I would never face but knew that I couldn't turn away from. Because I was the patrol medic, it was my responsibility to lead the efforts that would hopefully save Patrick's life.

The platoon commander took over my position at the mouth of the VCP and began managing the incident, blocking off traffic, securing the area, coordinating the other troops and trying to raise some help on the net. I took off running in the direction of the fallen policeman.

When I arrived at Patrick's body, I didn't know what to expect, and my instincts told me that he would probably be dead because he had flown in the air like a skittle when the car had struck him. He was lying flat on his back in the middle of the road with his arms spread-eagled by his sides. I immediately realised that even if he were alive, it would be vital that he wasn't moved because of the possibility of a spinal injury. I knelt beside him and went through the ABCs that I had been taught at Aldershot (airway, breathing, circulation).

There was a mixture of good and bad news: he was breathing, albeit very faintly and irregularly, and I couldn't find any external bleeding, but I had a grave concern that he might have internal bleeding that only a surgeon would be able to stop. I couldn't detect any broken bones, although it was difficult checking him over because I was worried about moving him. I pulled his shirt up and ran my hands over his ribcage feeling for indentations, and also looking for the telltale bruising associated with internal bleeds. Thankfully, there was none.

My initial assessment was that Patrick was most likely deeply unconscious due to the massive impact, and that he probably had some fairly nasty internal injuries, including a possible brain swelling. I was very concerned about him because when I peeled back his lids and shone my torch into his eyes, only one of the pupils responded, and the other remained stubbornly fixed and dilated, which is a strong indicator of brain damage. I was doing all I could, but it didn't feel like anywhere near enough, and I realised that the limits of my abilities meant the best I could hope for was to prevent him deteriorating any further.

I got one of the lads to take his jacket off and place it across Patrick to keep him warm, and every few seconds, I checked his pulse and pupils with my torch. Like his breathing, his pulse was agonisingly weak, and I worked out that the most effective way to check it was to shine my torch on his neck and observe the tiny pulsing of his carotid artery. I wasn't too concerned that Patrick was deeply unconscious, because sometimes that is a good place for a casualty to be, as it prevents shock and stops any thrashing around.

What did worry me was the possibility that he might slip into a coma. Once that happens, there is no guarantee that the patient will come round, and the chance of brain damage is greater. Patrick would make periodic groaning noises, so I made sure to speak into his ear and pinch his earlobes to trigger a pain response. Basically, I was doing all I could to keep him with us.

Another worry I had was that his tongue might slip down his airway and block off his breathing, as this frequently happens when a casualty is flat on their back. It is referred to as swallowing your tongue, but this is technically incorrect. What happens is the tongue relaxes and rolls to the back of the throat where it restricts breathing. Ideally, I would have liked to put Patrick into the recovery position, but it was too risky with a potential spinal case, so I had to settle for tilting his head back a little and making sure his airway was kept clear. I had to strike a balance between leaving him as he was and trying to keep him breathing freely, and I chose the latter. So long as I didn't bend his neck or twist it to the side, any spinal injury wouldn't have been affected. What I didn't want to do was put myself in a situation where I had to start performing a vigorous resuscitation, because with the fragile state of his body I reckoned that any more shocks would kill him.

While I was dealing with Patrick, the platoon commander had taken charge of the rest of the multiple and was frantically trying to summon help. He was doing his very best, but it seemed that everything that could go wrong was going wrong. The completely shit radio kits that we were issued with were breaking down – both our personal role radios (PRR) and the commander's more powerful system. (Through no fault of our own, and despite regular maintenance checks, our ancient kit sometimes let us down – this was known as 'bad comms'.) We were having real problems getting in contact with XMG, and so half of the patrol ran back on foot to alert them. While they were running through the square and being hassled by drunks, the remaining lads had to guide cars carefully past Patrick's body, and to my horror and disgust, a few bastards actually leaned out of their windows and laughed.

All the while, the clock kept ticking, and Patrick's chances of making a full recovery were diminishing rapidly. I could see that he was growing weaker and paler before my eyes, and the incredibly frustrating thing was that I could only sit back and watch it happen.

In medicine, there is a critical period called the 'golden hour', and if a casualty receives prompt treatment during this time, he has a good chance of making it. It was beginning to look like Patrick would not receive attention in time.

Before I dealt with that incident, I had fondly imagined that if someone got injured on a street patrol, help would soon arrive – I reckoned that it would be in the hills where there would be problems. However, Patrick had been lying on the cold concrete for over 20 minutes, and still we had no assistance. I asked what the delay was and was told by the patrol commander, who had managed to get one of the radios working, that the soldiers back at base couldn't get the Snatch vehicles or the Saxon ambulance to start, so they were having to come to us on foot instead. I shook my head in sheer disbelief, because the vehicles were checked over every day.

A Snatch is an armour-plated Land-Rover that was frequently used in the riots and mayhem of the '80s. They were great vehicles, but they hadn't been used regularly enough since the ceasefire took effect, and their engines were beginning to seize up. Obviously, ticking the engine over for ten minutes a day wasn't sufficient maintenance.

The Saxon armoured personnel carrier (APC) was another ancient piece of kit that was being used less and less, and consequently beginning to fall into disrepair, despite a rudimentary maintenance programme. If the Saxon ambulance had been working, we would have chucked Patrick into the back of it asap, drove him back to XMG base and awaited helicopter extraction from there. Thanks to our unreliable vehicles, that plan went out of the window.

Help finally arrived in the form of the medic. As we applied a stiff collar to Patrick and carefully manoeuvred him onto a spinal injury board, I briefed the medic on the care that I had applied so far. He was extremely professional and good at his job, but as he was assisting me with Patrick, I had a genuine fear that he was about to collapse. He was absolutely fucked and struggling to catch his breath after an exhausting run in the middle of the night; it had taken a lot out of him. But fucked or not I was just glad of his help and pleased that he had finally arrived. Between us we got Patrick strapped in and carried him over to a nearby field to wait for the doctor's arrival.

Because there had been a delay in getting help from XMG

security base, there was a knock-on delay in getting the doctor from Bessbrook Mill. I was getting more and more pissed off at all this waiting around, and Patrick looked as if he could have died any second. After a full 30 minutes, the doctor's helicopter finally appeared on the horizon, where it continued to hover and fly around in aimless circles. I asked why he wasn't getting his arse on the ground so we could extract the casualty, and I was told that the pilot wasn't allowed to land until a second chopper had arrived to provide top cover from the air. I thought this was a patently stupid rule, but I resisted moaning about it as it wouldn't have been helpful. Ten minutes later, the second chopper appeared, which had been scrambled from the quick reaction force (QRF) at Bessbrook Mill.

The doctor landed and asked us for an assessment of Patrick's condition and a debriefing on what had happened. I was amazed at the speed and skill with which the doctor assessed the fallen officer. Whereas I had been a bundle of nervous trepidation and had fumbled through my efforts with trembling hands, he was a model of brisk efficiency. Within the space of five minutes, the doctor had repeated all of my treatments and bunged in a half dozen more that I had neither the wisdom nor knowledge to understand.

One hour after his close brush with death, Patrick was airlifted to the main hospital. By the time he was on the operating table, almost an hour and a half had passed since his initial injury – so much for the golden hour.

We reformed as a multiple and were about to tab back into camp when the Snatches belatedly arrived to give us a lift. They might have been an hour late and had completely missed the drama, but I wasn't about to tell them to piss off because we no longer needed them. Thick smoke belched out of the exhausts, and the only way the drivers could keep them from stalling was by constantly revving them. The comedy of errors was compounded further when we climbed into the back and the vehicles promptly stalled. We all had to jump out and give them a push start, before madly diving into the back. The driver told us that the engine was so weak and the power so feeble that he didn't dare move out of first gear, and so that was how we crawled back to camp, with the engine howling and sputtering like an old banger.

There was no other way of saying it – the whole affair had been a fuck-up from start to finish, and the response time of the rescue team was woefully inadequate. The sergeant-major asked us to have a long hard think about what happened, because the next day there was going to be a thorough debriefing, and we would be walking through the scene of the crime with scene of crime officers (SOCO) from the PSNI. Already there were discontented rumblings and various theories being put forward about what had gone wrong, and most of them were coming from people who hadn't even been there. I didn't have the will-power left to argue, and, to be honest, I couldn't be arsed – it could wait until morning.

The next day, when we began our big debriefing, one of the points that was repeatedly raised was that the Skiball had failed to stop the speeding car, and it seemed some people were having trouble getting their heads round that. What they were really implying was that the lads on the Skiball hadn't deployed it correctly. Well, I had seen the whole thing, and I knew that theory to be a pile of bollocks. As soon as the shout had gone up, and whilst Patrick was still spinning in the air, the lads on the Skiball had run across the road and deployed it as fast as was humanly possible. The problem was, a car weighing well over a ton had been bearing down on them at great speed, and they didn't exactly have time to hang around and start checking for details. The vehicle had already knocked over one of their colleagues, and the driver was looking to do the same to them.

The lads actually performed very bravely, because by the time they had stretched the device across the road, the car was so close that they had been forced to dive into a ditch to avoid being hit –

and it damned near skimmed their heels at that! I don't know what more they could have been expected to do – perhaps they should have stood there a bit longer and let themselves be run over as well? I don't think so. No, we weren't going to let any blame be attached to our patrol, because the lads had performed brilliantly, and to say otherwise would have been a lie.

There were undeniably many failures on that dreadful night, but they had nothing to do with the soldiers' performances. Instead, the systems under which we operated were to blame. The SOCO investigation confirmed many of my initial suspicions about what had gone wrong, and it exonerated the soldiers from any wrongdoing. It turned out that the lads had deployed the Skiball correctly after all, but an inbuilt fault meant that when the driver went over it the spikes that should have ripped his tyres open ended up being flattened instead, and that was why he had been able to get away. The driver had also managed to get one side of his car up onto the grass verge and almost into the ditch (where the riflemen dived for cover), which meant that two of his wheels missed the Skiball entirely. There was nothing more the soldiers could have done to stop him, other than put a few rounds into his car, and in the current climate that was something you couldn't even contemplate doing.

A few days later, the car was found in a nearby field; it had been petrol bombed and completely burnt out. SOCO told us that the car had been reported stolen weeks before, and they had no idea who could have been driving it. They spoke to witnesses who had been in the area and managed to speak to the taxi driver who had also seen the Peugeot, but, as usual, they were met with a wall of stony silence. Patrick went on to make a full recovery, although he was off work for a long time and in a bad way at one point.

I know it would make for a more exciting story if the driver had been a masked IRA assassin wielding an ArmaLite assault rifle, but I suspect that the truth is rather more mundane. If the IRA had wanted to take out a few Brits or to ambush a VCP, I am sure they would have been a bit more professional and subtle about it, rather than barging into us like a bulldozer. The car was probably being driven by a couple of pissed-up joy riders, and rather than face arrest, they chose to mow down an innocent policeman and make for the border. I have no doubt that they wouldn't even have had a flicker of remorse for the man they almost killed, and, in fact, I suspect that they would have been rather pleased by it all. From their perspective they got away with it and had a good result.

However, what disturbed me most about the whole episode was how long it took for the rescue chopper to reach us. I have no doubt that if Patrick had suffered a serious arterial bleed, or perhaps severe internal bleeding, he would have died, and there would have been nothing I could have done about it. It got me thinking about what would happen if an IRA sniper shot one of us, and I had to conclude that we would probably die before help arrived.

The incident proved to me that since the beginning of the ceasefire, the army had let its systems get rusty and slack, and a lot of the previous efficiency had gone. Just because Patrick had survived and help had eventually arrived, people were viewing it as a success and 'no big deal'. But I didn't see it that way because I had been the one giving him first aid, and I knew that he had only been saved by a stroke of luck. The incident had been a failure, not a success. Of course, I had to keep my thoughts to myself, because senior commanders don't like being told where their systems are going wrong – and especially not by 'gobby' riflemen.

One positive that came out of the events of that night was that my confidence in the men around me actually increased. However, it decreased my trust and belief in the military way of doing things. It seemed to me that the army had fallen into the trap of presuming that everything would work out all right in the end – but in Northern Ireland, presumption is the mother of all sins.

As the clock wound down towards the end of the tour, it seemed that Patrick's near miss would be the only serious incident we would have to deal with. I wasn't complaining, and the lack of action suited me just fine. Crossmaglen seemed to have quietened down a bit in recent months, and apart from the occasional skirmish with the South Armagh Demilitarisation Committee (SAD), the streets seemed relatively quiet.

At the beginning of the tour, SAD had been the bane of our lives, and they had succeeded in surprising several of our patrols. Their favourite tactic was to wait until soldiers were on the ground, observe them from the local Sinn Fein office and at an opportune moment spill out of the doors waving banners and placards demanding that the troops leave. Another tactic was to hide out in various Transit vans parked around the square and then burst out of the back and try to encircle the troops. They liked to call themselves peaceful demonstrators, but they weren't above getting physical if they felt they could get away with it, and a few of the lads had received cut lips and black eyes during scuffles with them.

These minor encounters were nothing compared to the traumatic experience that I endured at the hands of SAD. On the day in question, we were on a foot patrol to a nearby estate, accompanying a couple of policemen as they made some enquiries about some cars that were being vandalised. I could never quite work out the attitude of the locals, and neither could the PSNI officers, but, for once, they were as nice as pie to us, and we felt like we had made some progress. As we made our way back towards the main road that would lead us to the security base, there was a good mood within the multiple, because, unusually, we hadn't received any abuse. I should have known our good fortune wouldn't last, and a moment later, a message came over the net: 'Watch yourselves. There is a crowd building up in the square around the base.'

The message went down like a lead balloon; the prospect of fighting off an angry mob wasn't in the least bit enticing. We hadn't yet got sight of the protesters, so we decided to go firm where we were and hope that the crowd would disperse. I admit that it was a case of wishful thinking, but, contrary to popular perceptions, we weren't about to rush into a fight. A message then came over the net that one of the multiples had managed to get back in unscathed, and although the second had encountered a bit of resistance outside the main gate, they too had managed to get back in. We were advised to stay put for the time being while an alternative route was worked out, which would somehow sneak us past the mob undetected. It was a sensible idea and nobody objected because we seemed well out of harm's way.

However, the members of SAD were a crafty and well-organised bunch, and if we were to outwit them, we would have to be very lucky indeed. They had been monitoring our movements for months, and they knew full well that we only ever went out in three multiples, so that meant there was another one still out on the ground somewhere.

Out of the corner of my eye, I spied a fat bastard dressed in a pair of filthy jeans breathing heavily, and I pointed him out to the PSNI officers. They recognised him instantly and informed us that we had just been 'dicked' so we had best start moving. The fat man waddled off to get reinforcements, and we ran across the road into an empty field. A second later, the message came over the net that a large crowd was moving in our direction.

The PSNI officers told us not to worry because they were going to use their local knowledge to outflank the protesters and guide us back into the base by the little-used back door. The idea was that as the mob was running towards the position that the fat man had pointed to, we would be running in the opposite direction across an open field that was shielded from their eyes by an industrial park. We would have to climb over a few small fences that led into a large scrapyard, but once we had cleared those obstacles, we would be able to cut through it, nip into the back alley and sneak in via the back gate. Well, that was how it was supposed to work.

We made our way across the field, and, I have to say, we were feeling the pace a bit. Most of it was an uphill run, and the weight of the ECM on our backs threatened to collapse us at any second. The fact that it was a baking hot summer's day didn't help matters either, but other than that, we weren't too concerned – yet. As infantrymen we were used to physical hardship, and it would take a lot more than a sprint across a muddy field to do us in. Besides, we had the PSNI guiding us, and they assured us that the shortcut through the scrapyard would save us bags of time. The PSNI men seemed supremely confident, and as they jogged across the field in their lightweight kit, they even found time to crack a few jokes. However, their mood darkened considerably when they got the message that the crowd was now pursuing us across the field and had also entered the security base's back alley.

It was a relief when we finally sighted the scrapyard. Once we had scaled the flimsy fences, we galloped into it at a breakneck pace. There were huge pipes, broken engines and lumps of masonry everywhere, and as we tripped and stumbled wildly over them, I was reminded of doing the steeplechase back at Catterick Garrison – only this time we weren't in a race, it was for real. At last, I caught sight of the road, and my spirits lifted as I anticipated seeing the men in front of me streak across it. But for some reason they had come to a grinding halt and were pacing about nervously while the PSNI men shouted and swore at one another. I didn't like the look of it and wondered what was going on.

The policemen who had been so certain of guiding us to safety had in effect led us into a trap. In their haste to sprint across the field, they had forgotten that it was a Saturday afternoon, and the scrapyard was closed. Instead of being faced with an open road, we were met by an enormous padlocked fence with barbwire and green spikes at the top. It must have been 10-ft tall, but it wasn't the height that worried us so much as what was placed on top of it. The message came over the net that we had best get our arses over the fence asap, otherwise we would be having a wrestling match with some of our friends from SAD.

You might wonder why a squad of heavily armed soldiers should feel the need to flee from a confrontation with protesters, so I will give you the reason: it is a soldier's worst nightmare that a crowd of yobbos will pin him against a wall and try to take his weapon from him – he simply cannot allow that to happen. But, in a cruel twist, neither can he use his weapon on the baying mob. Instead, he has to wait until their hands are around his neck and their fists are striking his face, by which time it is too late for him to use his weapon anyway, and the crowd will have probably snatched it from him.

The protestors knew that in the current climate a squaddie would not use his rifle against them, and there was always a chance that they could use this knowledge to kill him. A man's life is very fragile, and it would only take a few idiots in the crowd to get carried away for someone to be killed. Once a crowd saw a hated and bitter enemy trapped with his back to the wall, all rationality and thoughts of the peace process would leave their minds, and in a rage of furious blood lust, they could tear you to pieces. It has happened before in Northern Ireland, and given the right circumstances, it could easily happen again.

That is why our commanders observing the incident from the security base on the all-seeing CCTV cameras couldn't countenance a confrontation with the hostile crowd. And neither could we on the ground. We would just have to climb over the perilous-looking fence whether we liked it or not.

We went over the fence in our order of march, which meant I would provide rear protection while the rest of the multiple clambered over it as quickly as they could. Once the rest of the team was over, I would then start my own climb. I could see straight away that we would have difficulties clearing the fence, because the lads were finding it a struggle to get to the top and when they did, it was a precarious balancing act as they tried to avoid impaling themselves on the sharp, green spikes.

The policemen went over first, but it wasn't particularly hard for them as they carried no rifles and had no kit on their backs. Next up it were the soldiers, and that was when the problems started. Each man in the patrol had a thick webbing belt around his waist that was bulked out with magazines, water bottles, spare radio batteries and all kinds of other military paraphernalia. In addition to this, we were carrying heavy backpacks that contained ECM kit, helmets and riot gear. In my case, the huge Chubb bomb detector and extra med-pack increased the weight I was carrying even more.

Going over the fence one at a time was proving to be slow and cumbersome, and had we continued at that rate, the crowd would have been on us with within minutes. The decision was made to scale it in pairs and at opposite ends. It would mean that the fence would be wobbling like hell as two men struggled to clear it, but if we delayed it any longer, we would be in a critical situation.

I continued providing rear protection and was joined by a soldier from the intelligence corps who had been attached to us for the day. For some unknown reason, these men were called 'Conco' officers, and they often accompanied us on patrols. After a lot of cursing and desperate scrabbling, my colleagues at last cleared the fence, and it was time for me and the Conco to go over. I took the left-hand corner of the fence, and he took the right.

The owner of the scrapyard must have been paranoid about people breaking into his property, because after trying and failing to secure a grip on the bars, I realised that they were smothered in grease. It seemed that the Conco officer had discovered the same thing, and he began to shout and shake the bars furiously as he struggled to reach the top. It was possible to climb the fence, my colleagues had proved that, but you had to keep a cool head and choose your footholds wisely.

I decided to ignore whoever was rushing up behind me and apply all efforts to getting over the fence. I realised that going into a panic and flailing about like a madman wasn't going to help, so I took a deep breath and concentrated on trying to avoid the slick globs of grease that impeded my progress. The climb was exceedingly hard work, not least because the weight on my back was threatening to send me crashing back down.

But the hysterical reactions of the Conco officer were causing me the biggest headache of all, and I was worried that the man was on the verge of blind panic. I could have sympathised with him if he had had any real weight on his back, but the feeble specimen was only carrying a poxy little day sack that weighed about 20 lb. He was causing the fence to shake and sway so wildly that if he kept it up much longer, I reckoned the damn thing would fall down. From the way he was shouting, you'd have thought that an army of Zulus was about to overrun us. With every mad lunge he made he was threatening to tip us both off, and if he persisted with the wild man act, I doubted either of us would get clear.

I heaved my way to the top and started to edge my legs over the other side, taking extra care to avoid the sharp spikes and rusty wire that clawed threateningly at my trousers. My good friend the Conco was also making slow but steady progress; however, with each angry step, he continued to cause the fence to roll like a ship in a storm. As I perched on top of the fence and surveyed the drop, I tried to blot the swinging and swaying out of my mind and began to lower myself down, inch by inch. It was one hell of a height, and if I fell, I knew I would be lucky to get away with just a broken ankle. I had to worm my way down very carefully, because whenever I leaned back, the weight of the Chubb would threaten to send me sprawling to the floor. But at least I was on the right side of the fence, and it felt better to be going down instead of up.

I glanced across to the Conco and saw that he was hauling himself over the top – hopefully the journey down would be a bit smoother. I turned my attention back to my own progress and lifted a hand off the bars, intending to place it on a smoother section to my right. Suddenly, I heard a loud cursing and felt the fence veering crazily back and forth. My hand missed its intended target, and my body jerked downwards at an awkward angle. The weight of the Chubb and the sudden jolt threw me backwards, and I was falling into thin air.

The moment that followed was one of those surreal instances when time seems to stand still and offers you a split second to make a critical decision. The choice I faced was between a huge drop onto solid concrete – and the possibility of landing flat on my back and breaking my spine – or making a grab for the sharpened green spikes and ripping my hands to shreds. I chose the spikes.

As I was falling backwards, my left hand whipped out and caught hold of a spike, and my body crashed heavily into the fence, hanging from one arm. A split second later, I managed to bring my right arm round and secured that to a spike too. But the drama wasn't over yet, and as I resumed my descent, I was shocked to feel an intense stabbing pain in my left hand. I tried to remove it from the spike but found, to my horror, that it appeared to be somehow stuck.

When I managed to prize it free, I almost fainted and my mind struggled to comprehend what my eyes were seeing: my middle finger was almost hanging off, only attached by a few strips of skin, and my palm was gashed as if someone had taken a tin-opener to it. I realised that if I didn't get control of myself, things would only get worse. After a momentary pause, I somehow managed to lower myself down. As soon as my feet hit the floor, a stab of pain engulfed my hand, and my entire fist began shaking uncontrollably.

Although, from my perspective, the incident had seemed to unfurl in slow motion, in actual fact it had only taken a couple of seconds, and the guys on the ground had no idea what had happened. The multiple was formed up in its order of march and about to sprint away when I called a halt and approached the corporal. I showed him my hand and told him I was going to give my rifle to another soldier, because in my current state I couldn't keep hold of it if we were attacked. I told him that I had no problem with going through the crowd and was ready to fight, but he had to be aware that I would be about as much use as a feather duster.

The corporal took a quick look at my hand and pulled out a field dressing which he placed on my palm and told me to grip hold of. I could see by the expression in his eyes that he was as shocked as I was, but he covered his surprise well and remained as cool as a cucumber. He then moved me into the middle of the multiple to offer me some protection, and we bolted into the back alley.

My hand had swollen like a boxing glove, and the blood pumping out drenched my sleeves. Strangely, the pain then seemed to miraculously disappear and reduced itself to a tolerable throbbing. I can only presume that it was down to my body flushing itself with adrenalin in preparation for fight or flight. Whilst I was grateful for the pain subsiding, I was still very much aware that I was carrying a serious injury, and I was worried about how I would react if things got physical.

My greatest fear was that if the crowd was intent on violence, I would be the first one they would attack. Human nature is no different to that of animals when base emotions and passions are aroused. Whenever a pack of hyenas attacks a herd of animals, it is always the weak and injured that they pursue first. I had already made up my mind that if any of the bastards attacked us, I would just flip out and go crazy – it would be my only chance of survival in my current state. I still had a working right hand, and I would just have to make sure it was put to good use. But I also knew that I wasn't Superman, and if a strong and determined adversary got hold of me, I would lose the fight. What particularly worried me was what would happen if a nasty bastard clocked my injury and decided he was going to pull my finger off – because it was already hanging precariously, and it wouldn't take much force to remove it completely.

As we rounded the corner and entered the rubbish-strewn alley, I was relieved to see our sister multiple waiting for us at the top.

They were standing directly outside the back door and making it very clear that if we were attacked, they would wade in too. I spotted the main body of protesters about halfway up the alley; they were waving placards about and whooping loudly. I was relieved to see that the crowd wasn't anywhere near the size that we had been led to expect, and I estimated that there were only about 15 protesters. When we had taken to the fields, we had managed to split the demonstrators up, and I suspected that the remainder of them were still stuck in the scrapyard.

It seemed that we had got lucky: the protesters weren't looking for a fight but were just out to cause a little mischief. We deliberately slowed our pace as we walked past them and made a conscious effort to look each one of them hard in the eye. This wasn't bluff or bravado on our part but a deliberate military tactic. History has shown that large-scale demonstrations often attract weak and inadequate people who crave the security of a crowd to feel strong. We were always told to try and isolate individuals with our eyes and make them aware that we had seen through them. Basically, what you are saying to them is, 'Look mate, I know you feel strong in this crowd, but both you and I know you are weak.'

The demonstrators chanted the usual slogans of 'Brits Out' and 'Troops Go Home', but not one of them made a lunge for us. As soon as they saw the state of my hand they began laughing and clapping wildly and hurled a few insults, but I didn't mind just so long as they kept their fists to themselves. My stomach was turning somersaults, and my hand was throbbing, but I wasn't about to let the demonstrators see my discomfort. Everybody could see that I was fucked, and there was no point in trying to hide it, but if I showed any signs of weakness, it could be taken as an invitation to attack.

As we got closer to the base, we turned around and walked in backwards, never taking our eyes off our assailants. We stepped into the compound and closed the heavy steel door behind us. A split second later, a hail of missiles smashed into the door, and boots and fists hammered impotently on the steel. We ignored them and made our way to the unloading bay.

The initial danger had passed, and the pain in my hand returned with a vengeance. I was led to the sick bay, and the medic poured alcohol into the gaping wound and attempted to dress it. My finger was in such a state that he decided to leave it open until the doctor had arrived from Bessbrook Mill. The digit was almost hanging by a thread, and he was scared he might damage it if he bandaged it incorrectly.

One thing I was certain of was that my Northern Ireland tour was now officially over, and I had done my last patrol in Crossmaglen. The SAD demonstration had set out to aggressively disrupt and target our patrol, and as I surveyed my ruined hand, I had to ruefully admit that they had succeeded. Nobody had been more anxious than me to see our time in Northern Ireland come to an end, but the way it was finishing wasn't the happy ending I had hoped for.

The familiar sound of powerful rotor blades cutting through the air told me that the doctor's Lynx had arrived, and I breathed a sigh of relief. He strode in purposefully and laid out his briefcase beside me, where he opened it to reveal an assortment of grim-looking needles and syringes. Before he even said hello he was already stabbing my arm with some kind of powerful antibiotic and scrubbing my hand with iodine and a stingingly painful alcoholic wash. The general antibiotic he had put into my arm was merely a standard procedure and would provide only minimal protection from infection. In cases like mine, where the body has been pierced by rust and bacteria-laced steel, a more direct remedy is required. The doctor sighed heavily and drew back the torn skin on my hand so that his needle came to rest directly on the mess of blood and tissue. He then injected a dose of powerful antibiotics directly into the wound, and I jumped so high I almost hit the ceiling.

The doctor then told me that he was sending me off to hospital for an immediate operation. As the medic unlaced my boots and slipped me into civilian clothes, the doctor explained that I had suffered a partial 'degloving' injury, which basically meant that the skin on my hand had been pulled off like a glove. But not only that, I had also managed to virtually sever my finger, and all of the nerves and tendons in it had been destroyed.

On the flight to the hospital, the medical sergeant told me that I was to avoid telling anyone I was a soldier and that I wasn't to consent to any treatment until two bodyguards from the regiment had arrived. I was grateful for the treatment that had been given to me, but I had to stifle a laugh when the sergeant told me not to reveal my identity. How the hell was I supposed to keep it a secret when a fucking great Lynx helicopter was dropping me off at the gates of the hospital?

We arrived within 15 minutes, and the chopper began circling around the hospital looking for a suitable landing spot. The pilot announced that the only safe place he could set me down was near the car park, so I shrugged my shoulders and told him to go ahead. Whenever we were out on patrol, the Lynx helicopters would always swoop down like giant eagles, and we would dive out like fleas. However, in deference to my condition and our surroundings he hovered down at a gentler pace.

As the chopper descended, I looked down into the hospital complex and was met with a sea of curious faces and pointing fingers. So much for secrecy and a discreet arrival – it seemed that every window had a face in it, every doorway a huddle of bodies and every pavement a gaggle of gawping spectators. To top it off, a police Land-Rover sped towards us and a couple of coppers climbed out to greet us. I didn't want to be facetious, but I told the medic that we couldn't have announced our arrival any more openly even if the Queen was coming. I then jumped out of the chopper and made my way over to the policemen, who shook my good hand and escorted me into the hospital.

I could feel patients' eyes burning into me as we ran towards the lift that would whisk us out of sight. The policemen ushered me into a private room and told me that before I could receive any treatment they had to give me a security briefing. I felt like laughing whenever I heard the word 'security' mentioned, because any security I might have had was blown by my very public arrival. The whole hospital had seen me leap from the chopper, and I might as well have been wearing my uniform for all the difference it would have made.

The policemen gave me a fake address to memorise and told me it was to be used on my admission forms. I could still use my real name, because using a false one would only confuse things, but under no circumstances was I to divulge my occupation or the circumstances leading to my injury. They then said that they were going to introduce me to a security-cleared doctor who would perform my operation.

All of this talk about clandestine security made me feel like an extra in a James Bond film, but the effect was somewhat spoiled by the nature of my arrival. If they had been genuinely concerned about security and not just paying it lip service, I would have been dropped off in a nearby field and met by policemen there. The coppers would have then stuck me in the back of their wagon, given me a briefing and dropped me off at the hospital gates. Anyway, it was too late to worry about it, so I turned my attention to the doctor.

She was a stunningly beautiful woman with the most piercing blue eyes I had ever seen. She was so attractive that I even forgot about my injury momentarily and found myself being hypnotised by her gaze. As she poked and prodded at my hand and questioned me in her soothing Irish brogue, I began to wonder if she was a Protestant or a Catholic and what her feelings about the British were. I knew she was security-cleared, but that meant nothing: it merely confirmed that she was a reliable professional with no sectarian links. A security clearance couldn't account for the feelings in your heart or change where your loyalties lay; after all,

I was an anti-monarchist, yet I had taken the Queen's oath. It saddened me to think that this caring doctor who examined me with such tenderness and concern might actually hate everything I represented.

I asked her what her name was and she replied, 'Dr McCallion,' in a voice that I can only describe as neutral. I think she had noticed that I was attracted to her and felt embarrassed by it, so I made an effort to tear my gaze away from her intensely blue eyes and focused on my reddened paw instead.

When she was finished, she gently placed my hand back down and squeezed my arm. She told me that my hand was in a pretty bad condition and would require extensive plastic surgery. She said she would do her very best, but she couldn't guarantee that my finger could be successfully reattached, and even if it was, there was a risk it would be completely frozen like a lifeless sausage. My nerves had been avulsed (which is a medical euphemism for 'totally destroyed'), and my tendons had been torn in such a ragged fashion that their remains had rolled up inside my palm. Even if the operation was a success, I would need a couple of 'clean up' surgeries to recover.

Dr McCallion took me to a private room on one of the quieter wards, and I was prepped for surgery. I was relieved to see a couple of friendly faces from the regiment had arrived, and I told them I would see them when I got back. Minutes later and I was wearily closing my eyes as I drifted off into the blackness of anaesthesia.

I awoke from the sedative five hours later. The first face I saw was Dr McCallion's, and I could see in her eyes that she was the bearer of bad news. The operation had not been the success that she had hoped for, and I would be left with permanent and lasting damage. Dr McCallion apologised for not having been able to do more and explained that my finger would have to be amputated in a second follow-up operation at a later date. I told her that I was grateful for her efforts, and I appreciated and respected her skill, but, unfortunately, it was just one of those things. In the grand scheme of things, the loss of a finger and a bit of movement in your hand is absolutely nothing. I would have had cause to grieve if both of my hands had been damaged and I had lost multiple digits, because that would have been a life-changing event, but as it was, it really wasn't that big a deal.

Before she left, the doctor said she liked my attitude and wished that all her patients were as positive. I told her that I hadn't earned the right to wallow in indulgent self-pity when you considered that better soldiers than me had lost their lives and limbs in that pointless conflict. She gave me a whimsical smile, approached me and shook my hand to say goodbye. Her last words to me were that she didn't do politics and would never discuss the Troubles with a patient – before adding that she agreed with my assessment 100 per cent and hoped never to have to treat another wounded soldier. She was a remarkable woman, and I held on to her hand for perhaps a bit longer than I should have done, before releasing my grip and watching her leave. I never did see her again, but I never forgot her piercing eyes or the clear lilt of her voice.

I spent a week in the hospital, dosed up on antibiotics and going out of my mind with boredom. I was impatient and restless to start my rehabilitation, and I was constantly pestering the doctors about how long it would be before I could have my second operation. I thought about my friends who were still patrolling the streets of Crossmaglen or trekking across the beautiful greenery of the Irish border, and I realised how much I missed it all.

The life of a soldier is full of ups and downs and constantly changing fortunes. Only a week before, I had been a fully fit squaddie, capable of charging over assault courses and tabbing across steep hills for miles – now I was lying in bed and could barely manage to wipe my own arse. Reclining on my back and staring at the ceiling gave me plenty of time to reflect on where we had made mistakes on the patrol. The policemen had made a big error leading us into a dead end, and I think they had panicked a little in the heat of the moment. It was an understandable reaction, because they had seen rioters in Crossmaglen at their very worst, and they knew the damage they could cause. However, with the benefit of hindsight, I could see several different courses of action that we could have taken, and I cursed my luck we hadn't given any of them a chance.

If we had continued to move downfield for another 100 m, ignoring the scrapyard, we could have just walked through a thick hedge and been back on the road. Another option would have been to tab off towards the hills at breakneck speed and call in a chopper to pick us up. Even with all the ECM on our backs, there was no way a bunch of flabby protesters could have kept pace with us. Another possibility would have been to tackle the 'dicker' and hold him till the danger had passed. As a last resort, we could have just drawn our batons, closed ranks and hard faced it through the crowd. We could have tipped off the lads inside the base to be ready to bomb burst out of the gate, so if any of the mob had summoned the bottle to have a go, they would have found themselves quickly surrounded.

Mulling it over in my mind, I concluded that we had taken the worst possible course of action. I wasn't about to start getting all emotional and slinging accusations of blame about, but I privately held the view that my misfortune could have easily been avoided.

The coppers who had led us into the trap visited me in hospital and offered their apologies, but I told them it wasn't necessary and that it was just bad luck. I meant it, too, because they had made an honest mistake and clearly felt guilty about it. Nobody has made more mistakes in this life than me, and I wasn't in a position to pass judgement. When you consider that men were losing arms and legs in Iraq on a daily basis, for me to start tearing my hair out and whining would have marked me out as a prick and a coward.

Staying in the hospital gave me a good chance to get a feel for how the more sensible members of the public really felt about us. Dr McCallion was supposed to be the only person who knew I was a soldier, but without exception, every single nurse had already guessed as much. I never confirmed their suspicions or answered their questions, and I tried to adopt a kind of mute but friendly silence. Whenever a nurse came in to change my bedding or dress my wounds she would say 'Oh, are you the young man that came in on that chopper?' or 'So, what's it like being a squaddie over here?' It was an embarrassing and farcical situation, and not knowing what to say, I would just smile dumbly or change the subject.

My time in the army was drawing to a close, and I only had six months left to serve. Thanks to my injury I would be medically downgraded, and my time in Northern Ireland would be my last-ever tour. Despite the injury, despite my republican beliefs and despite all the hard work that had come before, I was glad that I had completed the tour. For a man of my age who had grown up watching the conflict unfold on the nightly news and who belonged to a different generation of soldiers than the ones he worked alongside, it had been a rite of passage.

As a restless teenager and a dissatisfied 20-something, it had always bothered me that while I was at home watching television, my contemporaries in the military were serving in NI in their thousands. Well, that particular circle had now been squared, and I felt comfortable and at ease with myself, because I had made my own small contribution to the history of the conflict. As I flew back to the UK in a RAF Hercules, I wished the people of Northern Ireland well with all my heart, but for me it was over – end of.

When I got back to Weeton Barracks, I was told that I could have a medical discharge if I wanted, but I turned it down. I hadn't joined the army to get medically discharged, and I had every intention of fulfilling my contract. Obviously, my abilities as a soldier were much reduced, and most of my days would be spent at the hospital receiving intensive physio, but I still felt that I had a contribution to make. After six months of extensive treatment my hand had recovered as much as it was ever going to, and I readied my mind for the step back into Civvy Street.

My return to civilian life had been something I had been relishing and dreaming about for over two years, even though at times it had seemed like a distant and unobtainable fantasy. The thought of leaving had sustained me in the sands of Iraq and endless border patrols of Northern Ireland, but as I prepared myself to retire from the army, I felt a shiver of nervous apprehension. For the first time, I understood why soldiers were often reluctant to leave the service, even when they wanted to, because, in many ways, it is scarier being out than in.

But I wasn't a fool, and I knew that the secret of leaving on a high note was never to outstay your welcome – no matter what job you do. I was a 33-year-old rifleman, and I was carrying some pretty nasty injuries; my time had passed, and it was the right moment for me to depart. If I had been ten years younger, I might well have stayed, but I had to accept that I had been lucky to squeeze in the service I had, and it was time to move on and do different things.

In any case, I had achieved my primary goal to recreate my brother's travels and take a short walk in his shoes. My time as a Green Jacket had been a sentimental journey that had taken me to the scorching deserts of Iraq and an invasion I never believed in, as well as to the back streets of a sectarian conflict that tore the heart out of the people and made cynics out of soldiers.

I left the Royal Green Jackets in early 2005, and I like to think that I made a mark in my own small way. I was the last-ever Green Jacket to pass out of Sir John Moore Barracks, and I was the oldest man to ever pass the modern-day Combat Infantryman's Course at Catterick Garrison. It is these two achievements that cause me to look back and smile more than any others. I also had the privilege of serving alongside some dedicated professionals and great soldiers, and I shall always remember their exuberance and friendship.

Before I left the regiment, I was awarded two campaign medals for operational service in Iraq and Northern Ireland and was handed a glowing testimonial, which referred to some of the actions I had been involved in as a soldier. If I am honest, I think the words made me out to be a better man than I really am, but it was nice to know that the work I did was appreciated, and it meant a hell of a lot to me.

As a child growing up, I had often fantasised that I would become a noble and heroic soldier. Well, if you have read this far, you will have realised that I never came anywhere near that ideal. The only excuse I can offer is that sometimes the dreams of childhood are outstripped by the harsh realities of the 'grown-up world'. But I am happy with what I did, and I feel pleased about the contribution I made. Perhaps the most honest way I can sum up my time in the army is like this: I was never a great soldier, but I was a good squaddie. That'll do for me.

GLOSSARY OF ABBREVIATIONS

1RGJ: 1st Battalion of the Royal Green Jackets
AGC: Adjutant General's Corps
APC: armoured personnel carrier
APWT: Annual Personal Weapons Test
ATR: Army Training Regiment
Capt.: Captain
CDT: compulsory drug testing
CIC: Combat Infantryman's Course
CO: commanding officer
Cpl.: Corporal
DOB: daily operational briefing
Eagle VCP: Eagle Vehicle Check Point
ECM: electromagnetic countermeasure
FFR: fit for role
Gen.: General
GPMG: general purpose machine gun (Gimpy)
IED: improvised explosive device
ITC: Infantry Training Centre
L/Cpl.: Lance Corporal
LSW: light support weapon

Lt.: Lieutenant
Maj.: Major
MBPC: mortar base plate check
NAAFI: Navy, Army and Air Force Institutes
NBC: Nuclear, Biological and Chemical Warfare
NCO: non-commissioned officer
ND: negligent discharge
NSP: normal safety procedure
OC: officer commanding
PRC: potential recruits course
PRR: personal role radio
PSNI: Police Service of Northern Ireland
PTI: physical training instructor
QRF: quick reaction force
RAF Regiment: air force infantry
RE: Royal Engineers
recce: reconnaissance
RGJ: Royal Green Jackets
RLC: Royal Logistics Corp
RMP: Royal Military Police
RPG: rocket propelled grenade
RSM: regimental sergeant major
RTA: road traffic accident
RUC: Royal Ulster Constabulary
SAD: South Armagh Demilitarisation Committee
Sgt.: Sergeant
SOCO: scene of crime officer
SUSAT: Sight Unit Small Arms Trilux
TA: Territorial Army
XMG: Crossmaglen